The subtitle to this book, *Critical Questions about Language in a Twenty-first Century World,* is well named as a quintessential book for all who wish to know why their language matters. Prieto has done remarkably well at informing the reader about everything relevant to the most important linguistic questions of our era.

Your Language Matters (hereafter *YLM*) begins with the surface level of language, the phonological (sound system), and moves on to lexicon (words), morphology (smallest units of words), syntax (grammar), semantics, and pragmatics (meaning and use). Discussions include the language-brain connection, or neurolinguistics, figurative use of language, metaphors, stereotypes, and finally, sociolinguistic variation and politeness functions in linguistic interactions. *YLM* brings these concepts to life, relating them to the readers' lived experiences. Key terms about language are at once symbolic, spontaneous, creative, effable, and arbitrary. Each chapter culminates with exercises in which students apply what they learned to reinforce those concepts.

YLM is straightforward and uncomplicated about all aspects of language. It is not limited to a specific language, but is relevant for any language, helping the reader understand that there is no "broken," "half-formed," or "wrong" way to speak. Prieto does an outstanding job of clarifying key language concepts, often through use of pop culture cartoons, like R2-D2 as a robotic language "expert," but then contrasting machine and human language. On-point visuals illustrate his points. His examples are up to date, focusing on twenty-first-century case studies, like how social media is changing the punctuation rules of written language, how Facebook interactions can lead to cyberbullying, and how doublespeak is a language tool used and abused by power structures.

All these aspects of *YLM* make it the essential introduction to language, its structure, systems, and use. A central focus of *YLM* is the fact that there is no "bad" language but that all language is organized, systematic, and can be learned. Language is also in a constant process of change, having progressed from Old English to Middle, Early Modern, and current Modern English usage. None of those varieties is better than the others, and where our English language is headed is anyone's guess. Beyond this, Prieto explores how we learn our first language and how best to acquire subsequent languages.

Dr. Prieto brings *YLM* to a conclusion with a "bang" rather than a "whimper." Indeed, it is a convincing narrative that everyone's language is worthwhile, and essential for understanding each other and bringing about harmonious global interactions. *YLM* offers the novice a fascinating view of everything we need to know about why your language matters, and as such, is an important contribution as an introduction to the field of linguistics.

Diana Boxer, PhD
Professor Emerita of Linguistics
University of Florida

Your Language Matters leads the reader toward a clear understanding of "the complex simplicity" of the analysis of communication. It is packed with useful hands-on information for linguists and scholars. The most compelling aspect of it is the author's writing style illustrated with examples and stories he recalls from his interactions with language learners. Figures, communication models, online tools, and exercises are a great addition. The book is a practical resource for language research purposes and for classroom use.

Liliane Toss, PhD
Professor of Modern Language and Linguistics (North Greenville University)
Adjunct professor of Arabic (University of North Carolina, Charlotte)

Dr. Victor Prieto's textbook on linguistics, *Your Language Matters*, is a journey of discovery into the various factors and dynamics that are involved in human communication.

It is a well-balanced overview of key terms in linguistics, and the history and complexity of language. It touches on every major component of language: phonology, syntax, morphology, semantics, pragmatics, and the lexicon. Clear examples are given to help the reader grasp the concepts. The chapter on Pragmatics, or the "playful" handling of language is both enlightening and entertaining to read—well summed up with Prieto's comment "words do not always mean exactly what they seem to mean." Prieto points out that real communication is not quickly mastered, it takes years of experience to perceive and correctly decode non-linguistic information which can completely alter the surface meaning of what is said.

We learn that communication is much more than just vocabulary and grammar rules, but also empathy, worldview, common sense, societal experience, speech register, temporal context, and social relationships—pragmatic issues unique to human communication.

Prieto also takes us on a tour into how the brain stores and processes information, suppressing non-relevant memories or sensory input and enabling a person to act or react appropriately.

Each chapter concludes with an exercise section that challenges the student's grasp of the material and, through further directed research, expands their comprehension beyond the pages of the book. Highly recommended!

David Paul Foris, PhD
SIL Global, retired

Your Language Matters

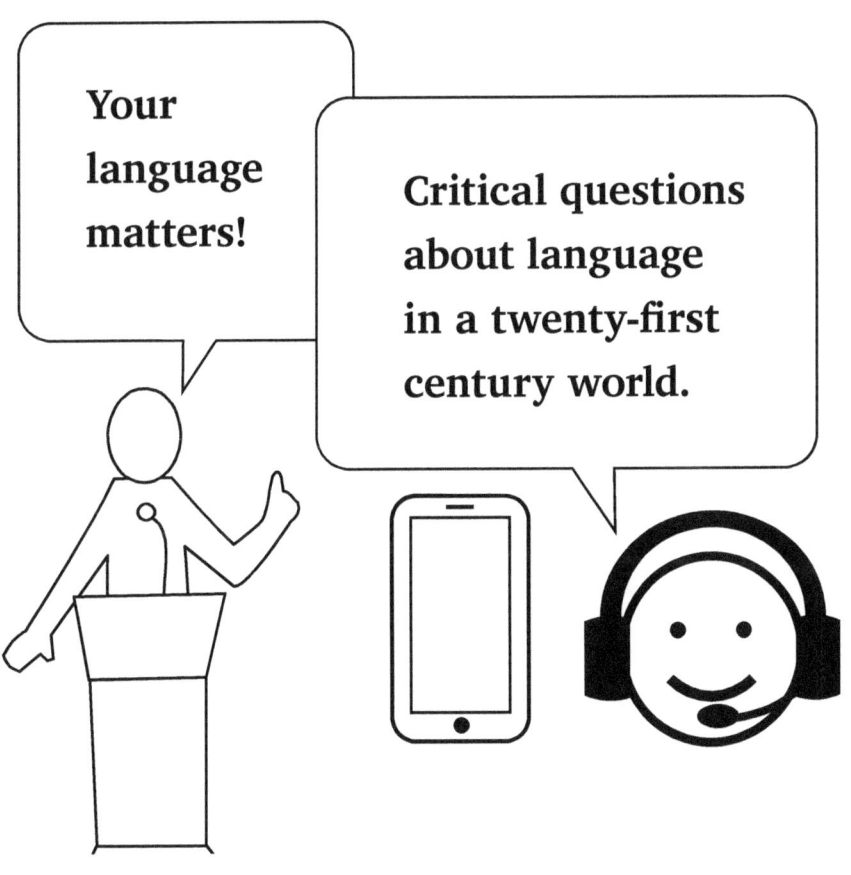

Editorial Staff
Susan McQuay, Editor in Chief
Eric Kindberg, Managing Editor
Linda Towne, Copy Editor
Eleanor J. McAlpine, Proofreader

Production Staff
Priscilla Higby, Production Manager
Judy Benjamin, Compositor
Barbara Alber, Cover Designer

Your Language Matters

Critical Questions about Language in a Twenty-first Century World

Victor M. Prieto

SIL Global
Dallas, Texas

© 2025 by SIL Global
Library of Congress Control Number: 2025941947
ISBN 978-1-55671-488-7 (pbk)
ISBN 978-1-55671-489-4 (ePub)

All Rights Reserved

No part of this publication may be reproduced, stored in a retrieval system, or transmitted in any form or by any means—electronic, mechanical, photocopy, recording, or otherwise—without the express permission of SIL Global. However, short passages, generally understood to be within the limits of fair use, may be quoted without permission.

Data and materials collected by researchers in an era before documentation of permission was standardized may be included in this publication. SIL makes diligent efforts to identify and acknowledge sources and to obtain appropriate permissions wherever possible, acting in good faith and on the best information available at the time of publication.

Copies of this and other publications of SIL Global may be obtained through distributors such as Amazon, Barnes & Noble, other worldwide distributors and, for select volumes, publications.sil.org.

SIL Global Publishing Services
7500 W Camp Wisdom Rd
Dallas, TX 75236-5629
publications@sil.org

Contents

Figures	xi
Tables	xiii
Preface	xv
How to Use this Book	xvii

1 Do We Really Know What Language Is?   1
  1.1 The components of language   2
    1.1.1 The phonological component: The sounds of a language   3
    1.1.2 The lexical component: Vocabulary   5
    1.1.3 The grammatical component: Rules to organize everything   6
  1.2 The features of language   7
    1.2.1 Symbolic   7
    1.2.2 Spontaneous   8
    1.2.3 Creative   9
    1.2.4 Effable   10
    1.2.5 Arbitrary   10
    1.2.6 Duality of patterning   11
    1.2.7 Displacement   12
    1.2.8 Complex simplicity   12
    1.2.9 Systematic   13
  1.3 The study of language: The field of linguistics   13

2 Do Animals and Robots Really Speak?   17
  2.1 Communication   18
  2.2 Human communication   19
  2.3 Animal communication   21
  2.4 Machine communication   23

3 Is Your Grammar Good?   27
  3.1 What we mean by grammar   27
  3.2 Grammar rules: Examples   29

	3.2.1 Rule 1: Phonology—There is structured order to sounds of a word	29
	3.2.2 Rule 2: Phrase structure—There is a structured order to words in a phrase	29
	3.2.3 Rule 3: Morphology—Word affixes carry grammatical meaning in a sentence	30
	3.2.4 Rule 4: Syntax—Word order carries meaning in a sentence	30
	3.2.5 Rule 5: Morphosyntax—Affixes and word order coordinate to change meaning	31
	3.2.6 Rule 6: Discourse—Context affects meaning in a narrative	32
3.3	Grammar options: Just options, not linguistic superiority markers	32
3.4	Grammar options: Worldview and culture trait markers	33

4 What Do We Mean When We Talk? — 39
- 4.1 Cognition and meaning — 40
- 4.2 Context and meaning — 42
- 4.3 Consensus and meaning — 43
- 4.4 Meaning relations among words (the "-nyms") — 46
  - 4.4.1 Meaning similarity, or synonymy — 46
  - 4.4.2 Meaning opposition, or antonymy — 47
  - 4.4.3 Meaning subcategorization, or hyponymy — 48
  - 4.4.4 Similar words, different meanings: Polysemy and homophony — 48
- 4.5 Meaning ambiguity — 49
- 4.6 Figurative meaning — 51
  - 4.6.1 The playful and esthetic/artistic use of figurative language — 52
  - 4.6.2 The explanatory purpose of figurative language — 52
  - 4.6.3 The compensatory function of figurative language — 53
  - 4.6.4 The face-saving function of figurative language — 53

5 Who Speaks English Better? — 57
- 5.1 Factors causing language variation: Sociolinguistic variables — 60
  - 5.1.1 The age factor — 61
  - 5.1.2 Gender — 61
  - 5.1.3 Social class and education — 62
  - 5.1.4 Region — 64
  - 5.1.5 Ethnicity — 65
  - 5.1.6 Register: Speech style per situation — 66
- 5.2 The role of politeness in language variation — 66
- 5.3 Final thoughts on language variation — 67

6 Did King Alfred Really Speak English? — 69
- 6.1 Forces behind language change (why language changes) — 73
  - 6.1.1 Economy (or "linguistic ergonomics") — 73
  - 6.1.2 Expressiveness — 74
  - 6.1.3 Analogy — 75
  - 6.1.4 Language contact — 75
  - 6.1.5 World changes — 76
- 6.2 How language changes — 77

7 Do We Mean What We Say? — 79
- 7.1 Language use: Beyond sounds, words, and grammar — 80
- 7.2 Contextual factors guiding language use — 83
  - 7.2.1 Situation (where and when) — 84
  - 7.2.2 Participants (who) — 84
  - 7.2.3 Ends (why) — 84
  - 7.2.4 Act sequence (what is next) — 85

		7.2.5 Key	85
		7.2.6 Instruments—nonverbal cues	85
		7.2.7 Rules	86
		7.2.8 Genre	86
		7.2.9 Competent linguistic interaction—Conclusion	86
	7.3	Language use as an inferential process	86
	7.4	Dangers in language use	88
		7.4.1 Doublespeak	88
		7.4.2 Unwarranted assumptions	89
		7.4.3 False advertising	92
		7.4.4 Language-related discrimination	92
8	**Is Language in Our Heart or Our Brain?**		**95**
	8.1	The brain as language storage	96
	8.2	Brain structure and its relevance for language	98
	8.3	The brain: Difference between human and animal communication	101
	8.4	Brain malfunction and impact on language	103
9	**Can Anybody Learn a Language?**		**107**
	9.1	L1 acquisition: Its nature	108
		9.1.1 L1 acquisition is natural	108
		9.1.2 L1 acquisition is innate	108
		9.1.3 L1 acquisition is universal	109
		9.1.4 L1 acquisition is gradual and sequential	109
		9.1.5 L1 acquisition is systematic	111
	9.2	Second language acquisition (SLA): Its nature	112
		9.2.1 L2 acquisition is non-compulsory	112
		9.2.2 L2 acquisition is sequential	113
		9.2.3 L2 acquisition is time-constrained	113
		9.2.4 L2 acquisition is systematic	113
	9.3	Suggestions for a better SLA experience	115
		9.3.1 Focus on communication in SLA	115
		9.3.2 Contextualize in SLA	116
		9.3.3 Exploit previous knowledge in SLA	116
		9.3.4 Orality before writing in SLA	117
		9.3.5 Multi-sensory approach in SLA	117
10	**Does Society Help or Harm Language?**		**119**
	10.1	Awareness of how society interacts with language issues	120
	10.2	Societal macro factors that shape language: Structure, dynamics, history, and beliefs	121
		10.2.1 Societal hierarchy	122
		10.2.2 History or past experiences	123
		10.2.3 Social etiquette	123
		10.2.4 Steady cross-linguistic interaction (languages in contact)	124
		10.2.5 Beliefs and prejudices	125

Conclusions   131

Appendix A: The International Phonetic Alphabet   135

Appendix B: Body-based Figurative Language   137

References   139

Illustrations Credits   151

Figures

Figure 1. What is language?	2
Figure 2. Texting—new writing strategies.	4
Figure 3. Language is a combination of symbols that point to a concept.	8
Figure 4. There are an infinite number of sentences in English.	9
Figure 5. A multilingual dog?	11
Figure 6. Meaningless units, combined purposefully, communicate meaning.	11
Figure 7. Language transports a listener or reader beyond reality.	12
Figure 8. Definition of linguistics.	14
Figure 9. C-3PO, a science fiction communicator.	17
Figure 10a. The Shannon mathematics-based communication concept.	18
Figure 10b. The interactive communication process.	18
Figure 11. Pronouncements by a judge are final.	20
Figure 12. Cyberbullying: Language used to hurt.	21
Figure 13. Monkey Communication.	22
Figure 14. Image created by binary code.	24
Figure 15. The unique metaphorical and social nature of human language.	25
Figure 16. Grammar = tools that combine the elements of language.	28
Figure 17. Good intuitive grammar.	28
Figure 18. Translation of the Latin.	30
Figure 19. Navajo geometrical sémantics.	35
Figure 20. Tuning up and tuning in for L2 acquisition.	36
Figure 21. Keep calm and …	37
Figure 22. Metaphorical connection to our cognitive universe.	41
Figure 23. Ambiguity in dialogue.	44
Figure 24. Jesus, the "Bread of Life" or the "Sweet Potato of Life?"	46
Figure 25. Laptop = computer, but not every computer is a laptop.	46

Figure 26. Subcategorization (hyponyms). 48
Figure 27. Cranes: Metaphorical connection, or homonym? 49
Figure 28. "The woman saw the man with the telescope." A case of structural ambiguity. 50
Figure 29. Sentences/intonation units as semantic mountains: One sentence/intonation unit = one idea. 51
Figure 30. Euphemistic or figurative language helps to avoid shaming others. 54
Figure 31. Use of accent to portray stereotypes. 59
Figure 32. Cross-generational miscommunication. 61
Figure 33. Abstract versus concrete levels of code. 63
Figure 34. Language areas of India. 64
Figure 35. Alfred the Great, speaker of Old English. 70
Figure 36. An Old English inscription. 70
Figure 37. Language and telephones—change over time. 73
Figure 38. We may be experts in our language, but not always its best judges. 79
Figure 39. Children and adults seem to talk in different dimensions. 81
Figure 40. Non-native speakers, like children, struggle with pragmatic competence. 82
Figure 41. Same question, different conclusions. 83
Figure 42. Hymes' speaking model. 84
Figure 43. Grice's Cooperative Principle (CP) of relevance in conversation. 87
Figure 44. Subtle linguistic manipulation using pronouns. 91
Figure 45. Subtle, or not-so-subtle, implications? 93
Figure 46. Victor, the "Wild boy of Aveyron": A language-deprived child? 96
Figure 47. Computer hardware components. 97
Figure 48. Information processing paradigm. 98
Figure 49. Baseline scan compared with prayer scan. 99
Figure 50. Anatomy of the brain. 100
Figure 51. Language centers in the brain. 101
Figure 52. Koko the gorilla is reported to have mastered around 2000 ASL signs. 102
Figure 53a. Wernicke's aphasia patients' speech. 104
Figure 53b. Broca's aphasia patients' speech. 105
Figure 54. Learning communication skills. 107
Figure 55. Language acquisition stages. 110
Figure 56. Baby Prince George learns to have its needs met. 112
Figure 57. Every language is equally challenging and accessible to children. L1 acquisition takes three-to-four years. 114
Figure 58. Effective L2 learners are good observers and great listeners. 116
Figure 59. A multi-sensory approach: (visual-auditory-kinesthetic-tactile). 118
Figure 60. Society's effect on language. 119
Figure 61. Society's judgments based on language used. 121
Figure 62. Social and linguistic hierarchies. 122

Figure 63. Sign in a pharmacy using euphemistic terminology: How societal norms
    shape language.   124
Figure 64. Living diglossia.   125
Figure 65. Sign in a Texas restaurant in 1949.   128
Figure 66. Languages and dialects.   129

Tables

Table 1. Adj-N phrase structure in English versus N-Adj in Spanish   29
Table 2. A syntactic English rule for basic sentence formation   31
Table 3. Agreement of S-V and N-Adj   31
Table 4. Body-based figurative language   42
Table 5. Language variance based on geography, society, and eras when spoken   72

Preface

Welcome to *Your Language Matters: Critical Questions about Language in a Twenty-first Century World*. This textbook is designed to introduce you to the fascinating field of linguistics and explore the pivotal role language plays in our increasingly interconnected global society.

In an era where communication transcends geographical boundaries and digital platforms shape our daily interactions, understanding the intricacies of language has never been more crucial. This book aims to equip you with the fundamental knowledge and analytical tools necessary to critically understand and examine language in its various forms and contexts.

Throughout the ten chapters of this text, we will embark on a journey through the core aspects of linguistics, from the basic building blocks of language to its complex societal implications. We begin by defining language itself and the scope of linguistics as a discipline. From there, we explore what sets human language apart from other communication systems, delving into the unique features that make our linguistic abilities so remarkable.

The heart of this book lies in its examination of language structure and meaning. We will unravel some intricacies of grammar, investigating how words are formed and sentences are constructed. We will then turn our attention to how meaning is encoded in language, before considering how context shapes our understanding of linguistic interactions.

As we progress, we will tackle some of the most pressing questions in the study of language. How do dialectal differences arise, and what are the consequences of linguistic prejudices? How does language change over time, and what forces drive this evolution? We will also explore the biological foundations of language, examining its neurological basis and the fascinating process of language acquisition.

Finally, we will consider the broader implications of language in society, investigating how it shapes, and is shaped by, our social world. Throughout the text, you will be encouraged to think critically about your own language use and the linguistic landscape around you.

This book is not merely a collection of facts about language, but an invitation to engage with the critical questions that linguists grapple with within the twenty-first century. As you read, you will develop the skills to analyze language scientifically, appreciate its diversity, and understand its profound impact on human experience.

Whether you are considering a career in linguistics, seeking to improve your communication skills, or simply curious about the language that surrounds us all, this textbook will provide you with a solid foundation and inspire further exploration. Remember, your language matters—not just as a topic of study, but as a fundamental aspect of your identity and your interactions with the world.

We hope this journey through the realms of language and linguistics will be as enlightening for you as it is for us. Let's begin our exploration of the critical questions about language in our twenty-first century world.

How to Use this Book

Over my 30 years of teaching linguistics and second languages at different universities and schools in the U.S.A. and abroad, I have encountered many contradictory ideas, misconceptions, notions, myths, and doubts about language from people around me. Some people have asked me questions about the origins of language and language use. On other occasions, based on peoples' misguided statements, I have asked them questions about language, to which they have frequently been unable to respond to their own satisfaction.

I have heard statements such as the following:

"We are from (such-and-such place) and don't speak English well," (this, from native speakers of English!).
"I know my grammar is terrible," (also from a native speaker).
"I don't speak a language; I speak a dialect," (from an Indigenous person).
"French is the most beautiful language in the world."
"British speakers sound smarter."
"Our ancestors spoke better English than we do."
"My puppy understands me when I talk to him, and I understand him when he talks to me."
"People from Spain speaks the purest form of Spanish."
"He is of this (ethnicity) *but* he speaks English well."
"I understand when I read something written in my heart language."
"People who use double negation are illogical."
"Languages without a writing system are primitive, not full languages."
"Sign languages are not true languages."

People have also asked questions like these:

"Why doesn't she just say what she means?" (from a frustrated husband).
"Can I learn a second language if I am 30 years old?"
"What is the best way to teach your children how to speak?"
"Should we speak two languages to our baby at home?"
"My son is two years old, and nobody understands him; should I be worried?"
"Why must I take a foreign language in college if my major is not language related?"
"Why do children interpret everything so literally?"
"Which country or social class speaks English better?"

"Can I lose language ability if part of my brain is damaged?"
"He asked me, '*How are you*?' and kept walking. Why did he ask me that if he didn't really want to know?"

These statements and questions constitute my motivation to write this book. These inquiries have been summarized in ten general questions about language, each of which makes up a chapter in this book. By responding to these queries or misconceptions, I aim to unveil the problems, dangers, and myths underlying statements similar to those given above. I also aim to give some fundamental responses to the questions given above or related ones. I encourage you to answer on your own the ten questions that are the chapter titles before you continue reading the text. Write down your answers in a notebook. After you complete the reading of this book, compare your original answers with your new knowledge to see if your answers have changed. These are the ten questions we address:

Do we really know what language is?
Do animals and robots really speak?
Is your grammar good?
What do we mean when we talk?
Who speaks English better?
Did King Alfred really speak English?
Do we mean what we say?
Is language in our heart or our brain?
Can anybody learn a language?
Does society help or harm language?

This textbook, then, has the purpose of introducing and answering fundamental notions about language. At times, the issues are presented with an exploratory or informative tone, but at other times with a more critical and well-researched view, including both creationist and non-creationist perspectives, views from the left and from the right, and from both popular knowledge and linguistic research. The author hopes that readers will be the final judge of such claims for themselves.

The book is the basis for lectures in the linguistics course, "An introduction to language" at the university level. It can complement any other textbook used in such a class or it can be used as the primary textbook for an introduction to linguistics course, for linguistics and non-linguistics students alike.

Your Language Matters contains theoretical content but also practice exercises for reflection on the part of the student. Some of the issues presented here are lacking in similar introductory linguistic textbooks, or not completely treated, and in some cases not revisited in recent decades.

A contribution of this book is that it re-evaluates decades-old hypotheses, and critiques language theories from a twenty-first century, media-based lens, making them relevant in linguistic interactions of today's society. We refer here to media-accessible information such as current websites, social media networks, and articles online to shed some light on the status of those linguistics principles in the current decades of this recent century. The reader will be able to associate with the testimonials and anecdotes of real people and experiences exemplifying the issues presented here. These current testimonials and examples narrate true incidents that clearly illustrate the points presented.

Apart from a look at theoretical information and its relevance to the twenty-first century, exercises and relevant questions draw the reader into dialogue with recent research to help them integrate the topic of study. It would be of unquestionable help to the readers in a university course to respond to these exercises while engaging with the corresponding section in the textbook.

1
Do We Really Know What Language Is?

The limits of my language mean the limits of my world.

– Ludwig Wittgenstein

Nicole was a freshman in my college classes in a small private university in South Carolina. She was born and raised on the island of Maui in Hawaii, hearing and speaking Hawaiian Pidgin, known merely as "Pidgin" in Hawaii, something her family always referred to as "slang." Growing up, Nicole and her brothers were taught to "turn it on and off" in the appropriate social situations, and they were encouraged to speak standard English in school, at the doctor's office, and in similar public places. However, at home and in more casual community settings, most of her family and friends spoke Pidgin. She told me about an incident at a family party in which her aunt told her: "Stop talking like a *haole* 'foreigner/white person'!" since Nicole was speaking English to her younger relatives. However, in the context of a family party, speaking Pidgin was inappropriate—offensive, yet funny—to the aunt. Nicole remembers an instance in one of my linguistics lectures when I asked her to read something in Hawaiian Pidgin aloud. She felt too embarrassed to do so, and not because of the normal speaking-in-front-of-the-class jitters, but something deeper. She later told me that to read Pidgin did not feel right since she was always told to speak standard English at school. For Nicole, it felt wrong to speak Pidgin even when specifically asked to do so, and on top of that, there were no speakers of Pidgin around to trigger a natural response to the use of the language. She told the class: "But it's not even a real language!" I looked at her and pointedly asked: "What is a language?" She replied that it had to have its own grammar and be spoken fluently by a new generation of speakers. I pointed out what was obvious to everyone else—that Pidgin does have its own grammar! Up until that point she had accepted the cultural bias about Hawaiian Pidgin. After this introductory class in linguistics and after covering topics covered in this book, she realized she did not have to be ashamed of using Pidgin anywhere. She realized it is a language and that she can speak her mother tongue anywhere since it is indeed a language! For many years, she didn't think that it was. Did Nicole really know what a language was? Do we really know?

What is language and what is *not* language? These may be basic questions, but most people do not stop to think about it. Some might ask: "Why should we care?" Our language or language capacity is typically taken for granted. It is such a common tool in our everyday experience that we may think we know what it is—or feel we do not need to know. Some argue that we do not need to know how a car functions to use a car. We do not know how an apple is produced, but we can still eat it and enjoy it. We could say the same thing about language: We do not need to know a lot about it to use it or even use it well.

Admittedly, we do not really need to study language to use it. However, like many things in life (e.g., cars, plants, and the human mind), we benefit from knowing more about what we take for granted. For example, the more we understand about cars and computers, the better we will use them and the more they will benefit us. Understanding language at a deeper level will help us understand and appreciate others better, communicate better, and appreciate who we are and who others are, and value the differences, differences that are observed in language use.

In addition, this knowledge of language will be a tremendous aid to those seeking to work in a language-related field, such as: language teaching, speech therapy, communication, law and criminal justice, computer language programming, education in general, social work and ministry, arts, journalism, professional writing, linguistics, language learning, interpreting, translation, and others. If we understand language as a tool that we can apply, then the more we know about that tool, the better we can use it. So, let us take some time to think more deeply about what language is and how it enriches our daily life.

You have probably heard expressions such as, "The language of love," "the language of music," "dog speech or language," "machine language," etc. We likely all agree that despite the variety of expressions, we still understand each of these "languages" in some sense as referring to communication or to a system of communication. We may mean communication through love, through music, canine communication, and so on. Linguistics, the science that studies language, however, defines language as a system of communication unique to humans. Oxford defines Language as "the principal method of human communication, consisting of words used in a structured and conventional way and conveyed by speech, writing, or gesture" (Oxford English Dictionary 2024). Elaborating on this definition is the focus of this chapter. We will study the components and features of language. In section 1.2 we define *language* for the purposes of this book. Secondarily, at the end of the chapter, we will study more about what *linguistics* is and does, and why linguists study language.

1.1 The components of language

Language, as described and defined here, is a unique and very complex, though natural, system of human communication that distinguishes people from other animate beings or from machines. At the most basic level, language consists of three major components: a set of sounds—the PHONOLOGICAL component; a set of words, or the vocabulary—the LEXICAL component; and a set of rules—the GRAMMATICAL component.

Figure 1. What is language?

1.1 The components of language

1.1.1 The phonological component: The sounds of a language

Every human language has a set of speech sounds that people articulate and combine to communicate meaning. For example, to express the idea of "cat," English speakers utter three sounds in this particular order: The sounds for *c*, for *a*, and for *t*. In linguistics, we represent these speech sounds, or PHONES, using brackets [ ] to distinguish them from the ORTHOGRAPHIC, or alphabetic, representation "*cat.*" The phonetic sounds for *cat* are [k], [æ],[1] and [t]—or [kæt]. The word *written* as *cat* is *pronounced* and PHONETICALLY TRANSCRIBED, [kæt]. See Appendix A, which gives the International Phonetic Alphabet (IPA) symbols.

Speech sounds in a language that distinguish one word from another, once analyzed and catalogued as unique in the sound system of that language, are called PHONEMES. The smallest units of speech sounds in a particular language, then, are considered its PHONEMIC INVENTORY. In English there are about 44 phonemes.[2] The calculation for number of phonemes changes slightly depending upon the subvarieties of the language.[3] As a comparison with English, in Spanish there are around 28 phonemes. A phoneme is written symbolically within forward slashes (//). Phonemes exist in a language whether it has a writing system or not. A three-year-old child can communicate very well with others orally (or via signs) without having ever learned to read or write. Many languages in the world today may not have a writing system but the speakers of those unwritten languages effectively communicate with each other orally every day. One criterion for an outsider to determine whether two speakers have the same, or different, languages, is a test of MUTUAL INTELLIGIBILITY using a recording and a word list. If the speakers understand each other, they can be assumed to speak either the same (or a related) language.

Thus, a language is viable—that is, considered linguistically to be a language—even in the absence of a writing system. *Writing is secondary to oral language use.* Linguists from the twentieth century stated this principle in different ways. One hundred years ago, Ferdinand de Saussure stated that "language and writing are two different systems of signs; the latter only exists for the purpose of representing the former" (1916:23). Almost two decades later, another renowned linguist, Leonard Bloomfield, explained it like this: "Writing is not language, but merely a way of recording language by means of visible marks." (1933:21). Similarly, a few decades later, John Lyons explained that "the spoken language is primary and ... writing is essentially a means of representing speech in another medium" (1968:38).

So, writing is secondary to oral language use. This fundamental premise points to the primacy of the oral language[4] over its orthographic representation. For languages with writing systems that use letters, or ORTHOGRAPHIC SYMBOLS, such as "c", "a", and "t", each letter or combination of letters represents a corresponding speech sound.[5] Since letters are symbols written to represent speech, the sound, i.e., phoneme, must exist first in the mind of the speaker. A similar phenomenon happens with punctuation.

---

[1] This is an International Phonetic Association (IPA) symbol, a phonetically transcribed symbol that represents the vowel sound in the words "bat," "cat," and "hat" in American English. See Appendix A for the IPA chart (2020).

[2] An online search gives various results, but many agree there are 44 phonemes.

[3] For comparison, the University of Oregon calculates that there are 40 phonemes in English.

[4] In sections 1.2.6 and 8.3 we will see that signs, used in sign languages for Deaf communities, carry the same function as speech in oral speech.

[5] A word of caution about confusing phonemes with orthographic or alphabetic characters: Sound/letter correspondence is not always consistent. A phone like [s], for example, is written with "s" (sir), the first "c" of (circle), or "z" (ritz). Similarly, the phone [k] is written "k" (kitten), "c" (cat), "ck" (sick), and "ch" (choir). In English there is considerable orthographic variance from the sound of a phone, making spelling difficult.

Typically, punctuation marks in writing reflect speech patterns: When we pause in speech, we use a comma or semicolon in text; when we complete an idea, we use a period; when we ask a question, we represent the query in writing with a question mark.

Although oral language is primary, writing is equally important in a technological world. Unlike a 100 years ago, or even 50 years ago, in today's technology-oriented twenty-first century context, a significant portion of human communication occurs in writing. Computers and cell phones have become primary modes of communication. This assigns to writing a crucial role, and we cannot minimize its value.

New codes and writing strategies have become popularized that just a decade or two ago were nonexistent. Emoticons, emojis, abbreviations in texting like "LOL" and "JK", use of capital letters versus lowercase, and other codes or mechanisms have become the norm in phone texting, email, chat, and in other social media.

Figure 2. Texting—new writing strategies.

Social media communication heavily influences writing style in today's world. Keris Suttles, a university professor colleague of mine, while conducting investigation for linguistics lectures, observed how the internet and "meme culture" is changing the use of standard punctuation. Since texting is so important for everyday communication, and because texting does not have extralinguistic help, such as a sound system, tone of voice, gestures, and so on, often texters resort to text symbols or conventions to convey things like sarcasm and discourse structure. Keris says that when she texts, at times she does not end her sentences with punctuation, as if inviting the person on the receiving end to join in and complete the thought. She sometimes interprets italics as sarcasm and refers to the use of capitalization in some cases as "sarcastic capitalization." She noticed that if a student mimics by text a teacher who said, "Where is your homework?" they might text it to a friend like this in the meme or message: "wHeRe Is YoUr HoMeWoRk?" Younger generations are compensating for oral expression using punctuation as an extralinguistic resource.

Although writing enhances a language, human communication exists—and a language is viable—with or without a writing system. Writing is not a requirement for language to be valid. Examples of many languages in the world today without a writing system can be found on the SIL Global *Ethnologue* website:

> The exact number of unwritten languages is hard to determine. [The] *Ethnologue* (28th edition) has data to indicate that of the currently listed 7159 living languages, 4,153 have a developed writing system. ... We don't always know, however, if the existing writing systems are widely used. That is, while an alphabet may exist there may not be very many people who are literate and actually using the alphabet. The remaining 3,011 languages are likely unwritten. (Eberhard et al. 2025)

The *Ethnologue* makes it clear that there are almost three thousand languages in the twenty-first century that do not have a writing system yet are recognized languages. They are not lesser or inferior languages. They are as valid linguistically, and as able to communicate a full range of speech, as do English, French, Arabic, Spanish—or any other majority language

1.1 The components of language

in the world. Even in languages with well-established writing systems, native speakers communicate in their mother tongue before they can read or write. You spoke English well before you could write it. Likewise, every language in the world can be spoken without an ability to express it in writing, and some minority languages exist without having had the development of a written phonological component.

With this in mind, we respect and value languages that don't have a writing system; they are not primitive or deficient, as some might suggest. At the same time, we appreciate the value of writing for those languages that have that facility as an essential secondary mode of communication. Oral societies without a written tradition may be devalued by those who don't appreciate the complex sound system, lexical collection, and grammatical organization characteristic of *all* languages.

At this point we turn from the phonological component and its orthographic representation to a discussion of the second general component that is part of the makeup of all languages: the lexicon.

1.1.2 The lexical component: Vocabulary

People cannot talk without words. Even though it is difficult to define every word in a way that satisfies all listeners, all speakers have an intuition regarding what a word is and how to use it. When we speak, if we are asked to slow down, we might speak deliberately, word by word. We learned that phonemes describe the smallest meaningful unit of sound; similarly, a word describes the smallest unit of meaningful speech. Bloomfield defined a word as "a minimum free form … the smallest unit of speech" (1933:178). A word is a linguistic unit distinct from other linguistic units. In writing English, we separate each word from others with a wider space separating words than the space separating letters within a word. Considering both oral and written use, a word is "a single distinct meaningful element of speech or writing, used with others (or sometimes alone) to form a sentence and typically shown with a space on either side when written" (*Oxford Reference* 2023d).

A word, again, is a communication unit that can stand alone. What defines a word when used differently, is relative. *Home* as a unique word in the sentence: "I went home." But consider the sentence, "I haven't finished my homework." In the second sentence, *home* is combined with another word to form a compound word. *Table,* in the sentence, "We are seated at a *table*," is a stand-alone word, but in "We are seated at tables," *table* makes up part of the complex word *tables.*

Thus, what is a root word and what is not, may be difficult to discern. For the moment, however, we will define WORD succinctly as "a distinct meaningful unit of speech or writing." Throughout our experience of life, we continually expand this set of meaningful linguistic units that help us refer to an entity, concept, or nuance of meaning, expressing precisely whatever it is that we may have in our mind. The collection of these linguistic units or words, is called a LEXICON. Each word in our lexicon is a LEXEME, or lexical item.

Within a lexicon, MORPHEMES are those words or parts that cannot be divided, that carry meaning by themselves. A morpheme is further defined as the "smallest unit which has meaning" in a language. Sometimes a morpheme is a lexeme and sometime a morpheme is a grammatical part that carries meaning. For example, *table* is a single word that is also a morpheme since the word *table* cannot be broken down into parts. However, although *tables* is also one word, it consists of two morphemes: the root word *table,* plus the plural marker "-s". (Since this little suffix has grammatical meaning, it is, therefore, a separate [grammatical] morpheme.) The human brain memorizes these small units of meaning, how they are applied, and stores them away for proper use. (In section 3.2.2 we will further discuss morphemes that are organized within the grammatical component.)

Languages can have very large vocabularies, certainly much greater than their phonological inventory (40–44 phonemes for English, as calculated in footnotes 3, 4). According to

Shipley and McAfee (2021:227), children between the ages of one and two can be expected to have at least 50 expressive words in their lexicon. In their Language Development Inventory surveys, where the normal register of linguistic behavior for children is reported, they note that 19–24 month-old normal children have an expressive vocabulary between 50 and 100 words, and a receptive vocabulary of 300 or more words (2021:256). Two- to three-year-old normal children have an expressive vocabulary of 50–250 words, and a receptive vocabulary of 500–900 words (2021:257). Regardless of how many words a person has in their lexicon, it is an ample lexicon, and it keeps growing throughout their lifetime.

Related to the lexical component, in chapter 4 we will consider the "meaning component." The meaning component involves the meaning *behind* words; the expressions, ideas or concepts that those lexical items express. These ideas or concepts are the SEMANTIC aspect of lexemes. Furthermore, people can "play," or interact, with words or expressions, expanding them to refer to secondary concepts. These metaphorical expansions of the original or literal semantic meaning is what is called the FIGURATIVE aspect of linguistic expression. Figurative language uses nonliteral meanings to convey a nuanced meaning or imagery, it goes beyond a literal meaning of the words themselves to convey a more abstract message. For example, figurative language is what allows us to use the basic word "foot" (a person's extremity) metaphorically, applying the word in a secondary sense, that is, as an increment of measuring, to calculate what is a *foot* long.

So, we have discussed the phonological component (units of sound in speech), the orthographic component (phonemes applied in writing), the lexical component, including words and morphemes (units of meaning in a lexicon), and semantics (the meaning that underlies vocabulary). But how does the brain organize all these core elements and their variations, such as figurative use? The system that allows the brain to keep track of all this information is called the GRAMMATICAL COMPONENT.

1.1.3 The grammatical component: Rules to organize everything

Since we have dozens of speech sounds or *phones* in our phonology, and thousands of words in our lexicon, we need a system to keep it all organized. That is the role of grammar. There is no way people could communicate, using thousands of linguistic elements, without systematic patterns to organize them. Chapter 3 will discuss how grammar helps speakers to talk and write fluently, so we will not elaborate much on the grammatical component here. Instead, we will consider how the system of rules is the glue to unify and coordinate all the pieces that belong to language; the phonological, lexical, and syntactic components.

A system of grammar is a set of rules, or standards, that every language includes that orders all the linguistic pieces. These "rules" are guidelines in the mind of the speakers of a language that allow the speaker to generate an acceptable word, phrase, or sentence in their language. Think of grammar as a blueprint or template for the complex words or phrases we use in speech or writing. For example, at the word level an English grammar rule dictates something like this: "To pluralize a regular count noun, add an "s" at the end of that noun." This rule allows the speaker to correctly generate the word "cats." At the sentence level, a rule orders how multiple words are put together to form a complete thought: A speaker of English intuitively follows the "SVO" order of words to produce a basic sentence such as, "Mary loves Peter." The subject (S), *Mary*, is the first word of the sentence, then the verb (V) *loves*, and then the object (O) *Peter*. The subject is the one performing the action, the verb is the action word, and the direct object is the entity directly affected by the action. If you change this SVO order, the sentence expresses a different idea (Peter loves Mary), or something nonsensical (*Mary Peter loves).[6] In Japanese, which typically has an SOV standard word order, *Mary* (S) comes first, then *Peter* (O), and the verb (V) last. Each language has its own grammatical rules.

---

[6] Throughout this textbook, an asterisk (*) at the beginning of a word or sentence indicates that this item is ungrammatical in English.

This word-ordering principle applies similarly to every language. Keep in mind that it is crucial to recognize these three major constituents of language: the phonemes, or speech sounds; the lexicon, or the words or vocabulary; and the grammar, or the mechanics or rules for ordering all three elements—phonemes, words, and grammatical parts—together.

Let us consider English and these three major language components. English has a set of phonemes or speech sounds relevant to communicating in our language. Some of these common sounds are [k], written as "c"; [æ], written as "a"; and [t], written as "t". These three sounds are part of the phonemic inventory of English. When we put these three sounds together in a certain order, we can construct the word "cat." The word *cat* has meaning and so is part of the lexicon of English. Finally, grammatical rules of the English language help us know that *cat* is a noun. As a result, we can use the word *cat* as a subject or an object in a sentence, but we cannot use it as a verb. For example, we cannot say: *"We want to cat." In English, a grammar rule specifies that only verbs follow the form of the verb, "to ..." (as in "to walk"), so "to," used as the infinitive form of the verb, cannot precede a noun. Putting all of this together, we see that the phonetic elements [k], [æ], [t] are combined to form the lexical term, written *cat*; we understand semantically that *cat* is an animal—a noun; and following grammar rules, we know how to use *cat* correctly in a sentence.

1.2 The features of language

Unlike any other system of communication, language is spontaneous, creative, predominantly arbitrary, and potentially infinite. For this exploratory introduction to the complex system of communication, we will polish our previous definition of "language." From now on our working definition for LANGUAGE in this book will be the following: *Language is a complex system of human communication that consists of a grammar and a lexicon.*[7]

Let's briefly discuss some features of language that make it unique. Take a few minutes to reflect about the features of language on your own. In your opinion, what are some of the features that characterize and constitute the communication system we call *language*? Can you call traffic signs *language*, for example? If so, why? If not, why not? Can you call the barking of a dog *language*? Is the term *language* used correctly in the book title: *The Five Love Languages*? Can music be considered a *language*? What can classify some of these as *languages* but not others? What are the criteria for correct use of *language* in your mind or the parameters you think others have? After completing this exercise, compare your initial ideas with the content of the following nine language features.

1.2.1 Symbolic

The first feature of language that we will discuss is the symbolic nature of language. Langacker states that "lexicon and grammar form a continuum of symbolic elements" (1990:12). His concept of SYMBOL from a linguistic perspective, is that a lexical item, even a grammatical rule, points us in the direction of an idea or a conceptualization. Words and rules are conventionalized notions of those concepts. A meaningful utterance then, according to Langacker, is a phonological signal of a concept. I follow this line of reasoning in my description of language as symbolic.

So, we can say that LANGUAGE IS A COMPOSITE OF SYMBOLS. Words are symbols and grammatical rules are pointers that, in combination, identify a notion. Nöth suggests that language is considered a semiotic skill because semiotics deals with the study of symbols (1995:17). The word *cat*, for example, stands for a certain animal with a set number of features. So, the word *cat* is an abstraction, or symbol, that points to this animal in the feline family.

---

[7] You may notice that the phonological component is not overtly included. Many linguists consider the speech sounds to be part of the grammar of a language. This is mainly a case of terminology. What is important for our purpose is that we understand what the major components of language are.

Figure 3. Language is a combination of symbols that point to a concept.

A century ago, Edward Sapir recognized language as "merely a conventional system of sound symbols" (1921:2). He then defined language as "a purely human and non-instinctive method of communicating ideas, emotions, and desires by means of a system of voluntarily produced symbols" (1921:7). Even earlier, Ferdinand de Saussure described words as signs of something else. He called each word or affix a *signifier,* and its meaning, or what it pointed to, Saussure called the *signified.* A SIGN here is understood as a symbol that refers to something other than itself, a form that stands for or suggests an idea or entity (1916:66–67).

So then, we use phonemes, words, and other linguistic tools at our disposal to represent and point to notions to which we refer. The word *cat* is not itself a cat, just a signifier of a signified object. People use words with relative freedom. For example, the word *fox* on the same day may refer to an animal but an hour later *fox* may refer to a person. Words are like balloons, not bricks. They are flexible in use and in the understanding of the implied meaning. We expand them, we stretch them, we use them in different contexts with different meanings; we exploit them as much as we can to communicate an idea. In the end, they are just symbols. We may even stretch the truth, and though both speaker and hearer are aware that a "fish story" is not technically accurate, it is understood in the context in which it is told, perhaps shared by the speaker in exaggerated terms and with a slight grin.

A further illustration of the symbolic nature of language is in the value assigned to it. A boy named John could have been named Peter by his parents without affecting his identity. However, once the identity is assigned, the name John points to this particular boy. Once there is consensus regarding the referent of a word, that name functions as an understood symbol.

The proper noun John must be elastic enough to be able to be used in reference to possibly millions of people, but at the same time, definite enough so both the speaker and hearer know what person is being referred to during a conversation about John. My colleague Keris uses as an example, the word "big." For small-town residents, *big* may refer to a four-story building, but for New Yorkers it would need many more floors to be called *big.* Once speakers negotiate the meaning of *big* in a particular situation, there is no confusion. Consequently, the New Yorker would be able to communicate with the small-town resident with full comprehension when the word *big* is used.

1.2.2 Spontaneous

Human language is spontaneous because, as Chomsky suggests, language is stimulus-free (2006:11). Many other systems of communication (e.g., animal "languages") are stimulus-bound. Humans are not restricted by their environment or prior action in their choice of speech. A person can, at any time, for example, enter a room and out of nowhere say, "Someday I will buy you the moon." Of course, unrealistic declarations like this should be spoken with caution; we might be labeled as unstable or irrational.

People typically speak in response to some type of stimulus, but that is an individual decision. The point is that stimulus—or lack of it—is not a restriction on our communication. A hypothetical statement does not need previous stimuli to express that creative idea. No other communicative entity (whether machine, animal, or something else) uses language

1.2 The features of language

spontaneously like people do. Reference to speech by non-humans is only used in a figurative sense.[8] For example, "My parakeet talks to me on sunny mornings," or, "My dachshund tells me when it's time to go for a walk". Cartoon images that show animals, machines or plants talking using speech bubbles, "humanize" or "personify" that non-human by attributing to them speech and thoughts as if they were human. Their "speech," of course, is fanciful communication imagined by the artist or author who created the character.[9]

1.2.3 Creative

The third feature of language is that it is *creative* and productive. Human language is open-ended because it can create new words, new sentences, and entirely new thoughts; and yet, communication is not disrupted and is not thrown into chaos when novel words are introduced. Because of the structured and systematic nature of language, words and sentences never heard before can be added to the English vocabulary and still be understood context.[10] For example, I am sure you have never read or heard the following before today: "This chapter of *Your Language Matters* was written thinking of you." Even though that sentence is entirely new to you, you still understood the meaning of the sentence without making a major cognitive effort.

Language is unlimited in scope since there are no boundaries in relation to the number of ideas or types of sentences a language can express. In contrast, languages have a limited number of letters in their alphabet. This roughly corresponds to the number of *phonemes* or speech sounds in a particular language that are considered relevant for meaning and are distinctive from one another.[11]

There is also a finite range of words at any one time in a language. Vocabulary in a language generally depends on the need for terminology to express what is in the context of the speakers of the language. In some languages the range of vocabulary is large and in others the lexicon could be significantly smaller. According to *Merriam-Webster*, both *Webster's Third New International Dictionary,* Unabridged and the *Oxford English Dictionary* "include some 470,000 entries" in English, although the percentage of those lexemes that are actually used by the average population is much smaller (*Merriam-Webster* 2024b). The point is that the number of *words* in any particular language can potentially be counted and catalogued in a dictionary. However, there can never be a dictionary of *sentences*—original sentences are created every day! And yet a listener or reader can understand any newly coined sentence, like the novel comment, "buy you the moon," as long as the statement is constructed correctly following the sound and structural rules of the language.

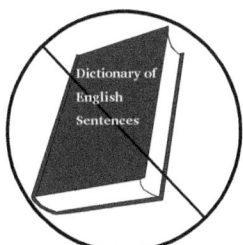

Figure 4. There are an infinite number of sentences in English.

---

[8] See section 4.6 for more on figurative speech.

[9] This type of personification is called *anthropomorphism* or *prosopopoeia*.

[10] See section 1.2.9 for further discussion of the systematic nature of language.

[11] A common assumption in linguistics and literacy is that ideally alphabetic characters emulate the phonemes of a language. For example, in a language with a letter-based alphabet containing 30 letters, it is likely that the language has 30 phonemes, or 30 speech sounds (phones). These oral sounds are innately recognized by the speakers of that language and, when combined according to phonological rules, are relevant for meaning and can be written distinctly.

Thus, we do not have or need a *Dictionary of English Sentences*. Can you imagine the size of such a work? And regardless of how big that collection might be, it would be incomplete. There are an infinite number of potential sentences in English, Spanish, Mayan, Navajo, American Sign Language (ASL), and all other human languages.

1.2.4 Effable

People need our system of communication to help us communicate anything we want to communicate. EFFABLE is defined as "able to be described in words" (*Oxford Languages* 2023)."[12] Katz stated the principle of effability when he claimed that "each natural language is capable of expressing the same body of thoughts" as any other language (Katz 1972:20). Even though this principle is debated, there is truth to it. People can express an incredible range of feelings, ideas, and information with the phonemes, words, and grammar that make up our language. Some thoughts that are difficult to convey in speech may be better expressed in a drawing or photo; every language has its limitations. And misapplying the rules of a language can result in unpronounceable words or utterances. Nevertheless, we can express the vast majority of the ideas or thoughts we need or want in our everyday communication. This is true regardless of what that language or variety of language it is that we speak.

1.2.5 Arbitrary

Since language is symbolic, as explained in section 1.2.1, the symbols used for a specific language are somewhat arbitrary. Thus, language is ARBITRARY because there is no connection, necessarily, between the sounds of a word, mostly a random combination of sounds, and the actual item it refers to in the real world. This is similar to how many first names of children are assigned by their parents. A child can be named anything, like *Bill, Philip,* or *Alexander*. There are no names that fit a specific baby; the name is totally arbitrary. Parents choose a name, it is registered on a birth certificate, and then it sticks with use. A girl named *Mary* could just as well have been named *Anna*, with no ill effects on her personality, life, and reputation. Both names would have been acceptable for this girl. Out-of-the-ordinary names that may affect life choices and experiences would not be ones chosen by the child's parents, a name such as *Lucifer*, for example. Parental choices for a name are more often based on family history, life experiences, and society dynamics than based on the sounds of the name itself.

Similarly, the English word *table*, is not more inherently related to an actual table or the concept of TABLE[13] than the Spanish word *mesa*, which refers to the same object. The combination of the sounds [m], [e], [s], [a] in Spanish[14] is based on an arbitrary consensus within a speech community. There is nothing table-like in this object requiring us to name this item a *table*, and not, say, a *flib*. In fact, if something innate gave an object its name, a logical outcome would be that every language would apply the same, or a similar, word for table.

Even ONOMATOPOEIA, or words that imitate the sounds made by an animal or object, are somewhat arbitrary from one language to another. English speakers represent a dog's bark as "bow wow" or "arf, arf," but Spanish speakers use the words, "guau, guau," to represent the same dog's bark. Since dogs cannot set us straight in this respect, both English and Spanish speakers will keep using what they perceive as dog sounds whether their term for dog "speech" can be acoustically proven or not.

---

[12] The adjective *effable is used most commonly as its antonym, ineffable.*
[13] An inanimate object with legs and a top, on which we put plates, books, and similar items.
[14] Remember that phonetic brackets represent the oral sounds, not the alphabetic letters.

1.2 The features of language

Interestingly, these onomatopoeias are the product of our language's phonemic inventory recorded in our brain and learned speech patterns. We process or interpret the sounds of nature through the ears of our phonemic standards. Sounds from nature (tree leaves rustled by the wind, animal "speech," and waves crashing on the shore) do not change regardless of the country in which they are heard, but people's description of these sounds in their mother tongue does vary. In Spanish, phonemic rules do not permit a word ending in "rf," so the onomatopoetic "arf" is practically impossible for Spanish speakers to say; "guau" does work. Thus, the expression of perceptions is at least partially arbitrary.

Figure 5 illustrates this arbitrary phonemic perception and verbal expression in different languages for the bark of a dog.

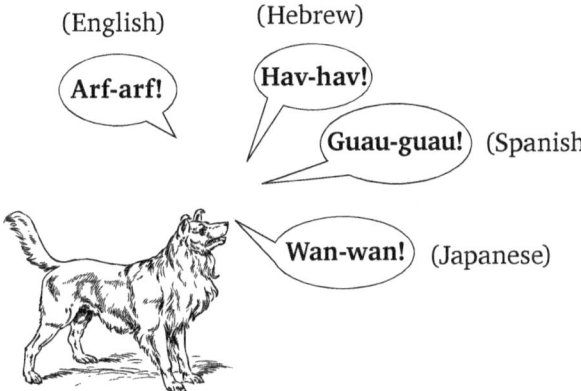

Figure 5. A multilingual dog?

1.2.6 Duality of patterning

Another amazing property of human language is that language is organized on two layers simultaneously. A dual structure combines meaningless units to form meaningful ones. The pattern of producing meaningful units starting from meaningless ones is known as "duality of patterning" (Hockett 1960:574). No species other than humankind does this. Every song of a bird, every roar of a lion, every whistle of a dolphin, is communication that is fully formed. Only humans combine meaningless units to form meaningful ones. This can be illustrated in both spoken English and sign language.

Returning to the example of *cat* in English, the [k] sound has no meaning on its own. The [æ] sound also has no meaning, and neither does [t]. Yet, when the three sounds are combined, we have meaning. A *cat* [kæt] is an animal that meows and is a pet in many homes in the U.S. Figure 6 illustrates how *cat* is spelled using ASL by means of three hand symbols—gestures which combine to spell the word *cat* in ASL.

Figure 6. Meaningless units, combined purposefully, communicate meaning.

This pattern of creating meaningful elements from meaningless elements constitutes an attribute of human speech alone; at least in its well-developed and complete sense of the expression "duality of patterning." Every basic-level element of the English language, whether phonemes or hand signs (in sign language), is meaningless. Yet, it is at this meaningless stage where English speakers start in our oral and written communication by means of language. All our foundational building blocks at the basic level are meaningless.

1.2.7 Displacement

Displacement is another feature of human language.[15] It involves the idea of referring to what is not present in the moment of speech. This means that humans can use language to refer to objects, concepts, and events that are abstract—either not visible to the listener at the moment of speech or a concept that cannot be physically discerned. We can displace ourselves using language. We can be transported to the past or to the distant future. We can travel to places we have never been before. We can be in heaven one minute and back on earth the following minute. We can visit the fantasy world of Santa Claus, Alice's Wonderland, the land of Pegasus, or a place where our TV superheroes live. There are no boundaries. Time and space are not limitations to linguistic expression and science-fiction experience.

Language allows us to displace ourselves from realities here and now; it takes the listener or reader to the future, the past, or the fantasy world of unicorns, flying reindeer, and beyond.

Figure 7. Language transports a listener or reader beyond reality.

1.2.8 Complex simplicity

Language is very complex. On one hand, it is so simple that a three-year-old can speak it effortlessly, but is also so complex that a foreigner, after years of learning a language as a second language, still may not master that language as fluently as a native speaker. Hundreds of books are written about just the suffixes and prefixes of the English language—and we do not yet know everything about affixes in English, much less other languages. As a native Spanish speaker who has learned English as a second language, this author's own 200-page PhD dissertation analyzed just two suffixes in Spanish, the diminutives and augmentatives (Prieto 2005). At the date of writing this book, significant translation errors continue to be

---

[15] Some have observed that there is some level of displacement in bee communication because they are adept at associative learning and communicate with other bees regarding the location and source of food, even hours later.

Yule explains this alleged displacement in bee communication this way:

> It is displacement of a very limited type. It just doesn't have the range of possibilities found in human language. Certainly, the bee can direct other bees to a food source. However, it must be the most recent food source. It cannot be "that delicious rose bush on the other side of town that we visited last weekend," nor can it be, … possible future nectar in bee heaven (2010:12).

Nevertheless, humans have total displacement available to them at any time and place, and at the tip of their tongue or their fingers.

made by software when translating from one language to another, even after multiple years of linguistic analysis and study in the field of computational linguistics. Machine translation will continue to improve and amaze us, but it is doubtful that computers will ever supersede our human, naturally complex, and potentially infinite linguistic capabilities.

1.2.9 Systematic

Because of the complexity of language, a well-developed system is required to marshal the rules of the phonological and grammatical systems and apply them correctly. Both the phonology and grammar of a language have complex organization of rules, patterns, and conventions. We discussed grammatical rules briefly when talking about the grammatical component in section 1.1.3. In a sense, the most important component of this organizational system is its grammar. We will discuss more regarding the rules and components of the grammatical system in chapter 3.

In addition to the nine features mentioned in sections 1.2.1–1.2.9, there are additional features of language studied by linguists. Charles Hockett in *Origin of Speech* (1960) investigated *design features*, or characteristics that distinguish human language from any other system of communication. Since the 1960s, other linguistic features have been added. Hockett includes both attributes of human language and attributes of communication systems observable in machines and animals. Although this book focuses primarily on human language, empirical evidence suggests that the nine design features are indeed features of non-human language. Like many theoretical visionaries, Hockett has been criticized by other linguists. However, all suggested features of language deserve further study. To that end, the exercises at the end of this chapter provide a way to consider these features using other people's perspectives.

1.3 The study of language: The field of linguistics

Fadua was born and raised in a mix of Berber, Arabic, and Spanish cultures, in Morocco, North Africa and in Spain. Due to her involvement in international projects, she also learned French and English. With these linguistic skills, she moved to the United States to study linguistics. She learned that studying language and linguistics helped her understand herself better. The interchange of languages and cultures had been confusing to her as a child. Due to her multiple cross-cultural and linguistic experiences, she had conflicting ideas of her own identity. When she studied language and linguistics more formally, that study of language helped her apply structure to her multicultural and multilingual awareness of herself and the world around her. She is now a successful professional in Europe, using these multicultural and multilingual skills, and maintaining a clear sense of self.

By now the reader should be convinced of the importance of language in our lives. If such a communicational and relational tool is so important, would it not be critical to understand it better? To do so requires study. LINGUISTICS is the domain in which language is analyzed and applied. It is *the scientific and systematic study of language and its structure*. Landsman describes scientific inquiry as the processes of research that involve critical "observing, questioning, gathering and learning background material, exchanging ideas and information, constructing or testing a hypothesis analyzing data, discussing findings, or drawing conclusions" (2005:ix). And that is what is involved in linguistic investigation.

> **What is Linguistics?**
>
> In a nutshell: Linguistics is the scientific study of language. Linguists apply the scientific method to conduct formal studies of speech sounds and gestures, grammatical structures, and meaning across the world's 6,000+ languages.

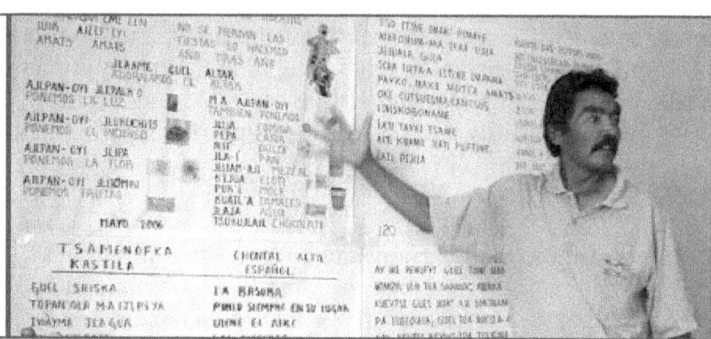

Figure 8. Definition of linguistics.

We study language for two basic reasons:
- to advance knowledge and science, and
- to improve important aspects of our lives.

The more we understand foundational communication as it relates to our lives, the more we will understand ourselves. That is how intellectual inquiry and science make a difference in our lives. We take for granted the study of our physical body (anatomy), our environment, our society, our history, politics, and so on. The study of language (*linguistics*) is equally important.

With a better understanding of language, we not only help advance scientific understanding in general but help avoid miscommunication between people. Some benefits of a better understanding of language and communication are that computers can be programmed to process language more naturally, and with improved translation software, people can overcome linguistic barriers internationally and transculturally; people with speech disorders can be assisted more effectively; and we can better understand how the communication centers in our brain function. The domain of linguistics began relatively recently, but the study of language by experts in other fields of science can be traced using a timeline, as the following exercise illustrates.

1.3 The study of language: The field of linguistics

Exercise 1: Timeline: language research (a brief history)

At the website: https://www.npr.org/series/5541690/exploring-language, scroll down and click on "Timeline: Evolution of Human Language Research." Following this pattern, list the main people, dates, and ideas developed, then draw a timeline to represent the chronology of the study of language. After completing this exercise, you will be able to identify some key names, dates, periods, theories, and works. This will give you an idea of the historical progression of the field of linguistics.

Person _____

Date _____

Idea _____

_____

Person _____

Date _____

Idea _____

_____

Person _____

Date _____

Idea _____

_____

Language and language research actually started well before the featured researchers in the timeline of exercise 1. Greek philosophers Aristotle, Socrates, and Plato, from the fourth and fifth centuries BC reflected on language. In fact, it is believed that Plato's renowned *Cratylus* is a treatise on language. Panini (an Indian Sanskrit grammarian who lived between the fourth and sixth centuries BCE), is the first to be considered a linguist and is known by many as the "father of linguistics."

Based on your reading of the article from exercise 1, you will have noticed that Rousseau, in the eighteenth century, is one of the first people officially recorded as a language investigator. During the nineteenth century, Broca and Wernicke did groundbreaking work in neurolinguistics. In the same century, Darwin gave his views on an instinct for language (further studied by Pinker in the 1990s). In the twentieth century, Chomsky, known as the "father of modern linguistics," gave us his *Theory of Universal Grammar* (UG) and his *Innateness Hypothesis* in the 1950s and 1960s.

There are many more linguists or language researchers with crucial investigative work on language. The following examples, like those from the timeline exercise, are commonly cited names in the field, whether in the field of general linguistics or its sub-branches: Sociolinguistics, psycholinguistics, syntax, morphology, phonology, dialectology, neurolinguistics, semantics, pragmatics, language acquisition, computational linguistics, and so on.

However, what we call modern linguistics did not really begin in earnest until the eighteenth century, as shown in the "Timeline" article studied in exercise 1. Apart from the philologists (linguists) mentioned in the timeline, others in scientific research combined their theoretical studies with linguistics, such as: Prussian ethnolinguist and philosopher, Wilhelm von Humboldt (1767–1835), who was elected as member of the American Philosophical Society in 1822. His linguistic notions were developed and popularized in the twentieth century. Lecture notes from Swiss historical-comparative linguist Ferdinand de Saussure, resulted in his *Course in General Linguistics* (1916). American structural linguist Leonard Bloomfield published his tome, *Language* in 1933. American Anthropologist-linguist Edward Sapir published *Introduction to the Study of Speech* (1921), which was the basis for the "Linguistic Relativity" hypothesis, or the "Sapir-Whorf Hypothesis," published by Sapir's student, Benjamin Lee Whorf, in 1956. Research in other fields related to linguistics include language acquisition (Lennerberg 1969), language teaching and learning (Krashen 1982), language in society (Labov 1994), computational linguistics, research in the language of medicine, and other similar lines of research.

The *linguistlist.org* website at Indiana University, a key source for current information about the field of linguistics around the world, lists about 30 fields of linguistic research for PhD dissertations. It shows that in the past two decades, linguistic dissertations continue to investigate traditional lines of research (e.g., morphology, syntax, applied linguistics, semantics/pragmatics, phonetics/phonology, sociolinguistics, historical linguistics, and language acquisition.) However, now we can also find many dissertations in less traditional fields such as: discourse analysis, computational linguistics, cognitive linguistics, and text/corpus linguistics. Even though many names and theories are not mentioned here, this gives an overview of the field of linguistics in past decades and in the current century.

Exercise 2: The benefit of studying language in your field.

1) The previous paragraphs give examples of other people who applied linguistic research to their field of study, and it was beneficial to them and the theory of their discipline. Refer to those examples and consider how the study of language can benefit you in your particular field of study, your dream job, occupation, or even a hobby. Write down your thoughts, giving specific examples.
2) Now, think of a friend, relative, or classmate who studies or works in a professional field or an occupation very different from yours (other than linguistics). How could understanding language better benefit or improve that field? Write down your thoughts as in the previous question but now for a field totally different from yours.

Exercise 3
1) Check the internet to find Hockett's *Language Design* features. Give a paraphrase of the *design* features that *only* belong to humans.
2) What evidence do you find that limits these features to humans?

Exercise 4
1) Now, compare your original thoughts about the "characteristics of language" (those you thought of before reading this section) with the ones described from the Hockett article. Which of the features you thought of match what is described in sections 1.2.1–1.2.9 and which ones do not?
2) If somebody tells you: "I listen to my puppy when he talks to me, and I understand him," what would you say about this statement based on the issues studied in this chapter?
3) Another student tells you, "My linguistics professor told me that 'the language of love' is not really a language." Would that be true—or false? How would you answer that person based on this chapter?

2

Do Animals and Robots Really Speak?

Every act of communication is a miracle of translation.

– Ken Liu

Figure 9. C-3PO, a science-fiction communicator.

In episode VI of popular science fiction "Star Wars," robot C-3PO, tells Han Solo, one of the main protagonists, that he is "fluent in over six million forms of communication." Due to this communication facility, especially as an on-the-spot interpreter, he is a key character in this saga. Wouldn't it be awesome to be able to communicate in so many languages? Even if C-3PO could interpret just six languages, that would be incredible! Thankfully you and I are at least fluent in one—and that is sufficient most of the time. We communicate, and we seem to express ourselves well. But, what, technically, do we mean by "communicate"? I have been using the term *communication* (and language ability) relatively freely, assuming you, as reader, share my understanding of the term. In this chapter, we will examine the nature and dynamics of communication more formally.

First, we will look at communication in general. Then we will describe three core systems of communication: Human communication, animal communication, and machine communication. The primary goal of the chapter is to contrast these different systems of communication and concurrently show the status of language unique to humans. In the process, we will discover that what animals and machines (and other non-humans) use to communicate cannot technically be called *language*, not in the sense of *language* from a scientific, or linguistic, perspective.

2.1 Communication

Communication is a miracle of interactive ability. As the quote by Liu says, we can introduce change in others and our surroundings in seconds by means of communicating. Animals, humans, and even machines communicate. Rosengren states that "all living beings communicate" (2000:1). He reminds us that etymologically, the word *communication* comes from *common*, asserting that "when we communicate, we make things common" (2000:1). In a basic, foundational sense, communication implies creating a *common sense*. A concept the speaker has is intentionally passed on to the hearer; the speaker may also receive a response from the hearer which creates a commonality. Feelings, ideas, messages, sensations are shared in common in the interactive process of communication.

Several decades ago, Shannon and Weaver (1949) postulated a mathematics-based model of communication which, due to its simplicity, has been critiqued as not representative of the dynamic and interactive aspect of communication. Figure 10a gives an approximation of that model.

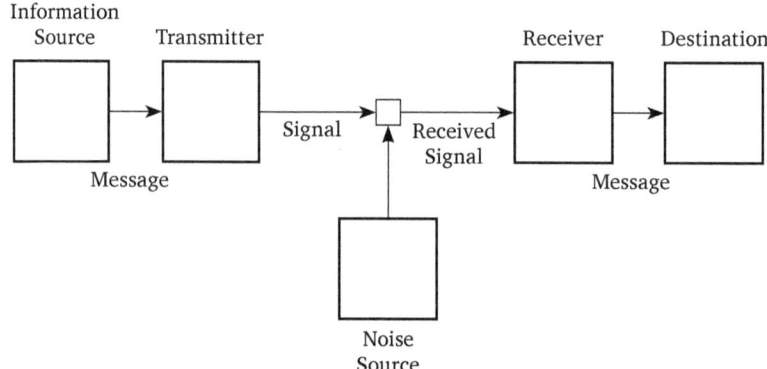

Figure 10a. The Shannon mathematics-based communication concept.

Today, communication is more widely understood to be more complex and interactive than simply one entity transmitting information to another via a common code. Figure 10b illustrates the lines of communication going in both directions, which better represents the interactive nature of communication.

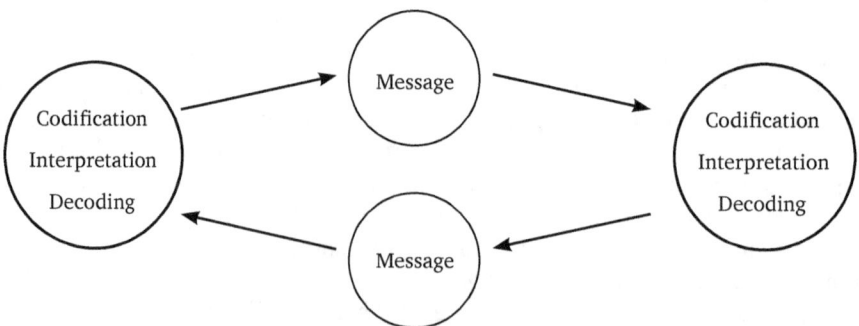

Figure 10b. The interactive communication process.

COMMUNICATION is defined as, "The result of any action (physical, written, or verbal) that conveys meanings between two individuals" *(Oxford Reference* 2024b). This implies a negotiated, interactive view of communication and allows for communication to happen both verbally and non-verbally. This book follows that general understanding and defines COMMUNICATION in its most basic sense as the interactive process between two or more entities where there is a sharing of ideas, information, and feelings, and an outcome of connection or community.

Following this definition, many entities in our world communicate. The question is, do we all communicate in the same way? We communicate because we need to and want to do so. Yet obviously each species does so differently. Notice that this sharing of information or ideas, messages, or sensations occurs by means of a mutually understood code of signs and symbols; otherwise, having information *in common* would rarely take place.

Some communication systems are more complex than others. For example, the system of communication used for traffic signs is simple compared to the Java computer programming language. The number of symbols and combinations of symbols is exponentially larger in computer programming language than for speed limit signs, stop signs, yield signs, street names, and the like. For a basic course on language programming, the number of rules and symbols to learn is significantly higher than the number of traffic signs a student driver needs to memorize to pass a written driver's license test. Regardless of their level of simplicity or complexity, both systems convey meaning and information from one entity to another. They each can be considered *systems of communication.*

Based on the content of chapter 1 and this section of chapter 2, we will see that human language involves the most complex system of communication imaginable, as compared with traffic signs or simple smoke signals, probably some of the least complex systems. The complexity of a system depends on the need and capacity of the entities communicating. Traffic signs are static and unidirectional. The driver does not interact with them to create additional meaning. Rather, they follow the model of communication described by figure 10a; their meaning is intentionally fixed and can mean only one thing. They are a rudimentary system of communication with only one specific purpose: control of road traffic. More highly developed systems are less restricted, and the range of communicative functions is significantly larger.

In sections 2.2 and 2.3, we will see that animals and machines can communicate, but not in the same way as humans can. Thus, when you see animals as animated characters such as Scooby Doo or C-3PO and R2-D2 speaking like people, you can be sure you are watching fiction or fantasy. Animal and machine communication cannot match the features of language described in chapter 1. Human communication (language) is intrinsically different from those other systems of communication. In linguistics, the term *language* technically refers only to the complex system of communication of humans. When people use expressions such as "machine language" or "my dog's language," people use the term loosely as a type of communication, but not as language, *per se*, as technically defined according to linguistics.

We will discuss more of the differences as we compare human communication with other systems of communication and will show the amazing complexity of human language. Some of these concepts were mentioned briefly when considering the features of language (section 1.2), but in chapter 2 we will expand further on the features of language in the general context of communication.

2.2 Human communication

Human communication occurs primarily via language, both oral and written. Although language is not the only means of communicating between people, it is the primary means. People also communicate using gestures, sign language, pictures, and so on, but these secondary means are much less in the public consciousness. Consider the examples that follow, which illustrate the amazing phenomenon of human communication via language.

In U.S. presidential elections, both in the Democratic and Republican primaries and later between the major parties, candidates take the stage to spar in nationally televised debates; likewise, volunteers supporting the major candidates take to the streets and phone for house-to-house or person-to-person campaigning. Additionally, ad campaigns promote the virtues of that party's candidate and disparage the opponent. The ability a candidate has to explain their agenda or outmaneuver the opponent orally often determines the basis for public support for that candidate, and the chance of winning an election often depends on the ability of one particular candidate to "win" public debates. Language is our primary tool for persuading others.

By means of speech, or language, (and at times, *only* via language), do we accomplish the following, expanding on what J. L. Austin (1962) suggests:

- Pass from the status of "single" to "married" by simple pronouncement: "I do", and "I pronounce you husband and wife." All that two people need are these statements, given in a specific context and by an authorized person, and *voila!*, they are married.
- Enter into war—in a matter of seconds—if the leader of a government says: "I declare war ...," a war begins. All a nation needs to become embroiled in war is a simple pronouncement by the head of that nation.
- Sentence people to death or life in prison. If a judge says, "This court sentences you ...," the accused person is held accountable to those words, whether condemned to death, to life in prison, or is granted freedom.

Figure 11. Pronouncements by a judge are final.

- Terminate the life of a patient with an incurable disease. Under certain circumstances, if an authorized relative gives formal written instructions to a doctor, that written permission is license for the doctor to disconnect the patient from life-sustaining machines.
- Accept or refuse an invitation or a position.
- Lie (with the potentially tragic consequences of that).
- Stay connected and interact with others by email, texting, Facebook, or other social media.
- Receive information that changes plans for one's life (a legal suit, a job offer, a legal summons).
- Initiate either a love relationship (a Valentine's Day card) or animosity (a notice of divorce).
- Discredit the reputation of another person.
- Compliment or offend a person, which may bring life-changing consequences.

Readers may be able to think of examples in their own lives where these suggested examples or similar ones reflect the life situations of someone they know. Featured in news reports recently, cyberbullying and name-calling illustrate how language has been used to harass and harm others. Demeaning language can permanently damage self-esteem, particularly of a young person. It is the cause of self-doubt, depression, even suicide. The prevalence of damaging language and personal attacks in social media is on the increase and the authorities do not yet know how to control it. One of the greatest but most fearful features of social media is potential for the newsbites to reach millions of the public in just minutes. Some people's fear of being discredited on social media can be overwhelming. A pejorative word like "ugly" connected to your name can be catastrophic. Words have power, for good and for bad. Yes, your language matters! Cyberbullying can be used with intent to destroy someone else's self worth. The example of figure 12 illustrates how language can cause others pain.

Figure 12. Cyberbullying: Language used to hurt.

I clearly remember an incident that happened 35 years ago when my mother, a retired nurse's assistant, said within my hearing: "I don't want any of my children to become a doctor or a nurse." I realize today that she said that out of frustration with the hospital administration where she was working, where she had repeatedly seen physicians and nurses be mistreated or judged unfairly. She did not want that for her children. When I heard her say that, right then and there I decided to discard my dream of becoming a medical doctor. Yes, words have power.

Language is intrinsically involved in most of the fundamental issues of life: professions, death, life, and love. Yes, language is important and must be used appropriately. A proverb in the Bible (Proverbs 18:21) says: "The tongue (language) has the power of life and death."

Oxford philosopher J. L. Austin (1962) states that when we use language, we "do things with words." By using language, we declare, we complain, we request, we invite, we promise, we accept, we refuse, and so on. These are what American philosopher John R. Searle called SPEECH ACTS. Both Austin and Searle established the foundation for what, in linguistics, is called Austin and Searle's (1969) "Speech Act Theory," the action the speaker wants to provoke in the listener (Nordquist 2019). Language is critical for our interactions, experiences, and resulting action as people. Human communication, then, unlike any other source or system of communication, presents the features and components mentioned in chapter 1 in combination with the functions and potentialities given in this section.

2.3 Animal communication

Even though animals do not have language, *per se*, in the strictest technical sense of the term used here, we cannot deny the fact that they communicate; and many times, they communicate in amazing ways. Each species of animal has a way of communicating among themselves. It is part of their instinct for survival.

Figure 13. Monkey communication.

In nature, we hear songs, hoots, and whistles; we see dances, exhibition of feathers, change of color; we smell unique odors, and we perceive many other aspects that are involved in communication among nature's creatures. But many of these may not be just odors or colors or songs, but ways in which many animals communicate. Humans may not understand the communication systems of that species, but there is communication taking place between animals all the time; and these systems of communication, like human communication can also be relatively complex and systematic.

Nature programs today clearly demonstrate animal communication. After watching videos on YouTube, National Geographic, PBS, and BBC, and answering the questions in examples 1–3, you should be able to draw a conclusion about how much of this animal communication can truly be called *language*. According to the Natural History Museum (2008:95), apes are the most intelligent of all great primates (gorillas, chimpanzees, bonobos, and orangutans). Of these, Koko, the Gorilla has been identified as the most developed animal in the world in terms of intelligence, having learned as many as 2,000 American Sign Language (ASL) signs and English words, by the age of 30. We will discuss more about Koko later. The Natural History Museum recognizes that there are records of these achievements, but these achievements come after much training, and is equivalent to language at a "rudimentary level" (Natural History Museum 2008:95). For comparative purposes, a five-year-old child can recognize up to 10,000 words in their receptive language. For children, this happens without any language instruction. Regarding children's receptive learning, O'Grady says that "the grammatical knowledge needed to use and understand language is acquired without the benefit of instruction" (O'Grady 2005:9). There is a significant difference between human and animal systems of communication, as will be re-emphasized later.

By means of these exercises you can draw your own conclusions regarding animal communication.

Exercise 1: Examples of animal communication:

On the internet, look for videos, audio recordings, text files, or websites that describe the system of communication of the following animals:

	Communication strategy	Message
Humpback whales		
Orcas		
Dolphins		
Apes		

Exercise 2: Is animal communication "language?"

For orangutans and others, and a deeper coverage on animals' communication, watch the "Contemplating Creatures" video from the Museum of Science of Boston or a similar one. This video is more than 60 minutes. It is academic and scientifically oriented, perhaps more than others. You don't have to watch all this video but at least watch the sections in which some scientists are apparently arguing for the animals' communication as "language." You can focus on minutes 11–13, 19–21, 23–25 and 26:30–27:30 particularly, where Dr. Rob Shumaker is arguing for a relatively "elevated cognitive capacity" of orangutans; based on "symbolic vocalization," tool use, and social learning. After you watch these sections, answer the following three questions based on what you saw.

a) Restate, in your own words, what Dr. Shumaker is saying.
b) How might that connect with "language" particularly?
c) Present your arguments for or against Dr. Shumaker's arguments.

I encourage the reader to think more deeply about the alleged "elevated cognitive capacity" of orangutans, based on "symbolic vocalization." Is this factor sufficient evidence to suggest they emulate human language?

Exercise 3: The "language" of apes:

Visit the website http://www.npr.org/templates/story/story.php?storyId=5541690. ("Exploring Language: What Lies Beneath," an NPR program on language). Listen to "A voluble visit with 2 talking apes." Would you call this "language?" Why or why not?

Geoffrey K. Pullum, a British-American linguist and co-author of The Cambridge Grammar of the English Language (2002), upon seeing the video, argued that the apes did not come close to demonstrating communication at the level of human language interaction. His point is that

> the apes in question (the bonobos Kanzi and Panbanisha) never utter a single sentence, word, syllable, or anything other than shrieks (their productive capacities, are limited to touching symbols on a board or a computer screen, usually to fulfill an immediate desire). And not one example was offered of the animals putting even two symbols together according to some linguistic rule." (Pullum 2006)

Pullum's arguments are shared by other linguists. This does not diminish the amazing complexity of animal communication; it is simply to keep in focus the fact that animal communication is far from what we know about human language.

2.4 Machine communication

Machine communication is technically and more accurately called "machine code" rather than *language* but the term "machine language" has been used a lot in relation to computers. Code is essentially the only language computers can understand. The *Encyclopedia Britannica* defines code to communicate with computers as a binary system of ones and zeroes. Computers do not understand a language as we know it, just ones and zeroes. According to this encyclopedia, to give a computer a command to add two numbers, it can look this way: "*0110101100101000.*" Since human language does not work that way, there has to be an intermediary or "translator" called the "assembly language." This sequence of zeroes and ones is roughly translated as "add pay; total."

Figure 14. Image created by binary code.

According to Bonnice (2014) computer programmers write code with instructions that people expect computers to follow, but in a way that computers can understand the directives. Examples of programming languages are Python, C++, and Java. They are logically sequenced step-by-step instructions, at some point using the binary 1-0 code. The computer cannot do more than follow the instructions it has been trained to follow. It will not make up new words or use more words or expressions than the ones that have been input into its Central Processing Unit (CPU).

In 2019, a group of robotics experts published a paper about their efforts to train the child-like robot *iCub* to say "no." According to them it was the first successful attempt for a robot (computer) or an Artificial Intelligence (AI) device to learn linguistic expressions other than nouns and verbs. The complication of negations like "no" results from the fact that it is a non-referential word; it has no visual or tangible referent, unlike nouns and verbs. This is a complicated area of communication in which computers, robots, and AI struggle. Typically, there is sensory-motor training for robots to learn language, but a word like "no," as simple as it is for children to produce, is a challenge for non-humans. As the paper continued to reveal, even after much research and work, they were successful most, but not all of, the time. This is not an issue with humans (Förster et al. 2019:24).

The robotics experts recognized that to be more successful in these efforts, a better understanding of the linguistic negation dynamics between humans is needed, more "detailed data on the precise dynamics [of] how prohibition in mother-child dyads is enacted." (Förster et al. 2019:24). Although Förster and others have accomplished a lot, AI devices are still far from creating, using, and processing human language as people do. If people are far from a complete understanding of human intelligence and human language, how can we create artificial intelligence and language that behaves like what is innate to humans?

The amazingly complex AI communication available in our world today is being improved rapidly. AI is "the study of how to make computers do things at which, at the moment, people are better." (Ertel 2018:2). Ubiquitous AI systems are even named, e.g., Siri, Echo, and Alexa; and Amazon.com personalizes Alexa: "Alexa is Amazon's voice AI. Alexa lives in the cloud and is happy to help .... Making Alexa part of your day ..."

These portable devices are available to us via a dedicated device, cellphone, and anywhere there is an internet connection available. ChatGPT and other modes of interaction with the technology now available, interact with people as prompted, delivering information to people who know how to harness it. Still, machine communication is a one-way prompt-response service, much as is illustrated in figure 10a, section 2.1. It is not creative, and depends entirely upon databases, electricity, code language, internet, and equipment, all provided by humans. It is not truly interactive since it cannot initiate a conversation, or dialogue with someone without a prompt. And it has no filters or sensitivity to emotion, nonverbals, figures of speech, pragmatic competence, and social register.

2.4 Machine communication

NPR Radio created a series of talks and programs about robotic language entitled, "What Lies Beneath" (beneath language rules, words, and sounds). After you read these stories as exercises, in combination with what is discussed in the rest of the chapter, you will have a good basis on which to compare systems of communication of machines and animals, with the complex, creative, and potentially infinite language ability that humans possess.

Figure 15. The unique metaphorical and social nature of human language.

Exercise 4 introduces Ripley the Robot, another example of robotic language, based on the following NPR Radio program:

Exercise 4: "Exploring Language: What Lies Beneath." (NPR program on language) http://www.npr.org/templates/story/story.php?storyId=5541690.

1) Read the story, "The Inner World of Ripley the Robot." What is similar and what is different between Ripley's communication and that of a seven-year-old child's, or a teenager's?
2) Read the article, "Autism Reveals Social Roots of Language". What does the article attempt to prove?
3) What is your opinion about the issues revealed in the previous two articles?
4) Based on what you read so far, and your own knowledge and experience, what are the ways in which human communication and machine communication are the same and different?

<u>Same</u>   <u>Different</u>

3
Is Your Grammar Good?

A man's grammar, like Caesar's wife, should not only be pure, but above suspicion of impurity.

– Edgar Allan Poe

"I won't hire people who use poor grammar," said Kyle Wiens, CEO of *iFixit*, a large online repair group and founder of *Dozuki*, a software company that helps other companies publish documentation. This article appeared on the *Harvard Business Review* website in the "Managing Yourself" section (Wiens 2012). Admittedly, Wiens has some good points in his article. No doubt that, for a company that manages document publication in English, complying with standard rules of the English language is crucial. However, Wien's pronouncement underlies a potential problem—and that may be related to what his view is of "grammar." What might be included in the *poor grammar* label for Wiens? Or what are the features of *good grammar* in Wien's opinion? Who gets to decide what the specifics are of this *poor grammar*? And what rules should the public abide by to avoid using that *poor grammar*?

A major, more pertinent question, emerges here: What do Wiens and others mean when they refer to *grammar*? It is possible that your views match Wien's, but it is also possible that you disagree with his views because, in reality there are different opinions about what constitutes *grammar, poor grammar,* and *good grammar.* This chapter explains the concept of grammar in the field of linguistics. We will exemplify it with grammar rules, and in this way reintroduce core areas of linguistics introduced in chapter 1: phonology, morphology, and syntax (see especially section 1.3).

3.1 What we mean by grammar

Both the chapter 3 epigram by Edgar Allen Poe and Kyle Wiens's idealism project high standards that we may feel we can't meet since the study of grammar may not have been a strong subject matter in grade school. High expectations by teachers in primary school may reverberate in our ears, their insistence that we speak and write using "correct grammar."

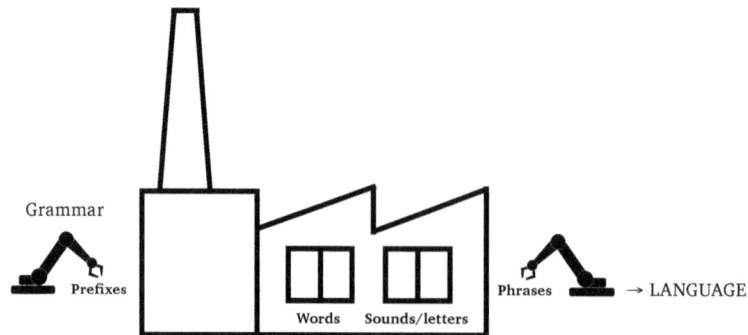

Figure 16. Grammar=tools that combine the elements of language.

However, as a native English speaker, you know intuitively how English grammar works. GRAMMAR is simply the *mechanics that correctly combines sounds, words, and phrases*. You learned all of those elements quite naturally, otherwise you would not be able to communicate orally. We absorb all these rules naturally, without formal instruction, by about three years of age. Yes, a normal three-year-old child may not be able to *explain* English grammar but *uses* grammar well. (Lust 2006:10).

The fact that you are reading this textbook and understand it shows that you know the rules of English; otherwise, even the title of the book would not make sense to you. You know the grammar of your particular variety of English. Maybe you don't know all the rules of higher-level formal English, or correct speech patterns of Irish English, but you know the rules of your own variety of English. That is a crucial distinction. And at times you can bend the rules of grammar for the sake of convenience.

Figure 17 illustrates that, at times, the rules of orthography or spelling may be modified. A person who is thinking, "You are my friend!" might text, "Your my friend!" due to the phonological or pronunciation similarities between you're and your, or simply to save time in texting.

Figure 17. Good intuitive grammar.

Of course, switching *your* and *you're* is not a good idea when writing for a class assignment in college but in non-formal situations this usage does not mean a person has intuitively poor grammar. Undoubtedly the youth in figure 17 could explain orally to you just what she meant in her text message.

3.2 Grammar rules: Examples

Do you know how many (intuitive) rules or patterns you need to express a well-formed English sentence? Again, you know these rules—at least subconsciously. You may not verbalize them formally in the way they are presented here, but you have these norms imprinted in your mind and use them appropriately when you talk. Let's discuss six of these rules.

3.2.1 Rule 1: Phonology—There is a structured order to sounds of a word

PHONOLOGY deals with speech sounds and how they affect meaning. A rule of phonology is that sounds follow a set order to convey a specific meaning. In any language the order of the sounds in a word must be maintained. As an example, three phones in English are [i] (pronounced "ee"), [d], and [r]. These can be given in any order as individual phones. However, if combined to form a word like [r] [i] [d] (*read),* the phonemes must follow that order.[1] If you reorder these phones differently, such as [dir] (*dear* or *deer),*[2] the word would mean something else entirely. Thus, the same sounds reordered create a word with a very different meaning. And reordered as **ird* or **idr,* the utterance[3] has no meaning at all. Phoneme order in a word follows a strict expectation for every English word, and for words in every language. This confirms what we studied earlier, that meaning can be built of meaningless units, such as phonemes. The [r] in *read* only contributes to meaning in connection with [-id] (*-ead),*[4] when spoken or written in that order. The same can be said for every word formed by the sounds in the phonology of a language.

3.2.2 Rule 2: Phrase structure—There is a structured order to words in a phrase

A PHRASE is a string of words with a head, either a noun (N) or a verb (V), and an optional modifier. In a noun phrase (NP) the head of the phrase is a noun, and an adjective (Adj) is the modifier. An example of a NP is *new book* (Adj-N), where *new* modifies or describes *book.*

In Spanish, the NP structure is N-Adj, with the modifier following the noun.

Table 1. Adj-N phrase structure in English versus N-Adj in Spanish

Adj-N phrase structure	new book
N-Adj phrase structure	*libro nuevo*

When the head of a phrase in English is a V, an adverb (Adv) is the modifier. An example of a verb phrase is, *read slowly* (V-Adv), where the V *read* is modified by the Adv *slowly,* or how the book is read. Phrase structure rules change from one phrase type to another within a language, and from one language to another. Even a dialect, or variety of a language, may have its own rules that vary from another variety of that language. In some languages, word order is less structured than English. These "free-order" languages have a different grammatical rules to avoid confusion, as we will see for Latin, in section 3.2.3.

---

[1] [rid] is the phonetic transcription of the verb "to read", as in, "I read the news daily."
[2] Dear and deer are homophones (different spelling, same pronunciation).
[3] An asterisk marks utterances or words that have no meaning or are not true words.
[4] Read ([rid] present tense) and read ([red] past tense) are homographs (same spelling, different pronunciation).

3.2.3 Rule 3: Morphology—Word affixes carry grammatical meaning in a sentence

MORPHOLOGY deals with the internal structure of a word. Some words have smaller parts that have a function or meaning. In addition to a structured word order most languages use affixes to change the meaning of a sentence. An AFFIX can occur at the beginning of a word (prefix), occur in the middle of a word (infix), or occur at the end of a word (suffix).

As was explained earlier, the word "tables" has two parts, or two *morphemes,* both *table* and the suffix *-s* have a meaning or a function within that word. Some languages do not have a fixed word order but depend more heavily on suffixes to change the meaning of a sentence; this complies with the morphological rule of that language—the notions of subject and object are carried by suffixes attached to a word rather than the word order. Classical Latin is an example of such a language. The Latin suffix *-us* indicates that the noun it marks is the subject of the verb, regardless of the position of the word in the sentence; whereas *-um* indicates that the word it marks is the direct object of the sentence.

In the following three-word examples in Latin, *canis* means 'dog', *domini* is 'master', and *amat* means 'loves'. The words in each of the possible sentences are given in a different order. Pay attention to the word order, the different internal parts of each noun, and the translation in English.

- *dominus canem amat* = the master loves the dog
- *dominus amat canem* = the master loves the dog
- *canem dominus amat* = the master loves the dog
- *canis dominum amat* = the dog loves the master
- *canis amat dominum* = the dog loves the master

Considering the meaning of the Latin suffixes in figure 18, translate what the Roman emperor said:

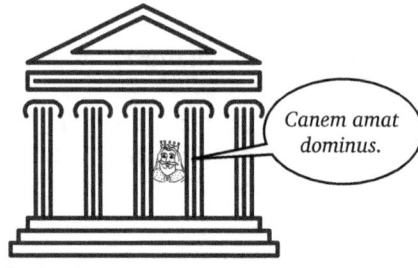

Figure 18. Translation of the Latin = _____.

Why is "The master loves the dog" the correct answer? It is because *domini* (master) ends in *-us*, a suffix that indicates that "the master" is the subject of the sentence. Each native speaker of a language learns intuitively and can correctly use the agreement rules that mark subject and object.

3.2.4 Rule 4: Syntax—Word order carries meaning in a sentence

SYNTAX is the area of grammar that deals with word order and structure at the phrase and sentence level. The following, as previously discussed, is the *syntactic* rule in English: the subject (S) of a sentence typically occurs at the beginning of a sentence, then the verb (V), and then the object (O). This is called an SVO language. An example of this sentence type is: "The students read the new book." If you change the order to "the new book reads the students," the sentence means something else, or nothing at all. This rule describes English and other languages like Spanish, but it is not the same rule for all languages. Some languages have

3.2 Grammar rules: Examples 31

an SOV order, which is the most common syntactic word order of all languages (Velupillai 2012:284). Languages like Japanese are SOV (Lehmann 1978:78). Other languages such as Classical Hebrew, are VSO (Lehmann 1978:416), and so on. Table 2 illustrates the SVO syntactic rule as it applies to English. You can use a similar breakdown of S, V, and O, and apply it to any language you have learned to see how they compare to English.

Table 2. A syntactic English rule for basic sentence formation

S	V	O
Subject	Verb	Object
The students	watch	the new movie
	The students watch the new movie.	

3.2.5 Rule 5: Morphosyntax—Affixes and word order coordinate to change meaning

If *morphology* affects the internal structure of a word and *syntax* affects how words are ordered in a phrase or sentence, MORPHOSYNTAX affects the meaning of a complete sentence based on a coordination of morphology (word suffixes) and syntax (internal sentence structure). Native speakers of a language have learned how that coordination affects meaning. In the present-tense sentence, "The students watch the new movie," if you want to refer to just *one* student, you automatically remove the suffix "-s" from the word "students." However, again in the present tense, you have learned that "*The student watch the new movie," is not a properly formed sentence and you add an "-es" suffix at the end of "watch," to structure the sentence correctly: "The student *watches* the new movie." There is the expectation of a match between the subject (S) and the verb (V) for a correctly structured sentence. This coordination is known as "agreement" or "concordance." See table 3,[5] which illustrates S-V concordance in English[5] and N-Adj agreement in Spanish.

Table 3. Agreement of S-V and N-Adj

S-V	The *students* watch the new movie
Agreement/concordance →	The student *watches* the new movie
N-Adj agreement, gender/number →	*Chicas buenas* 'good girls'
(Spanish)	*Chico bueno* 'good boy'

Other languages have other types of agreement. For example, it is common in Swahili (Kiswahili—a Bantu language in East Africa) to have O-V agreement; not only does the V agree with the S, but also with the object (O), or more precisely, the direct object. As illustrated in

---

[5] Note that the "-s" concluding the noun *students* doesn't have the same meaning as the "-es" concluding the verb *watches* (or "-s" in *reads*); they just happen to sound the same and have the same spelling. In fact, these are grammatically different suffixes in English, with different meanings that are consistent within their grammatical word class:
- An *-s* (attached to a noun, *students*) has the idea of plurality of a noun. If this (nominal) *-s* were attached to a different noun (like *book*), the *-s* still adds to the noun the idea of plurality (*books*).
- The suffix *-es/-s* (attached to a verb, *watches/reads*) contributes the idea that a singular subject is performing the action and that the action is occurring now. When this verbal *-es/-s* is attached to a different action, (*writes*), this *-s* suffix likewise communicates that the subject performing the action is singular (I, s/he, or it), and the action is occurring at this point in time.

table 3, many gender-based languages like Spanish have N-Adj agreement, where the N and Adj match in both gender and number; English, does not have Adj-N agreement.[6]

3.2.6 Rule 6: Discourse—Context affects meaning in a narrative

We have considered *phonology,* the sounds of a language; *morphology,* how affixes change the meaning of a word and sentence; *syntax,* how structured word order can change the meaning of a sentence; and *morphosyntax,* how morphology and syntax coordinate, affecting the meaning of a sentence. We will now consider a higher-level concept of grammar that people sometimes overlook when they study their own language, DISCOURSE.

If you were to delete the last article ("the") in this sentence, "The students read the new book," you would need an "-s" (plural suffix) to mark the noun, "book." The article *the* serves two purposes. It tells the listener/reader both that a) the book is singular and b) how definite or indefinite the noun is. *The* makes *book* definite, meaning that the book was previously introduced in conversation or is commonly known or understood by both the source (speaker/writer) and receptor (listener/reader). By use of the definite article it can be assumed that both the speaker and hearer know what book (or object) is being referred to. Otherwise, the speaker would give an indefinite article ("a"), which suggests that this is the first mention of *book* in the conversation or discourse.[7]

The concept of discourse structure is as innate as are the other grammatical concepts, just not as thoroughly studied in school. But the instinctive, natural way to organize grammar at a discourse level can be observed in your daily speech, in your writing, in any speech event or written communication in which you are involved. Imagine how unusual it would be if a friend came up to you, and out of the blue said: "Hey, I bought the car today!" versus "Hey, I bought a car today!" If there is no common background regarding "car," then in response to the first sentence you would probably say, "*What* car?" The first sentence sounds puzzling, whereas the second one sounds natural; however, if the topic "car" had previously been introduced and you knew what your friend was referring to, the first sentence would sound natural (you both know what *the car* refers to) and the second sentence would sound stilted ("Why is he saying *a car* when he told me about the car yesterday?").

Definiteness is just one example of discourse-level grammar. Average English speakers use the discourse grammar concept quite naturally. Perhaps you were never taught about discourse-level grammar before; if you weren't, even before discussing it in today's lesson, you still quite naturally apply discourse structure correctly when speaking.

3.3 Grammar options: Just options, not linguistic superiority markers

It is important to re-emphasize here that there is nothing superior about the rules of one language versus another, for example, Adj-N versus N-Adj order, both are valid grammatical options observed in different languages.

By the age of three, as a native speaker of English, you learned almost all the grammar rules for English, including others not mentioned in this book. You use these grammatical patterns, rules, and mechanics quite appropriately when you talk and when you interpret what other people tell you.

---

[6] Notice, as explained in section 3.2.1, that in Spanish the noun precedes the adjective, hence N-Adj; in English the word order is reversed, Adj-N.
[7] Indefiniteness may be indicated by a speaker either with an indefinite article or by making the noun plural: "The students read a new book," or "The students read new books."

All languages are characterized by a system of rules or grammar patterns, and there are innate restrictions on what is possible for human languages. This is what Noam Chomsky called Universal Grammar (1965). Some patterns seem to be common to all languages, like the distinction between nouns and verbs. As discussed, many languages have a syntactic pattern for organizing the order of the S, V, and O (SVO, VOS, SOV) and other parts. In other languages, the word order system does not seem to be as dominant and word order patterns can change for specific purposes (such as focus or emphasis). Lambrecht refers to this in his tome, *Information Structure and Sentence Form*. In Slavic languages, for example, "non-thematic constituents may occur sentence-initially," and this may have to do with the issue of emphasis (Lambrecht 1994:201).

Let me exemplify this diversity of grammar options with plural formation as well. The plural "-s" as discussed in 3.2.5, may not be used in other languages, like Mandarin, where there is not a bound suffix that indicates plurality because, unlike English, they do not need it; classifiers or measure words indicate number. In some languages, like Classical Hebrew, if the action expressed by the verb is performed by a female, then the verb requires a different marking than it does if the subject is a male; this is a grammar-gender marking rule. In (Ki) Swahili, there are noun affixes that indicate if the nouns refer to humans or non-humans, animate or inanimate entities.

A final example is about different grammatical options. As suggested earlier (section 3.2.3), what one language marks with an affix, another language might mark using a whole word, word order, or even phonological tone. The grammatical systems and patterns for every language is highly complex and of equal status as is English. Speakers of one language should never devalue or disparage another language or the speakers of languages different from our own.

Although English speakers learn English grammar as a child and master grammar rules quite unconsciously, there is more we can learn about our own language and how it compares with other world languages. There is value in continuing to learn and apply language skills in the context of institutions of higher learning, in professional contexts, and for putting your best foot forward in any situation. There is also value in learning about *other* languages and learning to speak other languages in our ever-shrinking world.

3.4 Grammar options: Worldview and culture trait markers

The grammar rules of a language may reflect the world around the speech community of that language. The Sapir-Whorf Hypothesis (Carroll 1956) includes the idea that our language (its structures and words) reflects the way we see the world. Typically, concepts, nuances of meaning, or communicational aspects that are marked in the grammar of a language depend on the cultural realities or the WORLDVIEW and dynamics of a particular speech community. Carole Lange suggests: "The way we express ourselves with words communicates our culture and reflects our character" (2023). Pointing to how the pandemic affected speech in 2020, and how the society crafted language that fit the times, Lange says:

> "Rhetoric," "misinformation," "disinformation" and a flood of words related to the pandemic, campaigns and social media dominate the press and conversations. Lexicographers around the globe chose "lockdown" as their 2020 word of the year because of its "unifying experience for billions of people across the world." …
>
> Whether in English or another language, words reflect events, discoveries, new products and changes in culture. Neologisms, sniglets and changing definitions are also subjects of this month's curriculum guide. The use of "they" to refer to a singular subject, punctuation gone wild, and the worldwide use of "okay" and "lockdown" make one wonder who is in charge of language use and acceptance. And make language purists cringe. …

"Rhetoric"—its classic techniques of persuasion and its more recent meaning of lacking substance—filled many print columns and airwaves this year. Promises on the campaign circuit, announcements of vaccines soon to arrive and crowds yelling at rallies are just a few of the many instances of rhetoric that reflect current culture and a country's character.

The vocabulary of the Eskimo-Aleut language family includes many words for snow, first analyzed by Franz Boas in the late nineteenth century. Laura Kelly explains the phenomenon of an environment that shaped a vocabulary, made possible due to their polysynthetic or fusional language. Where English might label types of snow using a descriptive phrase, the Innuit language may have up to 50 individual snow lexemes, including the following:

- *qanuk* 'snowflake'
- *kaneq* 'frost'
- *kanevvluk* 'fine snow'
- *qanikcaq* 'snow on ground'
- *muruaneq* 'soft deep snow'
- *nutaryuk* 'fresh snow'
- *pirta* 'blizzard'
- *qengaruk* 'snow bank' (Kelly 2021)

Spanish marks gender in nouns, in part due to the Latin history of the language: Latin is the root of the Romance language family that categorizes nouns by classes using specific suffixes—for example grammatical gender. One class of nouns is marked by gender; they include a feminine suffix in contrast to another class of nouns marked by a masculine suffix. (See table 3, section 3.2.5, for an example of the masculine versus feminine marking in Spanish.) The distinction between feminine and masculine gender marking is affected by biological gender when it refers to humans and animals, but also marks nouns that have nothing to do with biological gender. It is called *case* marking. When gender suffixes are used to mark a subject, the suffix marking that noun is called nominative case; when the suffix marks an object, that noun marker is called an accusative case. Additionally, if the subject is a masculine-class noun, it would use a different suffix than the ones used by the feminine-class nouns. Very likely, Spanish received the legacy of feminine versus masculine classification and marking from Latin. English is in the Germanic language family and consequently does not behave like Romance languages in this respect.

For some languages or cultures, like the ancient Native American language Haida (Boas 1911) and the Purepecha (Tarascan) language in Mexico (Friedrich 1971), the shape of an object appears to be important for everyday communication. In those languages affixes classify some objects according to shape. This is part of what Friedrich calls "geometrical semantics" or the semantics of shape. Shape is apparently a salient feature in some languages for certain objects or tasks. If you have experience in construction, you know that the shape of a board or 2x4 plank is critical. Likewise, the shape of an object might be more relevant for some people than others, and in some contexts more than others. Boas put it this way: "each language has a peculiar tendency to select this or that aspect of the mental image" (1911:43). In the case of the Purepecha ethnic group, they traditionally lived in the context of agriculture and ceramics. Shape for them is crucial. The shape of the pot, the shape of the field, the shape of the seeds they plant, and so on. As a result, they have several affixes marking shape, such as "longish," "bounded," "rounded," and the like (Friedrich 1971). Similarly, the Navajo language uses the affix *-á* or *-a* to categorize nouns according to a rounded shape. See figure 19.

3.4 Grammar options: Worldview and culture trait markers

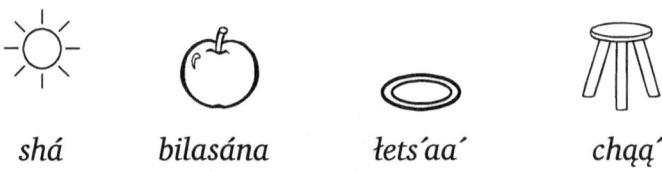

Figure 19. Navajo geometrical semantics.

What is common here? The solid, round shape. Navajo expresses that idea in the last "a" of each word.

In the Quechua and Aymara languages of South America, a pair of suffixes called *evidentials* mark how certain the speaker is of what they are saying, or of their data source (Hardman 1988). The two evidentials are -*mi* (assertive) and -*si* or -*shi* (reportative). If -*mi* is used e.g., *allillanmi* 'I am well', there can be no doubt the person speaks for himself. If -*si* or -*shi* is used, it indicates either that what the person says is reported speech *or* that it may not be reliable information. So, if a colleague says about his sick friend: "'*allillanmi,' nispa ninsi*," (the colleague reported), "He said, 'I am well,'" (sharing what his sick friend said who is not in the room). With -*si* used, there could be some doubt that the other person really is recovering his health.

Alexandra Aikhenvald explains further about evidentials, pointing to the fact that being precise and clarifying the source of a person's spoken information is important to both the language and culture in these Andean societies. Failure to use evidentials properly can diminish a person's social place in the community (2004:380). A Quechua ethical proverb teaches the importance of being truthful (and precise regarding one's source of information): *Ama suwa, ama llulla, ama qhella*: 'don't steal, don't lie, don't be lazy'. Accuracy of spoken information and source in speech is a high cultural value—and a precise communication tool reflected in the morphology of this Andean language.

Students or teachers of a second language (L2) can apply a principle related to understanding the grammar of that L2. While first learning to speak an unfamiliar language, the learner would do well to study features of the grammar of the L2 that are different from their own first language (L1) and focus on learning the rules of the grammar that are different from the learner's L1. For example, the subjunctive mood is a feature of Spanish that is not understood well by English speakers. It is one of three moods in Spanish, the indicative, the imperative, and the subjunctive. The subjunctive allows the speaker to give virtual information, as an emotional perception or bias toward something, instead of simply reporting factual information. Subjunctive use in Spanish is marked as a suffix on verbs. If a verb like "learn," is in the subjunctive mood in, "I hope you learn fast" (where a hope is expressed), then a subjunctive mood would be used, (*aprendas*). In contrast, when someone says, "you learn fast," *learn* (*aprendas*) expresses a fact; it is in the indicative mood. Spanish speakers make a natural distinction between these two verb forms by use of suffix differences. English speakers, however, do not distinguish the subjunctive use as a grammatical category; it is simply used as *learn* in both situations. As a native Spanish speaker and teacher of Spanish, I can recognize the potential for confusion and try to highlight this indicative-subjunctive distinction for non-native Spanish-speaking students and train them to discern this distinction.

Figure 20 illustrates a typical response when first attempting to teach the Spanish subjunctive to L1 speakers of English.

Español 201

Figure 20. Tuning up and tuning in for L2 acquisition.

For any person, then, the process of learning a second language (L2) different from their mother tongue can be very beneficial to tune their eyes, ears, and minds to those nuances of the L2 grammar that are not in their L1, or that are very different. Getting to know L2 native speakers, their reality and worldview, their history, and their environment may help in tuning into an L2, in the process known as second language acquisition (SLA).

Evaluate a language using the system and worldview of that second language, not using English. Expecting to see a definite article in your L2 simply because English uses a definite article is ethnocentric.[8] If you want to communicate with people of the language you choose to learn, speak like them, think like them, emphasize in their grammar whatever they emphasize and ignore what they ignore. (For example, not every language uses definite articles, or plural markers.) A great example of adaptability in life for an important goal, biblical author, Apostle Paul, once wrote:

> While working with the Jews, I live like a Jew in order to win them. ... In the same way, when working with the Gentiles, I live like a Gentile. ... I become all things to all people, that I may save some of them by whatever means are possible. (1 Corinthians 9:20–22 [*GNT*])

The following reflection questions will help you continue to think about these issues. Some do not have a right or wrong answer but provide food for thought. Some questions do expect a particular type of answer based on the discussion in this chapter. You are encouraged to go back and review these ideas. Open your eyes and ears to communication around you, physically or virtually, where these issues might be present, both overtly and covertly. The goal of the exercises is to think intelligently about these issues.

---

[8] Ethnocentrism = assuming your culture and language are the center of the world or the "default" system, and consequently expecting other cultures and people who speak other languages to accommodate to you.

3.4 Grammar options: Worldview and culture trait markers 37

For now, though, just...

Figure 21. Keep calm and ...

Exercises

1) Ask five people around you to define "grammar" for you. Report on these five definitions and write a conclusion paragraph where you report on the misconceptions you found, if any.
2) Ask these same people (or others) to give you one example of "bad English grammar" or "poor English grammar" used by native speakers of English, if they think there is such an issue. List those examples. Then, write a paragraph of your own opinion about this list. Indicate in that paragraph why you agree or disagree with them in relation to these examples of "bad" or "poor" grammar.
3) This week, while you are browsing the internet or interacting with people, in writing, face to face, virtually, or some other way, pay attention to examples of bad or poor English grammar on the part of native speakers of English. Write a paragraph with conclusions about your observation.
4) Interact with a non-native speaker of English somehow. Or browse the internet to find samples of non-native English speakers' writing or oral production. Indicate one English grammar rule that seems to be problematic for this person or these people. Based on what you studied in this chapter, hypothesize the potential reasons why this English grammar rule may be hard for them.
5) Write a paragraph about the status of your own grammar: Is it good? poor? bad? in between? Explain why you concluded this about your own grammar.
6) What are some of the limitations of language?
7) What are some of the advantages of language over other forms of communication?
8) Is the grammar of a teenager as complete as the grammar of a 40 year-old person? Explain.
9) When can native speakers of English say "ain't" or use double negation: never, sometimes, always? Explain.
10) What's one thing learned in chapter 3 that may have changed your view on anything?

4

What Do We Mean When We Talk?

*It's important to make sure that we're talking with each other
in a way that heals, not in a way that wounds.*

– Barack Obama

Rebekah, a former student of mine and a missionary kid (MK) raised in Guinea, Africa, came back to the United States for college. One day, during her first semester in college, she saw an older professor carrying a heavy box and she asked him if he needed help, and he said, "No, of course not!" and looked offended. She grew up surrounded by the Fulani culture in Guinea and the professor grew up in the U.S.A. What this question probably meant to the professor was: "You seem like you are not strong enough for that box," or even worse, "you are old, weak." Age-related implications such as these may be taboo in the American majority culture. However, in the Fulani culture, it is expected for younger people to offer help to older people. It is a way of honoring and respecting the elderly. In the mind of the MK, it meant: "I respect you and honor you, and that is why I offer my help." For the professor, it meant: "You are old and weak, and that is why I offer my help, my strength, my youth." If you had said that phrase in that context, what would you mean?

"What do you mean?" "I see what you mean." "What I mean is ...," and other utterances like these are expressions that tell you about our real need for language to mean something.

Yes, the main reason to use language is to convey meaning. That is what I mean! And that is the primary purpose of this chapter: To elaborate, at an introductory level, on what meaning in language or *linguistic meaning* is. This chapter will serve, then, primarily as an introduction to the specific subfield of *semantics*.

Interestingly, we may start our linguistic communication with meaningless units, but communication doesn't end there. As shown before, people can combine meaningless units, such as phones, to form meaningful units like morphemes, words, and phrases. A fundamental premise, then, is that language is used to communicate—to communicate ideas, messages, thoughts, feelings, information, and so on. If the words, morphemes, phrases, sentences, and expressions do not communicate anything, they are linguistically irrelevant. Thus, every word, utterance, or expression of language must mean something; it must comply with a communicative function. The specific subfield of linguistics that deals with meaning is SEMANTICS—the focus of this chapter. Another important subfield of linguistics that deals with meaning in language is PRAGMATICS (the focus of chapter 7).

Traditionally, semantics has been understood as the basic or core meaning of a word, morpheme, or expression. Pragmatics has been understood as the meaning of such words or expressions, but within a situation, social context, specific moment, or other context. In Prieto (2015), there is a cognitive explanation for language meaning creation and processing, specifically exemplified with Spanish diminutives. In chapter 4, we will continue summarizing pragmatics and meaning relations, considering cognition, context, consensus, ambiguity, and figurative language.

4.1 Cognition and meaning

Meaning creation and processing starts with people living their lives. People are born and start "capturing" the world through their eyes, ears, nose, hands, and mouth. Their bodies are the first and primary tool to connect with the world, experience it, and understand it (or attempt to understand it). Babies see, hear, touch, bite things, and smell because, in part, they are intuitively trying to learn about the world in which they live. All the experiences, events, activities, and sensations that enter human life via the five senses are stored and organized in the human brain. All of these stimuli are stored away as images, concepts, and thoughts. Depending on the relevance of such conceptualizations for the people who experience them, these can be represented by means of linguistic symbols; in other words, they can be *lexicalized*. Words or lexical items are linguistic symbols for those relevant conceptualizations. Which concepts are represented in language and which ones are not may change from language to language and speech community to speech community. Logically it must be so since not all people experience the same surroundings or the same customs and community life. However, since all people share the world (planet Earth), then it is also logical to think that there are many worldwide basic or fundamental concepts that every human or every language has lexicalized. One theory, not without controversy, has been suggested to explain these as core concepts in the mind of all humans (Wierzbicka 1996:14). Wierzbicka, more technically, calls these "Semantic primes" or "Semantic primitives," such as: "I/you," "someone/something," "where/when," "good/bad," "big/small," and "do/happen," among others. Even though not all experts agree on these being universal semantic primes, it is a theory worth considering.

This is related to a set of core words commonly found in most languages. Some linguists call this the "Swadesh list" in honor of the first linguist that formally accounted for this (Swadesh 1952), and others refer to the core words of a language as "kernel" words or lexicon of a language, making up 75 percent of its vocabulary (Wang and Wang 2004, and Jacob 2014).

One definition of linguistic meaning, then, is the *conceptualization represented or embedded in the linguistic symbol*, whether it is an affix or morpheme, a word, a phrase, a hand sign, or some other linguistic form. Because of the importance of the transparent liquid we drink, which helps us to live, all people or all languages have a word to represent it or refer to it: "*water*" (in English), or "*agua*" (in Spanish), "*eau*" (French), and maybe 7,000 other words in other languages. Now, every human can refer to this liquid by using this word. When we want to convey the meaning of that entity to others in English, we use the word "water." This is basically the same way all words and morphemes in a language work. Once this basic concept is established in the minds and the language of a speech community, this word now becomes a fundamental symbol or way to refer to this idea/entity, and this same word and concept can be extended for different communication purposes.

One of the clearest pieces of evidence that this all begins with our bodies connecting with the world (and/or basic things around it) is the great number of figurative language (non-literal language) expressions that are body-based. Some common figures of speech that use the body are metaphors and metonymies. You can think of a metaphor as an association or mapping of one (or a few) semantic features or properties of an entity (the source) with another entity

4.1 Cognition and meaning

of another semantic domain (the target) (Barcelona 2003). One meaning aspect of the target (typically a less basic domain such as spiritual issues) is illustrated or expressed using some meaning aspect or property or semantic feature of the source (typically a more basic concept or entity such as the human body). One example is "it costs an arm and a leg." We know, intuitively at least, the high value of arms and legs. Thus, this metaphoric expression illustrates the high cost of some object. Metonymy on the other hand is "a conceptual projection whereby one experiential domain (the target) is partially understood in terms of another experiential domain (the source) included in the same experiential domain" (Barcelona 2003:4). In other words, one entity or idea is illustrated, expressed, or explained via another entity closely connected with it in the realm of everyday experiences. One common example is, "Table three needs the menu." Clients at a restaurant, who typically sit at the table, are called "tables" by the waiters.

The human body has been a rich source of sub-conscious or conscious associations in metaphors, metonymies, and other figures of speech. There are many body-based metaphors, metonymies, or figurative language expressions we use every day, many times without thinking of them as metaphors or metonymies, as these words originally represented body parts. Table 4 (next page) and Appendix B illustrate many common expressions in American English that use body parts as metaphors, metonymies, or with an extended use. Of course, there are many more than these, but this sample serves to illustrate the point. It seems that every single body part commonly noticeable or familiar to us (unlike the less familiar ones such as liver, bladder, etc) is used this way. You can probably think of similar expressions with familiar body parts like head, hand, ear, foot, eye, nose, mouth, stomach, chest, neck, finger, toe, tongue, teeth, leg, arm, heart, knee, elbow, etc.

Some of these metaphors and metonymies are more obvious to us than others. For example, when we say, "we are all ears," we may quickly notice the metaphorical sense of the expression, and we see the body connection relatively easily.

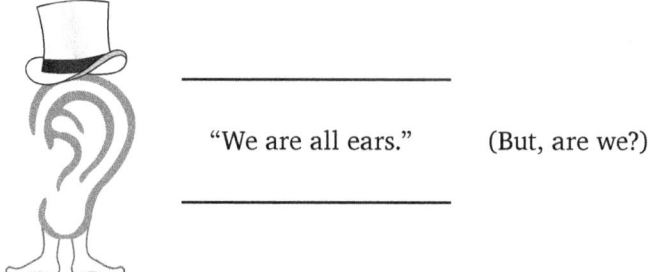

Figure 22. Metaphorical connection to our cognitive universe.

In other expressions, however, like "the back of the house," this metaphorical use awareness may not be readily present, and most speakers of English may not see that the word *back* came originally from the back of one's body—a metaphorical extension of the word that first referred to one's physical body. Lakoff and Johnson call these types of metaphors, "conceptual metaphors" (1980:3–4).

It is important to notice the connection and difference between general lexicalization processes and the development of metaphors and metonymies. Lexicalization is understood here as "the way experience is rendered into languages via the semantic content of lexical items that are used to express experiential categories" (Filipović 2007:1). In other words, crucial concepts in our life experiences connect with a word in our lexicons. This process involves the creation of a lexical item for a particular conceptualization. For example, if people consider the transparent liquid we drink as an important idea for our lives, then most likely languages will create or have an actual word for that. In English, we have the word *water*. In this way, we came up with words for basic concepts or entities such as *body, leg, foot,* etc. Once these fundamental lexicalizations have taken place, people may use those lexical items, already established in their cognition and lexicon, to explain, refer to, illustrate, or understand more abstract concepts. Here is where these metaphorical and metonymic expressions serve a fundamental purpose.

Table 4 illustrates the body as the foundation and the cognitive basis (*embodied cognition*, Shapiro 2011:4) that forms a significant part of our everyday language, especially found in idioms. Since the first concept we encounter after birth is our body, we then use bodily metaphors to understand many secondary concepts. Again, with our hands we touch and we feel; with our eyes we see, and we capture images; and so on. These images are stored in our brain and abstract conceptualizations emerge. Then we use these known lexical labels (like body parts) to define more abstract concepts, such as those given in table 4.

Table 4. Body-based figurative language

"The foot of the hills"	"The bare bones of a deal"
"The back of the house"	"On the tip of my tongue"
"The eye of the storm"	"Sticky fingers"
"The mouth of the river"	"Heads or tails?" (a coin toss)
"From your neck of the woods"	"The house needs cleaning from tip to toe"
"I don't have the stomach for it"	"Bad hair day"
"I hate your guts"	"We are all ears"

4.2 Context and meaning

Appendix B gives additional conceptual metaphors. These metaphors, metonyms, or figurative language are a common way to extend the meaning of literal words or expressions. For example, in the Bible, Jesus is referred to as "the Living Water." Bible readers know that it does not imply Jesus is the transparent liquid H_2O. In this context, it means Jesus is the source of life. Since people know, due to their experiential worldview, that a person cannot be a liquid, the meaning of "Living Water" is interpreted non-literally. This experiential worldview is referred to by Langacker as ones' "encyclopedic knowledge" (Langacker 1987:63).

This is how many semantic and pragmatic shifts happen. We start with a basic concept or semantic meaning, and then we extend the word or phrase to another context or meaning, and assign to it a different, related meaning.

Experiential worldview is applied in a contextual way that goes beyond figurative vocabulary. The question, "How are you?" initially is a content question seeking information about the hearer's wellbeing or health. This is the core semantic meaning of the question. In some contexts, however, this literal interpretation is restricted by the circumstances in which the "question" is posed. A pragmatic shift has occurred in which the context overrules the literal meaning. For example, imagine yourself running late for class and you see a friend in the hallway, and you blurt out, "How are you?" to the friend. Neither you nor your friend expect an answer other than, "Hi." or an equivalent greeting. "Hello," then, is an acceptable contextual or pragmatic interpretation of the "question." In that context, no one would reply with an explanation of their current wellbeing or health-related issues. That would be interpreted as odd by the first speaker.

In the movie, "The Night Clerk," Bart, the main protagonist has Autism Syndrome, a form of Autism-Spectrum Disorder. Whenever he is asked "How are you?" he responds: "That's a very complicated question and it could take a long time to answer," and he looks to the speaker to see if he really wants that long answer, or not. Most people can interpret the intention of the question without asking the first speaker if they really want to know.

In Prieto (2015), this semantic pragmatic shift is exemplified with the use of Spanish diminutives. Spanish has nominal suffixes that are called "diminutives". Typically, the diminutive '-*ito*' is thought to mean "little." However, apart from 'little', it has a wide range of meanings and functions. It can mean 'dear', 'inferior', 'very', etc. All these meanings somehow connect to the core idea or *semantic prime* (universal meaning) of "littleness" via extensions of usage and metaphorical associations. Regardless of how many uses or meanings it has, normally, Spanish speakers understand, in context, when -*ito* means 'dear', or 'little', or 'inferior', and so on. Speakers within a speech community have a consensus regarding these changes in meaning. Consequently, the appropriate interpretation is readily available. When the context is not established or does not seem to support an apparent meaning, there is a temporary communication breakdown. Sometimes, depending on the speaker's interest, willingness, and needs, there may be re-negotiation of meaning. Otherwise, there is no communication.

4.3 Consensus and meaning

The Humpty Dumpty character created by Lewis Carroll illustrates how important it is for linguistic expressions to mean something, and to mean something that both the speaker and listener can understand.

Let's extract this conversation between Humpty Dumpty and Alice from Carroll's famous novel, *Through the Looking-Glass*:

> "I don't know what you mean by 'glory,'" Alice said.
> Humpty Dumpty smiled contemptuously. "Of course you don't—till I tell you. I meant 'there's a nice knock-down argument for you!'"
> "But 'glory' doesn't mean 'a nice knock-down argument'," Alice objected.
> "When I use a word," Humpty Dumpty said, in rather a scornful tone, "it means just what I choose it to mean—neither more nor less."
> "The question is," said Alice, "whether you can make words mean so many different things."
> "The question is," said Humpty Dumpty, "which is to be master—that's all."
> Alice was too much puzzled to say anything, so after a minute Humpty Dumpty began again. "They've a temper, some of them—particularly verbs, they're the proudest—adjectives you can do anything with, but not verbs—however, I can manage the whole lot! Impenetrability! That's what I say!" (Carroll 1872:123)

Figure 23. Ambiguity in dialogue.

Typical dialogues in everyday communication do not normally go like this, of course. People do not want a lack of clarity or ambiguity in language. One reason we rarely encounter ambiguity in linguistic interactions is because the speakers share similar life experiences. The speaker and the listener both know how their world functions. They know how their language works and how their society is structured. They understand both the lexical meaning and the social meaning of words and expressions. They understand lexical meaning because they know the basic agreed-by-all concept embedded in a lexical item. For example, the word *dog* refers to a type of domesticated four-legged, barking animal. They also understand meaning beyond the words themselves—what we can call social meaning. In other words, concepts or nuances of meaning connected to words as shaped by the society they live in. A social meaning attached to the word *mister,* for example, is the social distance that the word maintains between two people. The lexical meaning of *mister* may be, a person of the male gender of a certain adult age, but its social meaning would be that of the social distance between the speaker and addressee. For a more detailed discussion and illustration of these concepts, see Zenner et al. (2019:sections 2, 3).

Consider another example. In most English-speaking communities, a student dosen't call a professor by his or her first name. But it is normal for the professor to refer to students using their first name. So, students who address their professor as "Dr. Jones," add a level of respect to the term of address, and students who call that professor "John" or "Ann" include a different social meaning, which would be clear to all parties involved if they belong to the same speech community.

A speech community lives in generally the same surroundings. You might have come across the "Yeah, no?" and "No, yeah?" apparent ambiguity in Midwestern speech communities. Residents of other regions might be confused by this, but Midwesterners are not. You can probably also think of an English teacher who says, "Double negatives are positive, but double positives aren't negative;" and then the student answers, "Yeah, right." Among students this "Yeah, right" means the *opposite* of agreement with the teacher's assertion. Thus, successful communication, even with apparently confusing expressions, occurs within the same speech community. Now and then, however, we may experience miscommunication, even within the

4.3 Consensus and meaning

same speech community. Miscommunication happens when some rules are not followed, the context is not well interpreted, or there is not 100 percent consensus.

Thus, a common background and a similar worldview is crucial for successful communication between people. Different backgrounds or different types of world experiences can render different meanings to apparently similar words. Let us consider abbreviations where this is easily noticeable. The abbreviation "SLA" is used commonly in linguistics, business, and the printing industry. If a student mentions "SLA" while at a linguistics conference, you will most likely interpret it as "second language acquisition." But if attending a business convention, you may interpret this to mean a "service level agreement." In the printing industry, "SLA" is a type of 3D printing technology. Librarians might interpret "SLA" to mean the "Special Libraries Association." How we interpret "SLA" is filtered through our common knowledge bank of language and experiences. In the course of conversation between a linguist and a freshman International Business student in university, the student may not know how to interpret "SLA" while the two are talking and the professor of linguistics mentions "SLA." The student might have to ask the professor what is meant by that since the student is not a linguist. Although the two speakers share much of the same background, their experience in that subject would vary, and so they cannot assume a shared understanding. Different backgrounds cause more "meaning negotiation" work, and there is no guarantee of successful communication. Therefore, a consensus via a common background and shared worldview constitutes a fundamental piece in human communication.

Communicating with people with different backgrounds may be tricky. We may need to communicate with people from other countries, other cultures, other races, other societies, or other language or speech varieties, even within our own state, city, or region. Getting to know the background of that speech community is crucial. If they speak another language, of course, we need to learn the words, sounds, and grammar of that language. In addition to that, we need to learn about their society dynamics: who is who in that society, what their expectations are, where they live, what the common topics of conversation are, what their common concerns are, and so on.

Virginia De Leon, of the *Spokesman-Review* newspaper wrote the story of a Spokane family who left the United States to serve as missionaries in a Southeast Asian country. The article reported on the problems they found in trying to communicate with people who had a totally different culture and language, and of course, with different backgrounds and worldview. The American family explained that translating the Bible is not just a case of finding an equivalent word in the target language. It also involves knowing the target culture, their history, their customs, their worldview, and their society. According to these former missionaries, the goal of Bible translation is to transfer the meaning of the Scriptural word or concept into a new culture, within their context. They gave the example of the biblical expression: "Jesus is the bread of life," explaining that a literal translation would not make sense to the Folopa since the Folopa people rarely eat bread. Their core diet consists of sweet potatoes, taro, yam, and sago. They decided to translate this phrase as, "Jesus is the sweet potato of life," which conveyed the core idea of the biblical metaphor in the Folopa context (De Leon 2007). This translation decision illustrates that communication between people requires a common understanding, a similar background, and a shared worldview at some level. Not having this common ground seriously complicates communication and can result in skewed or zero communication.

Figure 24. Jesus, the "Bread of Life" or the "Sweet Potato of Life?"
(It depends on the people group with whom you want to communicate.)

Without doubt there is dramatic difficulty in communicating transculturally and across speech communities because of unshared common background. This illustrates the fundamental need for consensus in human communication, and the potential pitfalls in the absence of shared meaning.

4.4 Meaning relations among words (the "-nyms")

Another way in which people convey or process meaning once words are established in the language is via word associations. Different words may connect with other words in different ways, and this contributes to the understanding of the message and the success in communication. Words or phrases have meaning relationships. For example, one word is similar to another in meaning, or one is the opposite to another, or one embeds the meaning of the other, and so on. The five most basic types of relationship of meaning referred to here are: Synonymy, antonymy, hyponymy, polysemy, and homophony. There are more, but because of the commonality and importance of these, we will briefly discuss only these five.

4.4.1 Meaning similarity, or synonymy

SYNONYMS are words or phrases that share similar meanings; they might clarify or illustrate the meaning of the other. For example, a *lady* can be understood as a *woman*, a *teacher* as a *professor*, a *computer* as a *laptop*, and so on. In the same discourse or conversation, it is possible that a person might say: "You know, I brought my laptop yesterday and I plugged it in, but it didn't charge. I've never had any problems with my computers until now! Oh man!" This is a plausible scenario in everyday communication. The interactants know that *laptop* and *computer* are synonyms, at least in this context—they refer to the same thing; the referent has not changed.

Of course, it is not possible to use both words indiscriminately all the time. For some examples, not every woman is a lady, but every lady is a woman; not every man is a gentleman, but every gentleman is a man; not every college teacher is an instructor, but every instructor is a teacher; and not every computer is a laptop, but every laptop is a computer.

Figure 25. Laptop = computer, but not every computer is a laptop.

Now, let us go back to the statement that synonyms are not synonyms all the time. Let's see some examples of this. For some reason, you really do not want to say: "Welcome, women and gentlemen;" you must say "Ladies and gentlemen," even though "ladies" and "women" are synonyms in some situations. There are typically subtle differences between synonyms. For example, the word "laptop" refers to a specific type of computer that you can carry around and that you can set on your lap, instead of on the top of your desk, as in "desktops." A "professor" typically is a teacher at the college or university level, so, a high school teacher is not a professor. "Lady" and "gentleman" imply some degree of social etiquette standards, which is not necessarily implied in the terms "woman" and "man".

This proves an important principle regarding synonymy in language: It is very hard to find 100 percent absolute synonymy in language. Even if you assume 100 percent synonymy, such as in the phrases jump drive, memory stick, USB drive, thumb drive, and so on (or any other similar grouping of synonyms), typically there are certain situations for one word or expression over the other. In other words, seemingly identical terms don't always apply in every context.

The correct use of synonyms conserve energy, resources, and effort. People tend to make the least effort for the most benefit, which shows up in language in the commonly cited "economy principle of language," originally implied in Whitney's words: "[We humans tend] to make things easy to our organs of speech, to economize time and effort in the work of expression" (1875:345). Thus, having two words or concepts that consistently overlap is not economical. When we have an apparent 100 percent synonymy, it may be due to a linguistic change in progress. One word may be going out of the language or being re-shaped in meaning.

Notice the crossover history of the words *happy* and *gay*. During the fifteenth century, these two words were synonyms. *Happy*, according to the etymological dictionary, etymonline.com, used to mean "with luck." It comes from *hap* or *fortune* plus the adjectival suffix *-y*. *Gay* in that same century, meant "full of joy." Later, the idea of luck (in *happiness*) changed into the idea of contentedness or satisfaction, and then the idea of happiness as most people understand it today. Around the eighteenth century, the word *gay* started having the meaning of a same-sex attraction, and today it is a commonly used term for homosexual, having gone through a series of somewhat-related meanings: light-hearted, carefree, lewd, lascivious, stately and beautiful, showily dressed, sumptuous, and so on. Today, in everyday Modern English, *happy* and *gay* that were originally synonymous, now have totally different meanings.

4.4.2 Meaning opposition, or antonymy

Two words or expressions may be *antonyms* having clearly opposite meanings, at least in one attribute or feature, if not all. In the realm of colors, we can see, for example, how *black* and *white* can be antonyms. They represent the two extreme ends of a continuum of color. *Husband* and *wife* can be said to be antonyms, at least in the feature of gender. *Rich* and *poor*, *good* and *bad*, *tall* and *short*, and others are examples of common antonyms in English. We use this antonymy in everyday communication to help communicate meaning: We explain opposite contexts as, "a black-and-white situation," "rain or shine," and similar phrases. These expressions are antonyms for communicative purposes. In a traditional wedding, a husband promises to love his bride in any situation, regardless of how opposite or contrary those situations might be: "I take you to be my wife, ... for better or for worse, for richer or poorer, in sickness and in health."

Notice, too, that even in a pair of antonyms, there are typically similar features in their attributes. Black and white are both members of the domain of color. In the idiom, "they are like oil and water," oil and water are antonyms. Both are liquids used in cooking but have the feature of separating when mixed. Thus, antonymy may compare two entities of a similar nature but that have opposite semantic characteristics.

4.4.3 Meaning subcategorization, or hyponymy

The issue of classifying or categorizing is crucial for compartmentalizing language. Subcategorizing is a fundamental cognitive category that, if examined deeply, becomes abstract and complex. For a point of entry, suffice it to say that people organize linguistic concepts in their minds in groups or categories. Lakoff was one of the first authors to formally observe linguistic categorization in his well-known work: *Women, Fire, and Dangerous Things: What Categories Reveal About the Mind*. He noticed how a certain ethnicity grouped together, grammatically speaking, the nouns that refer to women, dangerous things, and anything connected to fire. That people group perceived commonality among these three very different items, and this commonality became represented in their grammar (1987:93). Grammatical subcategorization is essential for human communication, as will be discussed further on.

When you meet a person for the first time, what goes through your mind? You may pose these questions: "Who is this person? Where is he from? Is he trustworthy? What is his occupation?" and similar thoughts. You might try to place the person according to race, political category, social class, or some other category you consider important. When you fill out a job application form, your interviewer may ask you to classify yourself according to gender, age, race, even religious preference. People tend to group things in their minds according to commonalities, classifications, or "prototypes" depending on the circumstances.

This natural need to categorize helps us make sense of the world. We may misclassify something initially, then re-evaluate and reclassify that object in our minds. If we see something fluttering around in the back yard, we may assume it is a bird; then, at a second glance, realize it is a cicada. Classifying and recategorizing helps us make sense of the world around us.

HYPONYMS are subtypes, a member of a larger class. A dog is a hyponym of an animal because it belongs to the *microcategory* of the larger category of animal. Other subcategories of animal are cats, cows, squirrels, deer, horses, or any other type of animal. If you are asked to write an essay about horses, then you are indirectly writing about one of the animal class. This is connected to Trier's (1931) semantic fields, Lyons' (1977) semantic domains, Freedman and Reynold's (1980) semantic mapping or webbing, and Miller's (1990) semantic networks. See figure 26 for an example.

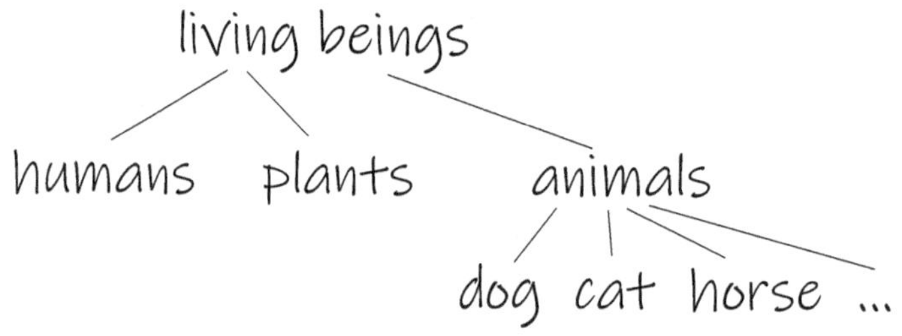

```
              living beings
             /      |      \
        humans   plants   animals
                         / | \ \
                       dog cat horse ...
```

Figure 26. Subcategorization (hyponyms).

4.4.4 Similar words, different meanings: Polysemy and homophony

You may have encountered the unfortunate fact in language that the same word, or lexical symbol, may refer to different entities or concepts. For example, the word *crane* may refer to an animal or a machine. How about the word *bank*? We can talk about my financial institution, the Bank of America, and the bank of the river. We can also use the word *school* for different meanings: a school of music and a school of fish. There are other examples like these: *bat*, the flying animal versus *bat*, a piece of equipment used to play baseball; the pool where you swim or the pool game of billiards.

4.5 Meaning ambiguity

This is a common fact not just in English but in human languages universally. Sometimes it is the product of a) an accident, b) a metaphorical association or extended uses of meaning, c) language contact, or d) chance. Remember, in English we have only 40 speech sounds or phonemes to produce an infinite number of ideas. What are the chances that we may end up using the same combination of sounds to refer to different objects? Even though the probability is not very high, the purely random chance of that happening still exists. So, chance is a potential reason for polysemy and homophony.

Some cases of polysemy can be explained cognitively and figuratively, as previously stated. In some cases, there is a connection of meaning resulting from an experience in the past. As mentioned, *crane* refers either to a construction machine or a bird, but the metaphorical connection can be explained perceptually since the two objects have a similar shape and movement. Metaphorically, then, the bird's name might have been borrowed to refer to the construction equipment.

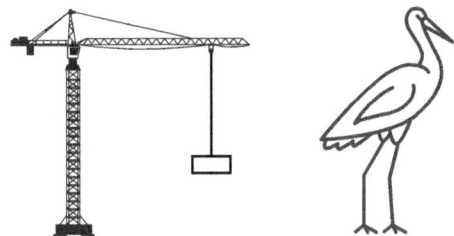

Figure 27. Cranes: Metaphorical connection, or homonym?

Why not vice versa? The answer has to do with the most natural or primitive explanation. The birds came into existence first prior to the machines; thus, the bird first, and then the machine. When we connect two words that share a characteristic but are of different semantic classes, we call this POLYSEMY, defined as, "different meanings but with a semantic relationship." There are other cases, however, when there is no semantic connection between the words whatsoever.

Words that have the same sound and spelling but have different meanings are called HOMONYMS, for example, "bat" (both a baseball and a flying mammal). Homophones are words that are pronounced the same but differ in meaning, and at times, in spelling, e.g., "son/sun." No semantic or figurative link exists between the baseball instrument and the mammal, or the male child and the star at the center of our solar system. Homonyms/homophones may be the product of accident or loans from other languages but, most likely, are a product of chance.

4.5 Meaning ambiguity

A certain level of ambiguity may be subjacently present in linguistic expressions. In this case, we are talking about expressions or words with two different potential meanings based on linguistic context alone. We also recognize that even though the linguistic context may render some level of structural (grammar-based) or lexical (word meaning-based) ambiguity, extra-linguistic context disambiguates such expressions.

In the field of computer language programming, or Natural Language Processing (NLP), the need for linguistic disambiguation has been most obvious. In search engines (e.g., Google, Yahoo), when you type in a phrase, words can have more than one meaning and the computer develops an algorithm to analyze the context and select the most probable meaning. Ide and Veronis state that "automatic disambiguation of word senses has been an interest and concern since the earliest days of computer treatment of language … [it is] not an end in itself, but rather [is] necessary ... to accomplish most NLP tasks. It is obviously essential for language understanding applications, such as message understanding and man-machine communication" (1998:1). It is evident in NLP that ambiguity is a hindrance to language understanding.

People naturally disambiguate because we need to communicate a message. Words or expressions with ambiguity may have two or more meanings. When we communicate something via language, we typically have a single message in mind, not two or three. Only in cases such as jokes, puns, riddles, or poetry, do we intend there to be two or more meanings, but in these cases the speaker is playing with language.

Let's do a quick exercise. When you read the following sentence in italics, think of its meaning quickly. Write down without thinking twice the first thing that comes to your mind.

- *The woman saw the man with the telescope.*

If you did this exercise as expected, and as people typically process language, you probably wrote one of these messages: a) "a woman, using a telescope, saw a man," or b) "a woman saw a man who had a telescope," or something similar. Even though there are two potential interpretations of this sentence, you most likely only wrote down one of those two, and you were okay with that response. Grammar rules in the English language allow for both interpretations; the correct meaning depends on the linguistic context in which those words appear. In that sentence, the grammatical rules of English permit this structural ambiguity because, in this linguistic context, the last prepositional phrase ("with the telescope") modifies either the direct object (the man) or the verb (saw). Thus, either the man had the telescope or the seeing was done with the telescope. Even though English grammar allows for both meanings, in everyday communication a listener typically processes just one interpretation.

Contextual cues are crucial here. Associative context may trigger one interpretation over another in word-sense disambiguation processes, according to the context availability model in psycholinguistics described by Kwong (2012). Context may not be the only factor in a word disambiguation process, but it is a major factor. And without a larger context there is no way to predict the "correct" interpretation for the sample sentence of figure 28.

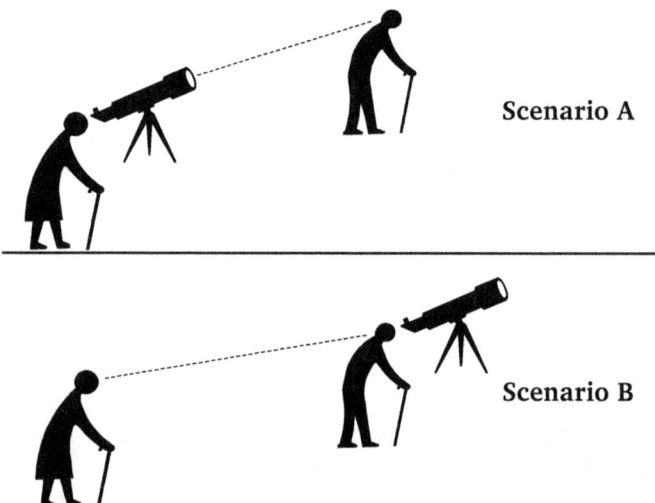

Figure 28. "The woman saw the man with the telescope."
A case of structural ambiguity.

Ambiguity can happen in the structure, or syntax, of a language and at the lexical-semantic level. A word alone can have two or more meanings, which is the case with homophony and polysemy. The word *crane* can refer to a construction machine or to a bird, and the word *play* can mean an action in a game or a theater enactment. Both are examples of ambiguity that is not triggered by the grammar rules of the language but by the multiple meanings of a word. Regardless of the source of the ambiguity, whether it is structural or lexical, we still tend to filter out incorrect interpretations. Either extralinguistic context, or discourse context, lead to selecting the "winning candidate," out of possible interpretations. If you are in a rental office for construction equipment, and you say: "I need a crane," everyone knows you are not talking about a bird. The listener who is aware of the contextual clues normally does not need to ask for clarification.

There is a critical, basic principle in language use, which we will call here, for lack of a better term, "sentences as semantic mountains" in a mountain range, or "one-sentence, one-idea." Theodore Bernstein, a former New York Times editor (and former professor of journalism at Columbia University), observes that writers only express one idea per sentence. He calls this the "precept of one idea to a sentence" (Bernstein 1958:98). Human minds benefit from this principle, not only when reading newspaper articles but in every instance of normal communication. Dealing with two or more ideas in a single linguistic utterance takes an unnecessarily high toll on a human mind and complicates efficient communication; it is as simple as that. We typically communicate one idea per utterance, or in the words of Chafe, one intonation unit in spoken language. Chafe hypothesizes that "conversational language appears subject to a constraint that limits an intonation unit to the expression of no more than one new idea" (1994:119), which is subject to how much information people can process at one time. He defines INTONATION UNITS as "brief spurts of language" that "verbalize a small amount of information" (1994:26) on which the consciousness is focused. This one-idea-per-sentence concept is the core reason we can disambiguate. As figure 29 illustrates, typically, a sentence in English, is like a semantic mountain.

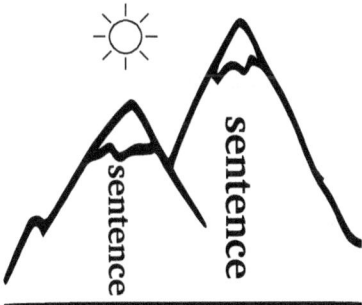

Figure 29. Sentences/intonation units as semantic mountains:
One sentence/intonation unit equals one idea.

4.6 Figurative meaning

Revisit the table of body-based figurative language expressions, table 4 (section 4.1), which lists idioms involving metaphors, metonymies, and other figures of speech. That table and Appendix B show that many expressions can be interpreted figuratively. We know, for example, that hills do not have feet; they cannot walk or do not have other common features of feet such as toes. The expression "the foot of the hill" must then be understood figuratively, that is, non-literally.

Figurative language helps us communicate in at least four ways:

- Playing with language or being creative (the "esthetic/artistic function")
- Illustrating complex concepts ("the explanatory function")

- Expressing thoughts for which we may not have words (the "compensatory function")
- Avoiding directness (the "face-saving function")

4.6.1 The playful and esthetic/artistic use of figurative language

At times, people use language for entertainment or pure enjoyment. This is very common in poetry, theater, and jokes. The following jokes show the humoristic function that switching between literal and figurative language can have:

- Q: "What did the chewing gum say to the shoe?" (A: I'm stuck on you.)
- Q: "What has a big mouth yet doesn't say a word?" (A: A river.)
- Q: "What animal can fly higher than a house?" (A: All animals can—houses can't fly.)

Wordplay has entertaining functions; it may help us to connect with others, to just hang out, or to pass time in social functions. It is important at least for part of our social lives. Poetry and similar arts are also used to entertain and often to convey messages in a more attractive or creative way. Consider Shakespeare's famous Sonnet #14, "Not from the Stars do I My Judgment Pluck":

> Not from the stars do I my judgment pluck,
> And yet methinks I have astronomy;
> But not to tell of good or evil luck,
> Of plagues, of dearths, or seasons' quality;
> Nor can I fortune to brief minutes tell,
> Pointing to each his thunder, rain, and wind,
> Or say with princes if it shall go well
> By oft predict that I in heaven find.
> But from thine eyes my knowledge I derive,
> And, constant stars, in them I read such art
> As truth and beauty shall together thrive
> If from thyself to store thou wouldst convert:
> > Or else of thee this I prognosticate,
> > Thy end is truth's and beauty's doom and date.

In this poem, most analysts see a rejection of fortune-telling and similar practices based on alleged astrological ("astronomical" in today's vocabulary) discoveries. Shakespeare seems to state that he does not gain knowledge or make decisions ("pluck his judgment") based on such practices. He gets knowledge from the eyes of the addressee of the poem (still unclear to many). He figuratively compares those eyes with stars. He also figuratively "reads the stars." Also at the end, he foretells (prognosticates) that beauty and truth will be doomed or die, figuratively, if this addressee does not have a child.

4.6.2 The explanatory purpose of figurative language

Figurative language can also be used to clarify or simplify abstract ideas. This connects with my explanation of the "cognitive basis of meaning." We start with basic realities such as our bodies. These entities or ideas that we are very familiar with help us understand more complex ideas or less familiar ones. For example, abstract concepts such as a "hypocrite" can be described as a "two-faced person." The idea or concept of face, familiar to all of us, can easily lead us to a new idea when hypocrisy is defined as two-faced. In the minds of many people in situations where Christianity or the Bible is somehow part of shared knowledge, God is conceived as Father and the religious idea of eternity is illustrated as heavens. The idea of respect for one another is expressed with the concept of "brotherhood" in many Muslim communities. It is common to see love commonly portrayed as a heart. Problems can

4.6 Figurative meaning

be seen as "barriers or obstacles on the road." According to Collins (2016), the Maya-Mam people in Guatemala relate concepts such as peace, happiness, health, and home with the idea of "center" or "centeredness". The common image of guilt is a burden on one's shoulders. Life is portrayed as a journey. In different cultures you may hear similar metaphoric associations. Figurative language helps us understand, express, and process higher-level thought and concepts.

Concrete objects such as "face," "father," "heart," "road," and "shoulder," may be considered PRIMITIVE CONCEPTS. These and similar basic terms in the list are very basic concepts with which we are very familiar. Most people readily recognize the idea represented in words used day-to-day such as *father, road,* and *body*. We readily connect one way or another with these concepts that are critical for daily life. Because of the fundamental nature of these *primitive concepts*, people can transfer these concepts to less tangible, more abstract concepts such as hypocrisy, marriage, life, and guilt. In a sense, *primitive concepts* illustrate or explain abstract nouns and complex concepts.

4.6.3 The compensatory function of figurative language

We seem to have more thoughts than words or lexical items. This may entail, admittedly, a philosophical and speculative debate. However, at some level, we have to agree that children without language or children from birth to one-year-olds, or children found in isolation, like "Genie" (Curtis 1977:5–6), do have some type of ideas or images in their minds, even if they don't have a developed language yet. This fact then can help us see how it is possible that we may have ideas, conceptualizations, or images in our minds for which we do not have a word yet. One way to portray these "hidden" thoughts is by using figurative language. Since we have fewer words than the things we may want/need to express, we may compensate with the words we have, and we can extend their use metaphorically. Of course, figurative language is not the only way to compensate for this, but it is a common way to do it.

Just recently, Dockrill's (2020) article on some new discovery in the bottom of the ocean came on *sciencealert.com*. The title of the news report was "Massive 'desert' exists in the middle of the ocean." The idea of a "desert" is used to convey this new discovery: A place with no sign of life, in the Pacific Ocean. This is in a sense a new concept for all of us, a new discovery: A place with no signs of living entities in the deep ocean. This concept is represented by the expression "marine desert."

Recently as well, the term "internet" came to the English language out of the necessity to refer to a new concept and reality that has changed our lives forever. This term uses the basic concept of a "net," but uses it metaphorically. We today refer to this cybernetic 24/7 connection via technology and computers with no time or space constraints, as a "net" of "inter"-connections through machines and technology.

4.6.4 The face-saving function of figurative language

Figurative language can help us with social etiquette as well. This use of figurative language is triggered by the fundamental principles of politeness and social norms. As human beings and members of a society, we are expected to follow certain norms of conduct and ethics. In 1978 and again in 1987, Brown and Levinson formulated and published what today in linguistics is known as POLITENESS THEORY (Brown and Levinson 1987:3). In this theory, Brown and Levinson suggest that much of linguistic interaction aims at preserving a certain degree of politeness between speaker and hearer. The *Oxford Dictionary* defines politeness as "behaviour that is respectful and considerate of other people." For many, this is fundamental in human life. Religious works worldwide propagate the courteous nature of humans created to be respectful, socially interdependent, entities. For example, biblical adherents read in

Genesis: "God said, "It is not good for the man to be alone. I will make a helper suitable for him" (*Gen* 2:18). There are similar narratives in the *Quran* (Islam), the *Torah, Nevi'im,* and *Ketuvim* (Jews), and the *Popol Vuh* (Guatemalan Mayans). The *Dictionary of Psychology* of the American Psychology Association (APA) refers to this as "social instinct," and defines it as follows:

1. The desire for social contact and a feeling of belonging, as manifested by the tendency to congregate, affiliate, and engage in group behaviors.
2. An innate drive for cooperation that leads individuals to incorporate social interest and the common good into their efforts to achieve self-realization. (APA 2023b)

According to the APA, SOCIAL ETIQUETTE is innate and generates in people not only individual interests but also the interests of others. Evolutionists, typically, also attribute a "social nature" to humans. Elizabeth Pennisi (2011), in *ScienceNow*, describes, "How Humans Became Social," from this view, "most likely because there was *safety in numbers*" (my italics). So, regardless of one's philosophical worldview, it is commonly accepted that humans are social and interdependent by nature and necessity. In this light, a politeness theory in language makes sense. Brown and Levinson open their treatise on politeness with a quotation from Durkheim (1915): "The human personality is a sacred thing; one dare not violate it nor infringe its bounds, while at the same time the greatest good is in communion with others" (Brown and Levinson 1987:37).

Saving face or the reputation and social image of others and oneself is crucial, then, for an acceptable social life in community with others. Taboos such as sex, death, and physiological needs, are a threat to this social image of individuals. Therefore, one way to minimize this threat to one's reputation is by using non-literal, euphemistic language. We may refer to "dying" as "passing away" or "putting a pet to sleep." We may refer to our physiological need to eliminate body waste as "number one" or "number two." We refer to a friend's erratic behavior as having a "bad hair" day. I might diminish the fact that I "totaled" my dad's car by saying, "I had a fender-bender." Euphemistic, figurative language is not the only way to save face in these contexts, but it is a very common and effective way.

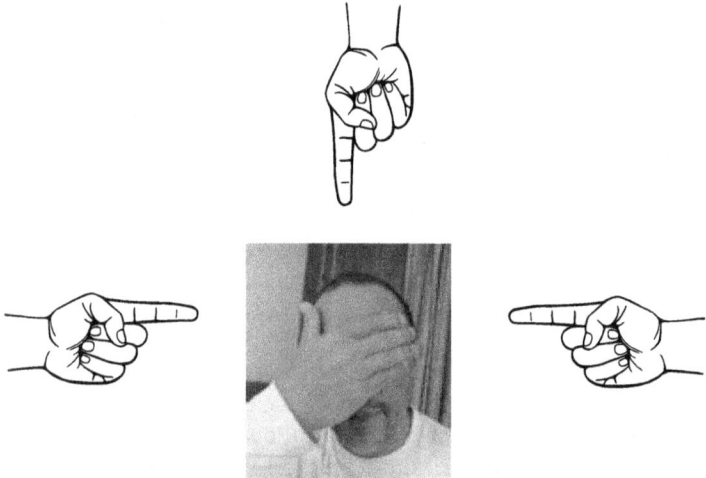

Figure 30. Euphemistic or figurative language helps to avoid shaming others.

Now, it is your turn to write answers to questions that will help you review the "cognitive basis of meaning," "polysemy," "figurative language," "ambiguity," and similar notions.

Exercises

1) **Cognitive basis of *go*.** The verb "go" is very productive in English, with many different uses, meanings, and connotations: "I'm *going* to class now," "Yes, they *go* to church—they're *churchgoers,*" "how's it *going?*" "It *went* well," "prices *went* up," "the bank *went* bankrupt," "I'm *going* to play," "don't *go* crazy!" etc. Based on the "cognitive basis of meaning" described, explain this multiplicity of meanings.

2) **Ambiguity and context (disambiguation).** Pick one example of structural ambiguity and one example of semantic or lexical ambiguity. Write the phrase/word. Identify its type of ambiguity. Briefly explain why you identified it as "structural/syntactic" or "semantic/lexical". Resolve the ambiguity, creating a potential scenario or context where only *one* interpretation is rendered plausible, and the other(s) are blocked.

3) **Figurative language on social media.** Pick two expressions with figurative language on your social networks. Write down these expressions. Explain why they are not literal language. Connect this use of figurative language to one of the four purposes of figurative language. If you cannot link it to any of these four, explain what other purpose it could have.

4) **Polysemy or homophony?** Read a website or article of interest to you based on your major or minor in college or a hobby or occupation. Pick one example of a word(s) written/pronounced the same but that could have different meanings. Is this polysemy or homophony? Why?

5

Who Speaks English Better?

You say either [iðər] and I say either [ayðər],
you say neither [niðər] and I say neither [nayðər].
Either [iðər], either [ayðər]; neither [niðər], neither [nayðər].
Let's call the whole thing off.
You like potato and I like potahto.
You like tomato and I like tomahto.
Potato, potahto, tomato, tomahto.
Let's call the whole thing off.

– Louis Armstrong's song, "Let's call the whole thing off."

Anita Henderson, an African American professional in Philadelphia, U.S.A., was relocating for professional reasons. The first time she decided to look to rent an apartment, she went to a large apartment complex to check it out. The manager told her that there was only one apartment available, and that it was the most expensive one, unfortunately. She could not afford it. The manager also told her that for the following month, that was going to be the case and that no other apartments would become available. The next day, using what she calls her "very best Standard American English" accent on the phone, she inquired about apartments in the same complex. Suddenly and "mysteriously," several less expensive apartments became available (Henderson 2001:2–3). She attributes this incident to the unfortunate link many people may make between physical appearance and accents or pronunciation. On the phone, she sounded different to whoever answered the phone; she sounded like a person that may match some abstract standards in the minds of the listener. She sounded, to this listener and apartment complex employee or official, like a person that could fit very well in that apartment complex and should be given the chance of living there.

For many, the way you sound and the way you look may have strong social meaning. Remember that social meaning involves our understanding of certain words or attributes based on society dynamics, history, and dynamics. Some accents have low prestige and others have high prestige. Dragojevic, Giles, and Watson argue that people form impressions of others when they interact with each other. They say that not only visual factors (such as gender, age, and ethnicity) play a role in these impressions, but also the way people talk. They explain that different ways of speaking (different languages, different varieties of a language, or different accents) have a certain degree of systematicity and reflect regional, social, and contextual differences.

For many, then, these language forms reveal the speaker's social identity; in other words, they may indicate or reflect a speaker's social face. That is why the way a person speaks "can convey a significant amount of social information about speakers, such as their geographical background, ethnicity, and social class, as well as stereotypes attributed regarding their traits" (2013:1–2).

In the U.S., for example, certain accents may have social implications due to what is considered low prestige. Mainstream accents, on the other hand, as heard on TV news shows, formal radio interviews, and government settings, tend to be attributed to a higher-prestige social meaning.

Each speaker of English communicates using a different accent, tone or stress, and grammar; we may each come from different regions where subvarieties of English are spoken. The primary goal of this chapter is to recognize these variations as acceptable linguistic phenomena. We will investigate, describe, and exemplify linguistic variation, considering its nature, dynamics, causes, and potential effects. The thesis of this chapter, then, is that people from all segments of society speak the same language in varied ways, and that is to be expected, and it is part of our beautiful diversity. Understanding that dynamic helps us avoid the linguistic profiling of which Anita was a victim.

Traveling in England brought me into contact with English spoken in an almost (to me) incomprehensible form. While visiting Southampton, it took my guide three times of repeating the same phrase before I understood it; he was just saying "turn right," but I kept hearing "ton royt" or something like that. I lived in South Carolina for 16 years. If a South Carolinian were to tell me the same phrase, I would not have a hard time understanding it. Southampton English sounds dramatically different to my ears than does South Carolinian English.

When in Spain, I need to pay attention to the different words, grammar, and different sounds, used locally, even though both they and I speak Spanish. Originally from Venezuela, after 27 years of living out of the country, when I go back to visit, even I sound different to them, and now Venezuelans use new vocabulary that I had not heard before.

While writing this book there was a worldwide epidemic of the Covid-19 coronavirus. We needed a new word to describe the virus, and other words were also created due to this unprecedented pandemic. I learned the phrase, "universal masking," which I had never heard before, but one with which the whole world is familiar now. Our language needs to adapt to changes in our world. Here is another example from Spanish.

Words are used more commonly or differently in one region or country than another. Some time ago, an Argentine newspaper reported on the weather conditions there. The article said that they had begun the day with *vidrios escarchados* 'frosted windshield/glass' (*Critica Sur* 2018). It took me a while to process this meaning from my Venezuelan worldview and variety of Spanish. For an Argentinian, in a Southern Hemisphere, four-season-climate country, *vidrios escarchados* is normal and a necessary term. For Venezuelans, living in a tropical climate near the Equator and without an ice- and snow-related climate, it is not. If Venezuelans used the word *escarchados*, it might refer to tiny, colored-paper sprinkles. It would be unfair on my part to criticize Argentinians because they use vocabulary different than mine. Similar examples of lexical differences between regions and countries are fairly common. An example in English is the word, *biscuit.* In the U.K., it means *cookie*; in the U.S. it often means *a dog treat*. Meanwhile, an American flaky biscuit closely resembles a British scone. You have undoubtedly heard similar examples of regionalisms in English.

The media sometimes uses language distinctions to portray stereotypes. For example, the Andy Griffith television show of the 1960s takes place in an imaginary town in the South called Mayberry. Andy Taylor (Griffith), the sheriff and voice of wisdom and discretion, and deputy Barney Fyfe (Don Knotts) are the main protagonists. The slapstick character, Barney, is portrayed with a whiney voice and an obvious West Virginian, mountain accent. Gomer Pyle (Jim Nabors), who has a heavy Alabama accent, is portrayed as an even more simplistic and naïve protagonist. In counterpoint, over the years of the show, it may be that you can detect a diminished Southern accent by the well-loved, folksy-friendly Andy. This use of accent to depict a protagonist's character is what Rowe and Levine call "Mock language" (2018:228). They maintain that purposeful use of accent to promote stereotypes can influence how people feel about the protagonists.

Figure 31. Use of accent to portray stereotypes.

At times, stereotypical accents are used to portray a language variety on the margins of society, belonging to a subset of society that contrasts with the language of the primary audience. Those stereotypes may even generate a distaste among the majority audience. Dobrow and Gidney examined ways in which children's TV cartoons make use of linguistic stereotypes to project antipathy toward the character (1998:106–107). They assert that "children use television as a source of information about members of other ethnic groups" (1998:106). And they remind us that often people use linguistic assessments of others to determine whether individuals are educated or not, intelligent or not, and similar types of judgments (1998:107). These authors noted that in cartoons many villains are portrayed with the accent or dialect of American English associated with low socioeconomic status, or have foreign accents, like "Italian American gangster" (1998:115). As late as the 1990s, "many of the villains in [their] sample used linguistic features that were recognizably Russian, Eastern European, or German" (1998:117). More recently, when Gidney was interviewed by the columnist Fattal of *The Atlantic* magazine (2018), he commented that in the animated movie "Lion King," Scar's minions, the villain hyenas, spoke with a marked nonstandard accent typical of marginalized Americans.

In Venezuela, protagonists with the most power or more prestige would typically come from the middle- or high-class neighborhoods of big cities such as Caracas or Valencia. Dangerous characters would normally come from the slums of those cities. Protagonists with less prestige would be characterized with accents typical of rural areas. The most prestigious protagonists speak with an accent known to be from Spain; that would automatically raise their prestige level in the show, characterizing them as one of the most intelligent protagonists.

My colleague, Keris, suggests that this should make all of us at least consider how a movie director may be trying to manipulate the audience based on the language style they assign to their characters. Similar to the Andy Griffith show of the 1960s, E. G. Anderson reports on one of the "X-Files" episodes from the 1990s to early 2000s that the "Sheriff Hartwell" character, sheriff of another small town in the South, is portrayed with "ridiculously overwrought accent [and] 'aw shucks' mannerisms" (2017:234).

Louis Armstrong's song (cited as the epigram for this chapter) and the content of this chapter show us that language varies and is exploited for effect. Yet passing judgment on different speech patterns may be creating a divide between "us" and "them" and passing judgment on others. In the same way that it is not wrong to live in one country or another or in one period of time or another, there is nothing intrinsically wrong with variation in language. In fact, is it fair to pass judgment regarding who speaks English better? Do people in England, the States, Canada, India, Australia, the Philippines, New Zealand, Trinidad, Jamaica, or any other English-speaking country speaks "better" than others from a different background and experience? And considering the regions within the U.S., do Westerners, Southerners, New Englanders, Midwesterners speak better? In England, is the King's English better than that of other people or groups? Or even, considering social classes, who speaks better? High, middle, or lower social classes? Then, regarding age, who speaks better? Older people or the youth? What about who speaks better English comparing women and men?

We will now consider some language variation with sociology in mind. Some factors that bring about language variation and change within our society.

5.1 Factors causing language variation: Sociolinguistic variables

The previous paragraphs mentioned major factors of linguistic variation. Here they are listed:

- Time (changes over historical periods)
- Age (differences across age groups such as older generations and younger ones)
- Gender (women's language versus men's language)
- Social class (higher social classes or castes versus lower social classes)
- Education (different levels of education and their impact on language use)
- Region (variation across countries or states or cities or villages)
- Ethnicity (African American Vernacular vs. Chicano English, for example)
- Register (formal versus informal language or speech style according to situation).

Of these eight variables, we will leave the time factor for further discussion in chapter 6, the chapter on language change. Language can vary across all these variables. Let us consider each of the other seven briefly, beginning with the age factor.

5.1 Factors causing language variation: Sociolinguistic variables

5.1.1 The age factor

Millennials (those born in the 1980s or 1990s) have distinct ways of communicating as compared, for example, to others born in the 1950s. Probably due to the technology era and their texting dynamics, abbreviations have become the norm in many instances of their communication. This is such a feature of this generation that it is becoming part of their oral everyday communication, not just texting. I have heard instances of "JK" when they mean to say, "just kidding". It is not uncommon to hear phrases such as *"ay, kay, ay,"* for "AKA," meaning "also known as," or *"ay-es-ay-pee"* or *"ay-sap,"* for ASAP, or "as soon as possible." You might have also heard the ironic *"bee-eff-eff,"* for "BFF," or "best friends forever."

Figure 32. Cross-generational miscommunication.

You can find many articles online now advising certain generations about words or phrases they should or should not use. For example, an online news article argues that people over 40 should not use these "millennial terms" or slang expressions:

- "yaaas" (for a strong "yes")
- "fam" (for someone like family but not real family)
- "bruh" (an exclamation of expression roughly similar to "seriously")
- "baddie" (someone in a small circle of friends that does not play by the rules)

The list continues, but, in summary, the article suggests that if a person is over 40 years old, that person may be better off saying "yes," "family," or "seriously" (*BestLife* 2020).

5.1.2 Gender

The best-seller book by renown sociolinguist, Deborah Tannen, *You Just Don't Understand: Women and Men in Conversation*, showed important distinctive features of what could be called typical "female speech" versus "male speech" in the speech communities of the U.S. during the last decade of the twentieth century and the first decade of the twenty-first century. Tannen (1990) shows, for example, how in the context of ordering at restaurants and similar settings, women tend to use more indirect speech than men. For example, a woman may order a coke by saying, "Could I have a coke, please?" or "Would you mind bringing me a coke, please?" A man, for the same purpose, might simply say, "I'll have a coke, please." This type of indirectness, Tannen argues, is a common characteristic of women's discourse but not of men's discourse in this setting.

This indirectness is not strange in linguistic interactions. As in many instances of our language use, we sometimes do not mean exactly what our words overtly suggest. This strategy has a purpose—it has pragmatic meaning. It is not that we are being dishonest. Someone may say, "Why don't you just say what you mean?" What is the person who says this doing? Is that person really asking us a question expecting that we explain to them why this is so? Is this person giving us a suggestion regarding what we should do? Is this person complaining? Even this person that is denigrating indirectness may be a protagonist of this indirectness without realizing it. Indirectness tends to be a way to show courtesy, according to Brown and Levinson's Politeness Theory mentioned earlier. Whether it is due to politeness or not, the reality is that this indirectness has meaning, and it sometimes distinguishes the language or the speech of a certain segment of the society in a particular context.

Considering current trends regarding the concept of gender differences, how might features of women's and men's discourse—which Tannen described in the later 1980s and early 1990s—be expressed in today's discourse? It is probable that changes have occurred regarding gender patterns of communication.

A 2018 news article compares the features observed by Tannen two decades previously. This more updated article suggests that these features are still prevalent in women's discourse; what might be changing is the perception of those features (Rafferty 2018). Bartholomew (as cited in this article) presents a defense of those feminine features, and argues that we should perceive them, not as insecurity or low confidence on the part of women, but simply an expression of the way women desire to connect with others. When women say, *sorry*, often they are not apologizing but building bridges. Thus, the article proposes, not seeing this *sorry* as a one-down or inferiority status for women, but a way of bridging relations. Some sociolinguists believe that it is likely that women may feel in a one-down status and have a low level of confidence in comparison to men, not necessarily because of their gender inherently, but because of global androcentric (male-dominated) environments (Wilson and Boxer 2015:6). Gender does appear to affect differences in language use, and we should recognize the characteristics of both male and female speech patterns and understand and value them.

5.1.3 Social class and education

Another crucial factor of language variation is social class, which could be a combination of different sub-factors such as education, last name or family heritage, economy, and political position. Basil Bernstein (1960) presents one of the earliest formal linguistic studies on this social class distinction in language. Bernstein observed that higher social class members develop an abstract and subjective mode of speech that projects superiority and exclusivity, possibly due to the types of work they have or the type of diverse situations where they study, work and live. This does not seem to be the case with lower social classes.

The main difference was that higher social class members had access to two different linguistic codes (an abstract code they consider theirs, and a lower-level code that is more concrete). Consequently, higher social class members tend to have a wider range of syntax structures and more complex sentences. Bernstein did not find differences in intelligence, so the higher social class members were not more intelligent than others but had higher expectation levels and opportunities for quality education. Look at the discussion in figure 33 that illustrates cross-code interaction.

5.1 Factors causing language variation: Sociolinguistic variables 63

Figure 33. Abstract versus concrete levels of code.

The more abstract, elaborate code used by the presenter on TV in figure 33, might be spoken by a college professor, a politician, or a media host. The level of sophisticated vocabulary and complex grammatical structures may be a linguistic code unfamiliar to people who have a lower level of education or members of a lower social class. Members of the higher classes, often with higher levels of education, can switch between a sophisticated version of English and the everyday language used by the average person. People from lower classes or with lower levels of education will typically have a more difficult time switching between these two codes.

Because of a strong connection between social class or socio-economic status and level of education, we are considering these two factors together and will not discuss linguistic differences based on educational level as a separate topic. Research has shown that members of a lower socio-economic status develop academic skills more slowly than do those of a high socio-economic status (Morgan et al.:2009). Aikens and Barbarin (2008) add that schools in lower-socio-economic neighborhoods generally lack funds and financial support from the government and communities, and this negatively affects students' academic success.

Note that what is referred to as "standard English" is typically synonymous with what might equally be called "educated English". Additionally, "standard English" tends to correspond to the speech of the socio-economically higher-class people. Thus, "non-standard" dialects or varieties normally refer to speech that may carry a stigma. But note that stigmatized English is not necessarily due to an educated linguistic analysis but is based on social dynamics or the society's taste or preferences.

People often judge language using sociological or society-based criteria. However, it is in bad taste to critique or ostracize others based on the use of what one may consider a superior version of the language.

5.1.4 Region

Traveling around the U.S., you can tell when you cross regional borders by people's speech. While in the Northeast once, I ordered "sweet tea," and the waitress looked at me like I was from another planet. She was not familiar with the term *sweet tea*. Sweetened tea is common in the South, and labeled as such, but is foreign to the Northeastern lexicon.

Regional differences have been studied and analyzed based on language subvariety differences. Kurath and McDavid (1961), for example, showed a regional distinction between the use of /w/ and /hw/, pronounced at the beginning of words like "witch," and "which," respectively. These researchers reported that in the early 1960s, the /w/ and /hw/ distinction existed in the North and South of the U.S. but not in the Midland, where people would pronounce "witch," and "which," as homophones. They also reported that the /hw~w/ distinction was completely absent in New York State, but was strongly maintained in Texas, particularly in the Dallas/Fort Worth area.

In the 1980s and 1990s, there was a push toward recording regional linguistic differences on maps, or more technically, linguistic atlases, that diagrammed isoglosses, or geographic boundaries of a certain linguistic feature, such as pronunciation of a specific phoneme or grammatical feature. In the early 2000s, atlases were published, such as the *North American English Atlas* by Labov, Ash, and Boberg (2006).

The linguistic map in figure 34 names some of the language families spoken in regions of South Asia. We see from this map that Bengali is spoken in eastern India, Hindi in central India, and Gujarati in western India. Other linguistic atlases show specific linguistic forms and their distribution across a region, country, or state. For an example, see Eberhard et al. (2025), the *Ethnologue*.

Figure 34. Regional languages of South Asia.

Some linguistic atlases show how linguistic variation is caused in different regions of the world. Chapter 5 gives examples from both English and Spanish which illustrate subvarieties of these major languages, spoken differently, even as an L1, between the English spoken in Australia, Canada, New Zealand, the U.K., and the U.S., etc., or the Spanish spoken as an L1 in Argentina, Spain, and Venezuela, etc. The same is true for other languages such as French and German, and the countries where they are spoken as an L1. Similarly, these major world languages are spoken as an L2 or LINGUA FRANCA in multiple countries. A *lingua franca* is a common language used in education or for economic, political, or cultural reasons, particularly between people whose local languages are not mutually intelligible.

In Africa, Swahili is also a major language. In the 1960s, Polomé (1967) described the regional linguistic situation of this language in the continent of Africa. He explained that, at that time, Swahili was an L1 for the African population in Kenya, the Tanganyikan coast and neighboring islands, Somalia, the Portuguese East Africa, the Mrima coast, and Mozambique. But millions of local people in East and Central Africa also use Swahili as a lingua franca or L2. In fact, he observed that many children in those situations may speak what can be called a "creole Swahili." A *creole* is an L1 developed from two distinct languages in contact with each other that the parents spoke as an L2.

This regional or cross-national (and at times cross-continental) diversity is true not only for major world languages but even more geographically restricted languages such as the Chinantec language family in Mexico or the family of Quechua/Quichuan languages in South America. The *Ethnologue,* published by SIL Global, recognizes 14 varieties of Chinantec. Quechuan languages are spoken by ten million people in Bolivia, Colombia, Ecuador, and Peru, by 44 different-but-related linguistic varieties (Eberhard et al. 2023). Regional differences in speech, both minor enough to be considered dialects of a language and major enough to be classified as distinct languages within a language family, have been demonstrated for most of the 7,159 living languages today.

5.1.5 Ethnicity

Another factor that may cause linguistic variation is people's ethnic backgrounds. Many people in the United States, for example, have different ethnic backgrounds, in part due to waves of migration to the U.S. of people from different continents and countries worldwide. Ancestors of millions of North Americans alive today came from Europe, Asia, Africa, or Latin America. These immigrants along with Native Americans are part of the "melting pot" that is America today. People of multiple ethnic origins have had an impact on the English language of twenty-first century America. A blending of ethnicity affects a combination of speech patterns obvious in accents, grammatical patterns, and intonation. The English spoken by Hispanic Americans, for example, includes a sprinkling of words from Spanish. Hispanic Americans talking among themselves may include Spanish vocabulary in their English speech, or jump from English to Spanish sentences, and back to English. This is called CODE-SWITCHING, a linguistic characteristic of many English speakers with a distinct ethnicity. Some companies capitalize on ethnic population concentrations by advertising products to a specific ethnic group in the U.S. by having bilingual Spanish-English speakers code-switch between languages in TV commercials, as reported in "Code-Switching among U.S. Latinos" (Toribio 2011).

Labov (2009), in his classic book on the linguistic diversity in America, describes what he calls African American Vernacular English (AAVE, formerly called "Ebonics"). He asserts that "AAVE is clearly a dialect of English rather than a separate creole language." As an example, Labov describes the substitution of "-in" for "-ing" as a common phonological feature. So, the word *working* is pronounced *workin'*. AAVE also presents a high incidence of dropping a final "r" (e.g., [paak] the [kaa] 'park the car'); and copula "be" deletion (e.g., "he good."). In the *Babbel Magazine,* Devlin (2024) describes what many call Hawaiian English. He says that some of Hawaiian English features include the absence of the interdental fricative phonemes "th," [ð], and [Θ]. Some Hawaiians pronounce "the" as [da] and "with" as [wit]. This pronunciation is influenced by the Hawaiian language and Hawaiian Pidgin language.

These examples illustrate speech forms originating from ethnicity-related factors. Some factors portray an ethnic identity for which speakers gain a certain in-group pride, called COVERT PRESTIGE, as described by Chambers and Trudgill (1998:85); other (mainstream) people may have a sense of pride based on their use of a standardized form of the language that is associated with power or status. This is known as OVERT PRESTIGE (Chambers and Trudgill 1998:85). Compare with section 5.1.3.

Ethnicity is combined with factors related to region. These ethnicity-region features have been used for advertising and for political advantage. In July of 2020, a newspaper article was entitled, "How Democrats aim to win Latino votes." the Associated Press (AP) reported that the Democrats hired Spanish speakers for political campaign commercials to win Latino votes. The Democratic campaign advisors believed that commercials broadcast in Spanish would attract these voters. Three Spanish speakers with different region-based accents were hired. "The narrator for the version that aired in Miami had a Cuban accent. In Orlando, Florida, the accent was Puerto Rican. And in Phoenix, it was Mexican" (*AP News* 2020). Regional language use, "micro-targeting," is perceived to attract ethnic groups specific to that area, as a way to exploit race and language for political reasons.

Regardless of the prestige level a language variety may have, ethnicity is frequently a player in the unique linguistic form in which that variety is spoken, and that may have secondary ramifications. This may have been a contributor to the experience Anita had at the beginning of this chapter.

5.1.6 Register: Speech style per situation

Finally, the context or situation where you speak may also influence language variation. There are formal (e.g., a university conference), semi-formal (e.g., an office), and informal (e.g., home) situations in which we adapt our speech, depending on to whom, and where, and when we are talking. REGISTER is the term used to categorize the way a person speaks in relation to their audience, or the style used in a specific social situation. Registers include at least a formal register and an informal one. This is similar to the discussion on *social class*, in section 5.1.3. When a young college student talks to their friends or classmates, they do not talk in the same way as when they talk to their college professor. Also, they may talk to the professor differently in the classroom context than in the lunchroom or in the professor's office. On some college campuses, addressing your college professor for the first time as simply "John," instead of "Dr. Jones," might get you started on the wrong foot in that class and in your relationship with the professor. In this case, *register* may overlap with *age,* section 5.1.1, and *education,* section 5.1.3.

Zwicky and Zwicky (1982) decades ago accounted for the effects of contexts and situations in language styles, or registers. They argue that *register* is a dimension in language variation, in this case, illustrated with *register* in the written form. For example, an author chooses wording differently for a newspaper article than for a kitchen recipe, or for a text by phone.

5.2 The role of politeness in language variation

Violation of appropriate linguistic norms can cause serious breakdowns in communication. In the *Handbook of Sociolinguistics,* Kasper (1997) defines the idea of LINGUISTIC ETIQUETTE, which she categorizes under the umbrella of the POLITENESS THEORY, a human need to save face, following an approach by Erving Goffman ("On Face-work" [1955], "The Nature of Deference and Demeanor" [1956], and *Interaction Ritual* [1967]). For example, the need for indirectness

5.2 The role of politeness in language variation

in some public social contexts is part of these etiquette norms, and addressing another person using their first name, or not, with respect to social distancing, is another example of social appropriateness. Imagine speaking during a court case without being granted permission by the presiding judge. The offender could be held in contempt of court. And if they continue, the judge has the authority to have the person arrested.

In May of 2013, the John A. Hartford Foundation reported that "The U.S. Department of Health and Human Services (HHS) has released the Enhanced National Standards for Culturally and Linguistically Appropriate Services in Health and Health Care." If working for the HHS, caregivers would need to pay attention to the linguistic etiquette under which they work. Violating the language etiquette standards could have irreversible consequences.

Linguistic etiquette standards are rapidly changing in the political sector. Leandra Bernstein, an NBC journalist, reported about the state of incivility in political discourse. Regarding the results of polls in reference to the then-upcoming 2020 presidential campaign and elections, she observed, "The vast majority of Americans believe that divisions in the country are getting worse and the national dialogue is breaking down … the average voter believes the country is two-thirds of the way to the brink of civil war … most voters lament the sad state of political discourse" (Bernstein 2019). Based on a Georgetown University's civility poll, Bernstein continued that, finding a balance between linguistic etiquette and political debate is now more difficult since, "[national] leaders … [are] regularly violating the norms of political civility with … personal attacks on … critics."

Cillizza (2018), a CNN editor, wrote an article on twenty-first century politicians' assault on political correctness. He cited part of a "Meet the Press" speech during a presidential campaign: "'We have to straighten out our country, … political correctness is just absolutely killing us as a country. … Anything you say today, they'll find a reason why it's not good.'"

Cillizza cites politicians having "lowered the overall bar for what is considered acceptable discourse among politicians and other leaders in the country." He comments that, likely due to an intentional disregard for linguistic etiquette in public political discourse, cases of hate crimes, including public anti-Semitic threats, significantly increased in 2017. It is difficult to discern any more what norms are appropriate in the register of public speech, and how hate speech should be handled.

In 2020, after a presidential election, the losing candidate criticized the process by referring to "fraud," a "destroyed system," "rigged elections," "illegal voting," and "stolen elections." Comments like that eradicate the established etiquette in this context; in fact, as has been borne out, they can be very dangerous. *USA Today* debunked the misinformation and the alleged fraud that energized the strengthening of violence and conspiracy theories (Sadeghi and Kochi [2022]). Without question, linguistic etiquette norms underlie our linguistic interactions and have a place in maintaining social equilibrium.

We see the rise of social etiquette norms in recent *netiquette* (social etiquette for internet use) policies. California State University, Fullerton, along with many other universities, lists these, among ten netiquette norms:

- Remember the person: Put yourself in the other person's shoes.
- Maintain the same standards of ethical behavior online as in real life.
- Respect others' time and privacy.
- Make yourself look good online: Know what you are talking about and make sense.
- Keep flame wars under control: Appropriate use of language and tone.
- Forgive others' mistakes: Be patient (*Netiquette* 2023).

Appropriate online behavior is an essential requirement for building a healthy community of online users and learners within a given course.

5.3 Final thoughts on language variation

In summary, language differences in society allow for natural and rich variation in accent, pronunciation, social heritage, and ethnic diversity. Variables affecting language variation include diachronic time factors, the age of a speaker, gender, social class, education, the region from where a speaker originates, ethnicity factors, and register. Often, there is a crossover of some of the factors affecting language use and the perception of language use. For example, ethnicity and region combine to affect forms of speech. In other cases, gender and class may overlap, determining language use and perception. Educational level has a bearing on social class and register, and there are other factors that come to bear on perception and actual use of any language. These factors may contribute to a pride in one's own language, or perhaps a sense of inadequacy. And linguistic competency in a language can be exploited for personal or political gain. Recent erosion of public etiquette at a highly public level has given rise to the establishment of internet standards to help safeguard social etiquette within the context of universities.

In conclusion, language varies widely. It varies from country to country and from region to region; it varies among society groups in the same region; it varies across gender, ethnicity, age, social class, and context-register. In the following exercises you will have the chance to review some of these factors and their impact on language variation. Write out these exercises in a descriptive, objective way.

Exercises

1) Based on the English varieties described, what variety or varieties of English do you think characterize(s) you the most, if any? If none, explain why. If any, explain why. Think of any of the factors mentioned: Is geography a most distinctive factor for you? Or ethnicity? Or social class? etc.
2) Pick a TV personality who speaks English differently than you do. Answer question (1) again regarding this person.
3) Do you think that Deborah Tannen's description of gender differences in language is true for today? Exemplify and explain. Do an online search if necessary.
4) This week, while you are interacting with others (in class, at a restaurant, at home, in church, at the gym, etc.), see how any of the factors mentioned (region, gender, social class, ethnicity, register) impacts language from what you observe. Report your observations.
5) Pick a TV show, movie, YouTube video, or something similar, where you believe there is an overt or covert portrayal of some type of dialect/accent/variety. Comment on the appropriateness or not of that media strategy. Does it perpetuate stereotypes?

6

Did King Alfred Really Speak English?

> Uren Fader dhic art in heofnas
> Our Fadir that art in heuenes
> Our Father who art in heaven
>
> Sic gehalyed dhin noma
> Halewid be thi name
> Hallowed be thy name
>
> To cymedh dhin ric
> Thi Kingdom comme to
> Thy Kingdom come
>
> - Ira Maurice Price, *The Ancestry of the English Bible* (1911:228)

Alfred the Great (see figure 35) was the king of Wessex, an Anglo-Saxon kingdom in the South of Great Britain, during the years 871–899 AD; he was probably the most famous of English kings who lived during the period when the English language spoken then is now referred to as Old English (OE). The first line of the three stanzas of the epigram and the inscription (figure 36) belong to this period. What you are reading in this textbook is Late Modern English (LME). So, comparing scripts, you can see that English has significantly changed over time. OE was also used by the authors Bede, in *The Venerable*, reported to be the main historical source for the Old English era; Caedmon, considered to be the earliest OE Christian poet; and the author of *Beowulf*, one of the most famous writings of the period.

This chapter focuses on critical issues surrounding language change over time.

Figure 35. Alfred the Great, speaker of Old English.

Figure 36. An Old English inscription.

It is difficult for readers of LME to understand texts written in OE due to the significant change in the English language over time.

Look closely again at the OE words in figure 36: *Her swutelað seo gecwydrædnes ðe*. According to OE analysts, the inscription means, "Here the Word is revealed to thee." It is engraved in the arch of the south porticus (portico) at St. Mary's parish church in Breamore, Hampshire, England. King Alfred would undoubtedly have understood what the OE words meant. Most average speakers of English in the twenty-first century struggle to grasp that meaning, even knowing what the individual words mean. This OE text would have been written between the fifth to eleventh centuries AD. OE was spoken 400–1000 AD; the English of the Middle Ages, known as Middle English (ME), was spoken 1000–1400 AD; Early Modern English (EME) was spoken 1400–1800 AD; and the English we speak today, called Late Modern English (LME), has been spoken since 1800 AD.

Change happens to all of us in every arena of life. Describing how and why languages change over time is the goal of chapter 6. In a sense, this chapter is an introduction to the history of the English language, but it is also a commentary on change that occurs in all languages.

A text that spans the four eras of English is recorded in the Bible. It is known as "the Lord's Prayer," taken from Matthew 6:9–13. The OE, ME, and EME, are from Cook's (1891) evolution of the Lord's Prayer in English. These are contrasted with a LME rendition, dated 1992.

The Lord's Prayer

Old English
Fæder ure şu şe eart on heofonum,
si şin nama gehalgod.
to becume şin rice,
gewurşe ğin willa,
on eorğan swa on heofonum.
urne gedæghwamlican hlaf syle us todæg,
and forgyf us ure gyltas,
swa we forgyfağ urum gyltendum.
and ne gelæd şu us on costnunge,
ac alys us of yfele soşlice.

Middle English
Oure fadir that art in heuenes,
halewid be thi name;
thi kyndoom come to;
be thi wille don
in erthe as in heuene:
gyue to us this dai oure breed ouer othir substaunce;
and forgyue to us oure dettis,
as we forgyuen to oure gettouris;
and lede us not in to temptacioun,
but delyuere us fro yuel.

Early Modern English
Our Father, thou that art in heavens,
be thy name hallowed.
Come thy Kingdom.
Become thy will in earth as in heavens.
Give us today our daily bread
And forgive us our guilts
as we forgive our offenders.
And not lead thou us into temptation.
But release us from evil. Be it so.

Late Modern English
Our Father in heaven:
May your holy name be honored;
may your Kingdom come;
may your will be done
on earth as it is in heaven.
Give us today the food we need.
Forgive us the wrongs we have done,
as we forgive the wrongs that others have done to us.
Do not bring us to hard testing,
but keep us safe from the Evil One.
Mt 6:9–13 (*GNT*)

As discussed in chapter 5, language varies geographically and, as seen in the samples of the "Lord's Prayer," also varies over time. Language change happens, not just from millennium to millennium, but even from decade to decade. Change is part of the natural dynamics of language, as is true in every area of our lives. The COVID-19 pandemic demonstrated that the world as we know it can change rapidly. Likewise, language change can occur rapidly. My colleague, Keris, put it this way: "Language must serve the user, not the other way around. If times change and you need a new way to say things, then language needs to be flexible enough to serve the users in new ways." Language change is not only natural, but also useful.

In the religious or sacred life, there can be tension between the vernacular language (the language used by average people in their day-to-day lives) and the formally recognized official language of that religious domain. Religious language is sometimes described as "classical language," "sacred language," "church language," or even "God's language." In the Arabic world, there are two major types of Arabic: Classical Arabic, which is used in the Qur'an, the primary religious book of the Muslim world; and vernacular (common) Arabic, which is spoken in the home, and normally varies by country. In Jewish communities, a similar tension exists between Classical Hebrew and other forms of language spoken by Jewish people in the marketplace, among themselves.

In Christian communities in the U.S. and English-speaking countries worldwide, there has been a long-standing debate regarding what version of the Christian Bible to use. For millions of Christians, the most common version or translation for decades, has been the *King James Version* (*KJV*). Some churches in the U.S. advertise on their websites or church marquis as a "King James only" church. Some *KJV* proponents today have a pejorative view of recent translations or versions. In many Christian communities in Spanish-speaking

Latin America, a similar tension exists between proponents of the traditional version of the Christian Bible, the *Reina Valera (RV)*, and those who use more modern versions. Some sectors of society prefer a traditional version for the reading of sacred books or for liturgical use. But there are extreme cases where the average person may not understand the "sacred" language, yet adamantly defend it as the only permissible language at church. For example, until the Second Vatican Council (1962–1965), when the Roman Catholic Church endorsed worship in local languages, the Church administered the Mass in Latin (the official language of the Roman Catholic Church), even though Latin was understood only by the clergy, not the average congregant.

A common factor about these classical or "church-proper" languages is that they are older versions of a language, yet they were once the everyday vernacular. For example, Classical Hebrew was the spoken Hebrew thousands of years ago. The language in the *KJV* was the version of the English language spoken in everyday communication during the time of James I, who authorized the original *KJV* translation in 1611. The Spanish language used in the original *Reina Valera* was, likewise, the way Spanish was spoken in 1569, at the time that translation was published. Much of the vocabulary and grammatical forms are archaic in today's spoken Spanish. Yet religious purists argue for the use of these archaic linguistic forms for sacred books, liturgy, and hymns in church. Some people seem to believe in a golden age of language and assume that modern use of the language is less appropriate when used in the formal context of the church.

Timothy George suggested in *The Nature of God*, that "one of the great temptations in all religious cultures is to localize God, to so contextualize God within a specific place, time, idiom [language] that he becomes captive to the whim and desires of those who conceive of him in these limited ways" (2014:199). Does God prefer one version of a language over another, or one language over another? Is one form of a language more pure or sacred than another? In reality, the "sacred languages" of today are merely an earlier stage in the development of a language. Language from one era cannot be considered more, or less, pure than that language spoken during another era. The form of the language has merely changed. We prefer to say that language *adapts*, instead of language *evolves*, to avoid the illusion that a previous version of the language is inferior. For the sake of analogy, we will call these time-capsule varieties, *eralects*.

Table 5. Language variance based on geography, society, and eras when spoken

Geolects of English	**Sociolects of English**	***Eralects of English**
Geography-based varieties	*Society-based varieties*	*Temporal-based varieties*
Southern American	African American English	Old English (OE)
British English	Standard American English	Middle English (ME)
Midwestern American	Nonstandard English	Early Modern English (EME)
Eastern American	Urban American English	Late Modern English (LME)

Each eralect of English was valid historically in its own period. Idealizing (or disdaining) forms of English spoken in a different era ignores valid linguistic change that has occurred over time. Similarly, we should not idealize any *geolect* of English (e.g., Australian English, British English, etc.) or any *sociolect* (e.g., Urban American English or any other variety of the language spoken by a segment of the whole).

But why and how did these history-based varieties emerge? Why and how did the language change? In section 6.1, we will consider some reasons behind language change (the "why"), and in section 6.2, some of the ways in which language changes (the "how"), with examples from the twenty-first century.

6.1 Forces behind language change (why language changes)

Languages may change simply because speakers of that language change. Change to our speech patterns reacts the same way that change to a tool or media affects developments of a medium itself. Figure 37 illustrates what happened to the telephone over time, due to new inventions, adapted expectations, and needs. Similarly, language change is as natural and as expected as changes in human taste, behavior, social environment, and need.

Figure 37. Language and telephones—change over time.

Deutscher points out that "in essence, the motives for change can be encapsulated in the triad economy, expressiveness, and analogy" (2005:62). He rejects other reasons for, or factors of, language change, or else he embeds them within his three major categories. However, as shown in the next sections, there may be more factors than this triad of economy, expressiveness, and analogy. We will cover each factor, beginning with Deutscher's three, but then include additional forces behind language change. The order of presentation here does not indicate a hierarchy or level of importance. Often there is a fusion of motivating forces driving change.

6.1.1 Economy (or "linguistic ergonomics")

Deutscher's reference to *economy* takes us back to Whitney's (1875) long established "economy principle of language" described in chapter 3. People are essentially practical regarding the use of tools and tend not to waste energy and effort unnecessarily, taking the shortest route with the highest possible benefit. Recently, Hagura, Haggard, and Diedrichsen (2017) studied human decision-making based on the path of least resistance. Even though not a language-based study, nor about language choices, the study demonstrates a pattern or human tendency that presents itself in many areas of life. The subjects in the study demonstrated a bias toward taking the path that, for them, represented the least effort. The cost involved in a decision influenced the choice they made. People seem to be wired to take the path of least resistance.

Are you familiar with Aesop's fable about the fox and the grapes? In the fable, a fox sees some good-looking grapes on a vine and wants to eat them, but the vine is too high for the fox to reach. After several attempts and failures, the fox concludes that the grapes are probably sour, contrary to its first opinion. Similarly, people tend to reject expending too much energy if the benefits are not obvious or guaranteed. Like the fox, people choose the path of least resistance—which also holds true regarding our use of language. Why say ten words if just three words can communicate the idea? Why follow a grammatical rule if the nuance of meaning is no longer relevant to our reality?

Even though the connection between the human tendency toward taking the path of least resistance and language efficiency may be debatable, frequently in decision-making and language choices, people do prefer a less costly path, with a high preference for maintaining efficiency in our speech. It is related to a twentieth-century concept, *ergonomics*. The Greek prefix *erg-* 'work', combines with *-nomics* (as in *economics*). ERGONOMICS is "an applied science concerned with designing and arranging things people use so that the people and things interact most efficiently and safely" (*Merriam-Webster* 2024a). With respect to language, we can consider *linguistic ergonomics*, our accommodation of language for the highest benefit with the least possible effort.

Linguists Sperber and Wilson (1986) argue in their Relevance Theory (RT) that when we process linguistic information, we attempt to gain the most cognitive effects while expending the least possible processing effort. In other words, we process what is relevant, and what is relevant is what results in the highest possible cognitive gain, with the least amount of expended effort. For example, when deciphering an ambiguous sentence, we disambiguate the multiple meanings, by selecting the interpretation that requires the least effort—which is also the interpretation that carries the most information relevant to the context or situation.

The sentence "Did you see the crane?" is semantically ambiguous because, as was shown in section 4.4.4, "crane" has more than one meaning. However, only one interpretation would be relevant considering the context, the purpose of the utterance, and the type of participants involved. In a zoo, the most likely interpretation would be in reference to a bird rather than a machine or equipment at a construction site. That interpretation requires less cognitive effort.

In conclusion, linguistic change can be the product of our need as people to be more economic or ergonomic in our use of language. Some examples of linguistic change due to economic reasons in English include, from phonemes to our English lexicon and grammar:

a) loss of phonetic sounds, e.g., [k], and [x] for "gh," in knight;
b) loss of words, e.g., hither, thither, thee, and thou;
c) neologisms (newly coined words), e.g., Venmo, ghosting, doxing; and
d) changed grammar, including suffixes and word order, as a historian of the English language explains:

> Old English was a very complex language, at least in comparison with modern English. Nouns had three genders (male, female and neuter) and could be inflected for up to five cases. There were seven classes of "strong" verbs and three of "weak" verbs, and their endings changed for number, tense, mood and person. Adjectives could have up to eleven forms. Even definite articles had three genders and five case forms as a singular and four as a plural. Word order was much freer than today, the sense being carried by the inflections. (Barker 2024)

6.1.2 Expressiveness

Deutscher uses the term *expressiveness* in the context of language change to refer to our need to "achieve greater effect … and extend range of meaning" (2005:62). He demonstrates this with the negation *no*. He makes the point that in many cases, just using the word *no* is not enough to express all necessary nuances of meaning. In that case, we might say "no way" or "not at all" to express negation more emphatically. Some people reduplicate the use of *no*, saying, "*no, no*, I'm fine." It is possible that the constant use of one of these other "more expressive" *no's* will become used frequently enough to eventually replace a simple "no" in our lexicon.

Use of these other more expressive *no's* seems to contradict the economic force mentioned in 6.1.1 by adding words to a simple *no*. But less effort expended in an expression in some contexts may lose the emotional gain we want, and so we add words for that additional expressiveness.

Some more expressive options may find wide acceptance and become a preferred option. Some adverbs these days have gained an expansive use due to expressiveness. "That's awesome!" or "It's great!", or "Wonderful!" instead of a simple, "good" or "nice." The expanded use of the adverb *literally* is heard commonly, too. *Literally* is used as hyperbole and for dramatic effect. For example: "I literally flew from there when I saw the cops coming!"

Merriam-Webster suggests that *literally*, contrary to its original meaning, is used figuratively in many cases. This figurative use of *literally* is "a statement or description that is not literally true or possible. … It is pure hyperbole intended to gain emphasis." (*Merriam-Webster* 2024c).

6.1 Forces behind language change (why language changes)

In a 2020 Reddit (reddit.com) blog interaction, a teenager wrote: "I'm 19 and I feel like I am literally going to explode." The teenager was exuding anger and frustration due to previous schooling experiences.

In the next generation of English speakers, the word *literally* may be used in the United States as an intensifier like "very much" or "really", in which the secondary, metaphorical use replaces the primary meaning of "in a literal or exact manner." When the literal meaning of a word falls into disuse, another word or expression replaces it.

6.1.3 Analogy

Analogy involves the comparisons of two unlike items or concepts that share a particular aspect. By analogy, the first item clarifies or explains the second item by means of the shared similarity, often in the form of a metaphor or simile. The use of analogy has been crucial in language change. (Fischer and Olbertz 2019:253).

Deutscher (2005:62) argues that one of the areas where analogy is obvious regarding language change is in the regularization of language patterns. Although languages have many irregular forms (e.g., irregular verbs, irregular nouns), languages have a strong tendency to form a regularity of patterns. It is predictable, then, that most verbs in English are regular. Most verbs in English, for example, form their past tense with the suffix -ed: work/worked, stay/stayed, open/opened. The minority are irregular: go/went, do/did, write/wrote. If a new English verb was adopted into the language, speakers would likely form the past tense of this hypothetical verb with -ed, following regular grammatical pattern. Nouns also have a standard pattern of regularization, in which they generally form a plural using an -s suffix, e.g., books, cars, computers; but a few have an irregular form, e.g., feet, men, deer, and sheep, in which the plural form has become regularized as such.

The trend in language change is to regularize the grammar rather than to diversify. In a study comparing irregular verbs in OE with LME, there has been a decline over time. "Of the 177 irregular verbs that existed in Old English, only 98 are still irregular today" (Al-Hussein 2018:100).

Of course, how analogy relates to language change goes far beyond morphological regularizations. Analogy also spreads to phonological, syntactic, and semantic changes. Metaphors and metonymies are key in semantic changes. One common example of metonymy has to do with naming a part for the whole or a whole for the part, such as saying, "I have many mouths to feed" (a part for the whole), or "Argentina defeated Brazil in the 2021 Americas Soccer Cup" (a whole for a part). In soccer, when the ball touches any part of a player's arm it is called a "hand ball." Traugott and Dasher in *Regularity in Semantic Change*, suggest that "in semantic change … a term for a part will become a term for a whole, but not vice versa" (2004:29).

6.1.4 Language contact

Weinreich has established the foundation for formal studies on language contact. He originally defined language contact as the use of two or more languages by the same person. In this scenario, Weinreich explains, one language very likely introduces elements of its lexicon and grammar into the other language (1968:1).

Bull explains that the most basic description of a language contact situation is when two languages, language A and language B, exist in close proximity, creating a third linguistic variety, either a new language or a new variety of one of those languages. He exemplifies this with a variety of a Norwegian language in northern Norway. In this case, in one city, the Finno-Ugric language, Finnish, is in contact with Norwegian, a Germanic language. Bull says, based on his studies, that we can "assume that in multilingual surroundings, even a majority language … will be subjected to … influence from minority … languages" (1995:16). He concluded that the structure of northern Norway dialects is at least partly a product of language contact. Bull says that one linguistic example of this change in this contact situation is the marking of gender. Monolingual Norwegian speakers and most dialects of Norwegian that are not in language contact mark three genders—masculine, feminine, and neuter—but most northern Norwegian dialects have lost this three-gender distinction due to prolonged contact with languages that don't have a gender distinction (1995:24).

In many Spanish-speaking countries today, the Spanish names for sports are borrowed from the name in English (with a phonemic adaptation): baseball → béisbol, basketball → basquetbol, and football → fútbol. In English, the "g" in "rouge" sounds today like the "s" in "vision," but, according to Lehmann, that fricative sound did not exist in Middle English or before. Lehmann points out that this sound was adopted by the English language due to the influence of French loanwords like rouge (Lehmann 1992:187). In fact, due to extensive contact of French in England, when the highest classes used French in discourse, 30 percent of Modern English vocabulary is directly borrowed from French. The French language influenced the grammar, pronunciation, and writing of English. Consider the words used in everyday English like, cliché, faux pas, and déjà vu that have not even been adapted into standard English phonology patterns.

6.1.5 World changes

As our language changes, so does the world around us. New realities require new words such as internet, blog, coronavirus, and others. At the same time, other items or situations are becoming irrelevant, leading to the disappearance of archaic words and expressions. The words "thou" and "thine" are now archaic; you can see them in older versions of the Bible. The verb "to dial" is now rarely used in the sense of calling a phone number, since we have hardly any dial telephones anymore. Similarly, using the expression "answering machine" instead of "voicemail" quickly reveals that you belong to an older generation.

On the other hand, new realities require new words or expressions. I already mentioned words like "voicemail." The word "text" is now used as a verb, meaning sending a text message over the phone, a means of communication that did not exist a few decades ago. In the twenty-first century, people text, blog, surf the internet, and tweet. Even presidents communicate regularly by means of social networks.

Political correctness and changes in society influenced the way we communicate. New social expectations and new moral values discourage the use of some words, encourage the use of others, and create new vocabulary. Today there is pressure to use inclusive language due to political correctness. This movement started in the late twentieth century and became popular, in part, thanks to works such as Thorsen and Becker's *Inclusive Language Handbook* (1996) and the APA *Inclusive Writing Guidelines* (APA 2023a).

The result of peer pressure and inclusive language expectations in society, is that we have new or redefined words that are now more popular or more used than before. Twenty years ago, it was common for an English professor to ask a class of male and female students, "Did everybody bring *his* homework?" Currently, that is considered an inappropriate use of the pronoun. Instead, it is politically correct to say, "Did everybody bring their homework?" Meyers refers to a survey in 1985 which found that most editors in the U.S. were opposed to a singular *they* (Meyers 1990). Two decades later, however, the Modern Language Association's (*MLA*) guidelines for formal writing establish that "singular *they* is widely accepted" and that *they* is also used "as a generic third-person singular" form (*MLA Style Center* 2020). Similarly, due to the inclusive language movement we now say humankind instead of mankind, chairperson instead of chairman, server instead of waiter/waitress, etc. But language changes due to political correctness go beyond avoidance of sexist speech.

The focus on respecting and or re-dignifying marginalized groups of society affects references not only to gender, but to factors such as disability, social class, ethnicity, and other social distinctions. The term *disabled* is now "differently-abled," ethnic names or references are removed as team names, e.g., in 2020, *ABC News* announced that the NFL Washington Redskins retired their team's name amid the "Black Lives Matter" movement, which sparked a cultural awakening (Sanchez 2020).

Section 6.2 is about *how* a language changes, that builds on the concept of *why* a language changes.

6.2 How language changes

Some of the critical driving forces behind language change include the factors discussed in section 6.1. Language economy, a desire for expressiveness, analogy—using the language to explain itself, language contact with other languages, and social issues in our world that effect change on language cause speech and expression changes to language by influencing components of language to adapt or restructure. The changes occur in every component of language: phonology, syntax, morphology, semantics, pragmatics, and the lexicon.

English speakers notice the loss or gain of words, as discussed above in the gain of "voicemail" at the cost of losing "answering machine," or the gain of "flight attendant" at the cost of losing "stewardess." But the gain or loss of vocabulary or morphemes is only one way language changes. We readily observe changes in semantics, or meaning of words, when they assimilate or lose meaning. Changes can be observed in phonology upon a close examination of the gain and loss of phonemes due to language contact and assimilation. Change is also apparent at the morphological and syntactic levels of grammar due to linguistic ergonomics and expressiveness. For example, to accommodate the times in which we live, English has added the prefix *e-* for "electronic," as in *email, e-signature*, and *e-vite*, currently often assimilated in spelling with no hyphen, as *email*, and *evite*. A suffix used in the technology world as a descriptor in our computer-based society, is *-ware*, used in *software, hardware, malware,* and *ransomware*. Changes in language like these can best be analyzed over a span of time.

In exercises 1–3 you will see what some linguists said decades ago about the history of language and languages in general.

Exercise 1: PBS aired the video, "In Search of the First Language," in 1997. Both the video and the transcript are found on this website: https://www.pbs.org/wgbh/nova/transcripts/2120glang.html.

1) Why is the Bible passage mentioned at the beginning of the video?
2) What does the analogy of trees and branches tell us about language or languages?
3) Give examples of "obvious connections" among languages (refer to the Hebrew and Arabic comparison).
4) Name the lawyer-linguist who first discovered connections between English and languages of India (and others).
5) Write down the most famous statement given by this lawyer-linguist.
6) What are the major languages he compared?
7) What does the example of the use of [t] in English and [d] in Hindi tell us?
8) What do we call this method in historical linguistics?
9) How many branches of Proto-Indo-European (PIE) are there? Name some.
10) What Bible passages were used to compare OE with ME?
11) Name the languages in the Sino-Tibetan family. Give the region(s) in which they are located.
12) How are they trying to reconstruct the "Proto-Sino-Tibetan" language?
    Is Thai one of the Sino-Tibetan languages?
13) Words are similar across languages for one of three reasons. Name them.
14) Approximately how many language families are there in the world?
    Name others not previously mentioned.

15) Name three major language families in North America (according to Greenberg).
16) Name a North American language that shows the problem of language loss and reconstruction.
17) Name the four major language families of Africa.
18) What is "Kernel Vocabulary?"
19) Define "linguistic isolate." What language in Europe is an example of this?
20) What is the relation between genetics and historical linguistics?
21) Give examples found by Labov that demonstrate language change in Philadelphia (and the U.S.A.):
22) Name some linguists who believe the Nostratic Hypothesis.
23) What is "water" in PIE? What is "water" in "Proto Nostratic"?
24) Why is "10,000 years" a critical point?
25) What does the word "milk" show?
26) Do most linguists believe that all languages come from a single source? What does (academic-traditional) science say? What do you think?

Exercise 2: Summarize the argument on this website: https://www.icr.org/article/mystery-human-language/.

Exercise 3: Compare any of the OE texts in this chapter to your version of English today. Describe at least three differences. Make sure you pick differences in different linguistic areas. For example, one difference can be phonological, another syntactic, another morphological, another lexical, etc. For the sake of this exercise, assume that the orthography reflects pronunciation. Use that to come up with phonological differences.

7

Do We Mean What We Say?

A diplomat who says 'yes' means 'maybe,' a diplomat who says 'maybe' means 'no,' and a diplomat who says 'no' is no diplomat.

– Charles Maurice de Talleyrand, 1754–1838, French statesman and diplomat

After giving a lecture as a visiting professor of linguistics at a university in Peru in the summer of 2012, a student came to me feeling frustrated. I had just lectured about how people speak between the lines, indirectly, just giving hints, and not overtly saying what they mean. She disagreed that, in her case at least, this was not true. She claimed she always said what she meant and meant what she said. I asked her, "Always?" She responded, "Never in a million years would I beat around the bush! I'd kill myself first!" or something equivalent in the Spanish language. I asked her, "A million years? Kill yourself? Do you really mean that?" We both laughed. This encounter showed me two things. First, this re-emphasized, to her and to me, that people indeed play with language in many ways. We have hidden messages in what we say or do not say. We often do not say overtly what we mean for various reasons. Second, it helped me realize again that we are experts in our own language, but not always its best judges.

Figure 38. We may be experts in our language, but not always its best judges.

This chapter will describe linguistic meaning beyond words themselves and the rules of grammar. This is linguistic meaning in context, sometimes called PRAGMATICS, or the use of words in a concrete, practical sense.

This chapter complements chapter 4, which discussed basic semantic meaning. So, this chapter will describe how people play with linguistic meaning in light of the context in which that language is used. Let us look at how people use language in the arena of meaning, beyond the analytic discussion of phonology, vocabulary, and grammatical form. Then we will see how context and meaning interact and inferential processing takes place in the mind, giving shape to meaning.

7.1 Language use: Beyond sounds, words, and grammar

Language can be defined as a system of communication that consists primarily of phonology, a lexicon, and grammar. However, language is much more than sounds, words, and grammar. If language were limited to a lexicon and a grammar, very likely computers would be carrying on a two-way conversation with us. It would only require inputting the lexicon and the grammatical rules into the appropriate computer code.

However, as discussed in chapter 2, it has taken experts multiple years, a lot of research, and many hours of instruction and programming to train non-humans, such as animals and machines, to achieve one-way noncreative, limited communication. And, although there have been incredible advances in training them to speak human languages satisfactorily, they are far from an ability to speak correctly 100-percent of the time. Admittedly, researchers have achieved much in voice recognition, in syntax-interpreting rules used in language programming, in machine translation, and in similar AI tasks. Yet, if you compare the most advanced robot or computer with humans in this respect, its adaptive, *creative* linguistic ability would be non-existent, even when compared with a seven-year-old child. This contrast would be even more obvious if compared with post-puberty teenagers or adults, who have a more developed abstract communication ability via language.

In chapter 1, when discussing the complexity of language as one of its features, we considered an example of machine translators and their limited capacity to achieve an acceptable translation of a relatively simple phrase. The question remains, why can't computers do this job satisfactorily or adequately? The major reason is that computers cannot interpret voice inflection, stress in speech, contextual clues, and nuances of language use, aspects of communication considered normal by people, and to which they are very accustomed. Computers can effectively process sounds, words, alphabets, rules, syntax, and other mechanical tasks, but cannot deal with non-mechanized aspects of language. For example, in speech, people play with humor, with double meaning of words, use figurative language, express irony, say one thing even though they mean another, use incomplete phrases intentionally, fill in gaps in what others say, read the contextual clues, and so on. These nuances are beyond the adaptability allowed in data sets required by AI used in computer feedback to a prompt. AI depends upon a human source to feed it the data required, like a lexicon (dictionary), a set of grammar rules, and an immense amount of data. However, more than data manipulation is required to interpret and process the "playful" handling of language.

"Language use," referred to in this section as pragmatics, is a major focus of chapter 7. Chapter 4 introduced the meaning of language in general, more properly referred to as *semantics*. Here, we expand the concept of semantics to include PRAGMATICS: How context contributes to implication and relevance in meaning. At times, we will refer back to semantic meaning in order to compare the literal understanding people attach to words and expressions—with pragmatics, that goes beyond basic semantic meaning.

Pragmatics, of the various components of linguistics, such as syntax, morphology, phonology, and semantics, is the skill set that is last learned by children, due to the high level of abstract processing that is required. Papafragou points out that children's ability to infer what others mean matures with age and experience. This is true for basic inferential processing of vocabulary, requiring a more refined degree of awareness to process pragmatic meaning.

7.1 Language use: Beyond sounds, words, and grammar　　　　　　　　　　　　　　　　81

For example, it takes inferential skill to interpret, "How are you?" at its most basic meaning, i.e., "Tell me about your pain," or "Are you still feeling sick?" But the pragmatic use of this expression, as a greeting, requires a higher level of inferential processing.

Papafragou observes that many phenomena that require the hearer to imply or infer meaning, or phrases that express ideas indirectly, such as irony and metaphor, present difficulty for children (2018:167). This was illustrated for me one day, when my son was about five years old. My wife said to him, "Stay here and do not move a finger." When I arrived on the scene and told him to follow me, he said, "Mom said I can't move." He looked like a robot and had no intention of moving without her permission. My wife, my son (now 26), and I now laugh at the incident, but it was terrifying for my son at the moment. My wife was trying to protect him by telling him to stay in a safe space, but he interpreted the requirement literally. Young children often find it difficult to process figurative language. Why do adults often "say what they don't mean," and "not mean what they say!"

Figure 39. Children and adults seem to talk in different dimensions.

This level of complexity for pragmatic competence also manifests itself in second language acquisition (SLA). Just as children struggle with understanding meaning beyond the words, or to "read between the lines," foreigners learning another language experience a similar challenge. Internationals learning English often miss a joke or the point of a certain phrase even though they have mastered the words and the grammar. When I moved from my first home country of Venezuela to the U.S. 27 years ago, I was invited to sing in an English-speaking church. I thought I knew English fairly well. My BA was in English education, and I had done well on my speaking-proficiency test of English as a Foreign Language. At the program, when I was walking to the stage, a new friend at church whispered to me, "Break a leg!" I was so angry! It was hard for me to even speak to him again. How could he say such a crude thing at a moment so important to me, my first time singing in English in front of an English-speaking group? I certainly knew what "break," "a," and "leg" meant. I knew the grammar rules that combined the words. I understood every phoneme. But I didn't understand the meaning of the idiom (see figure 40). People who are learning a language as an L2 (and young children) may decompose an idiom into individual words instead of processing it as figure of speech. It is pragmatic competence that will give this expression its idiomatic, non-literal sense. Language use requires more than a lexicon and an understanding of the grammar.

Later, I found out that my new-found—and quickly-lost—friend was just wishing me good luck! So, I reconnected with him.

Figure 40. Non-native speakers, like children, struggle with pragmatic competence.

Here is an example of English speakers learning Spanish. In 2019, I took a group of English-speaking college students to a university in the Yucatan Peninsula, Mexico, for a Spanish study-abroad summer trip. Nearby, there were a few *cenotes* 'underground springs' in a sinkhole, which, in the hot and humid climate, quickly became popular among the students. They would swim in the cenotes almost every day. Spanish speakers use the word *bañar* for both swimming and for taking a shower or bath. My students of Spanish had learned the word, but with the more standard meaning of "showering/bathing." They were soaking wet from a swim when a local Mexican taxi driver picked them up from the cenote and asked them, "*¿Se bañaron?*" which can be interpreted both, "Did you go for a swim?" and "Did you take a shower?" The friendly cab driver was not really asking for information, since the answer was obvious. It was just a way to connect socially with his passengers. One of my students (excited and proud of herself that she had understood the question) replied with a confident and enthusiastic, "No!" The puzzled taxi driver repeated the question a couple of times. But, to his disappointment, he received the same answer each time.

In this case, different factors were at play. On one hand, the two semantic meanings (polysemy) of the word *bañar,* were not apparent to the English speaker. She thought of only one possible meaning. On the other hand, the driver was asking a *rhetorical* question (not seeking information, since the answer was obvious). The driver, pragmatically, was just connecting socially, not asking. The student also did not see the pragmatic meaning of this "question," to the driver's disappointment. For his part, the taxi driver may have interpreted that the young ladies did not want to talk to him—and that was the end of the conversation.

If you have been around speakers of English as a second language (ESL), you may have encountered examples like this. If you have studied a second language (L2) yourself you may have also experienced something similar. Your experiences illustrate the point of this chapter: words do not always mean exactly what they seem to mean. That is, a question doesn't always seek an answer, a statement is sometimes a question, a question is sometimes a command, a *no* might mean *yes*, and so on.

A person who knows a language well will be able to master these secondary meanings hidden beneath the words. In other words, a good language user has pragmatic competence in the language they are learning. Consider figure 41 and make a connection between the image and the topics of this chapter.

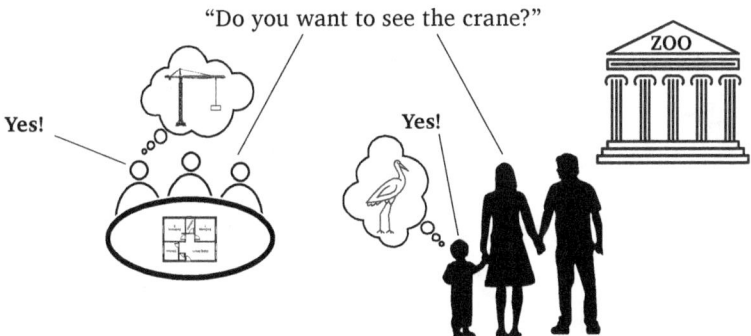

Figure 41. Same question, different conclusions.
(Context and experience determines the correct interpretation!)

For pragmatic competence in a language, knowledge of the lexicon, the sounds, and the grammar of the language is insufficient for full competence. Many other factors accompany the words that impact meaning—again, what people can read between the lines. When talking, open your eyes and ears, not just your mouth.

The "How are you?" example above further illustrates the point. How do listeners decide what response is appropriate? In milliseconds, based on extralinguistic clues, they need to interpret what the speaker intended to say. The literal words and grammar rules of the phrase don't make sense based on the nonlinguistic signals, so they depend on their wider experience. They calculate the time, situation, who is asking what, to whom, with what intonation the question is being asked, and other contextual factors. If it is a doctor talking to a patient, then it is likely a question about the patient's health. If it is a friend and classmate one minute before the beginning of class, then it is just a quick greeting due to the hurried circumstances. In the earlier example with the word *bañar,* a native Spanish speaker wouldn't interpret the meaning to be "taking a shower or bath" in the situation of a lake, pool, beach, or *cenote*; inside a house, it would rarely be interpreted as "swimming." Context and extralinguistic information matter. Context includes situation, time and place of interaction, and related factors. In section 7.2 we will examine these contextual factors further.

7.2. Contextual factors guiding language use

In this section, we focus on the pragmatic issues guiding language interpretation, or processing. Hymes's (1974) model gives the eight context-based factors that contribute to the use of language. The acronym SPEAKING spells out those extralinguistic factors that describe *context*. They are **S**ituation, **P**articipants, **E**nds of an interaction, **A**ct sequence, **K**ey, **I**nstrumentalities, **N**orms, and **G**enre. We will now discuss each of these factors.

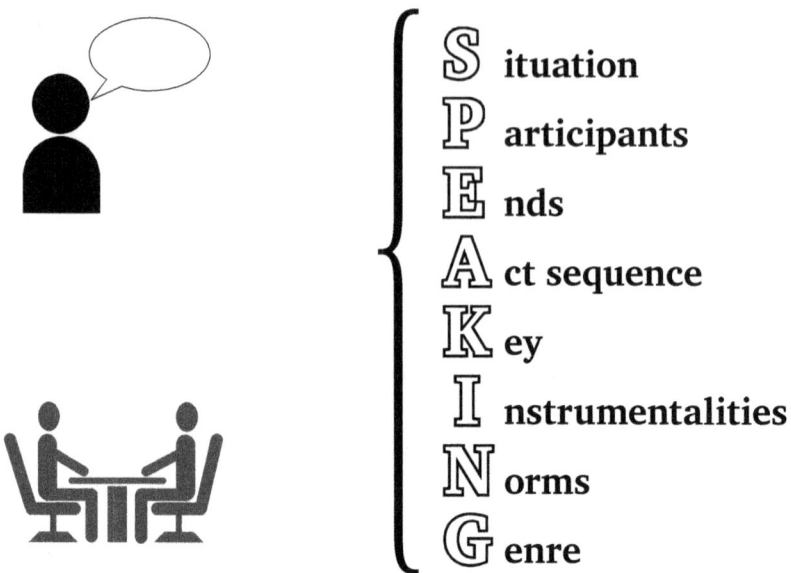

Figure 42. Hymes' "Speaking" model.

7.2.1 Situation (where and when)

Situation refers to the place and time of an interaction, the where and when it takes place. That is crucial to know before we interpret any utterance or linguistic expression satisfactorily. "I'm good," can mean many things in different contexts. Apart from the most basic meaning of "I am not bad," as in, "I am not a bad person," it may also intentionally convey different messages. At a tennis match, if the referee or umpire asks you, "Do you need to warm up more, or are you ready for the game?" "I'm good," may mean, "I'm ready." But speaking to the host at your friend's house where you went to eat a meal, "I'm good," could mean, "I'm not hungry, thanks," or "I'm full."

7.2.2 Participants (who)

Information about who the participants are also impacts our interpretation of what is said. We need to know, not only when and where something happened, but also who said what to whom. Knowing the participants' relationship and role is critical. Again, in the "How are you?" example, if a patient says it to another patient, it most likely means "Hi," but if the doctor asks the patient the same question, he is inquiring about the patient's health. If I ever say: "I declare war against X country," most likely you would laugh, but if the president of the United States made that declaration, nobody would laugh. The president of a country has the authority and oversight to make such a claim—with obvious serious consequences.

7.2.3 Ends (why)

The term "ends" in this context refers to the goals or final objective of a linguistic interaction or discourse. Not only do we need to know the *when*, the *where*, and the *who* of the interaction, but also the *why*, or its purpose. When we go to the doctor, the purpose is to be checked by the doctor and to find out about our health. Keeping that purpose of the doctor-patient interaction in mind helps a patient correctly interpret the doctor's question, "How are you?" more accurately. Imagine the scenario in which the phone rings, the name of a salesman displays on the cell phone screen, and the dad tells his seven-year-old daughter to answer and say that he is busy now. So, the daughter says to the salesman, "My dad told me to tell you he is busy." If the daughter understood the purpose of her dad's directive, she would answer the phone differently.

7.2.4 Act sequence (what is next)

Interactions normally follow a certain sequence; Schank and Abelson (1977:38) call it "scripts," or an interaction or domain with a relatively fixed expected sequence of events. People often act in relatively predictable patterns. An example of this is what Schegloff and Sacks (1973:295) call *adjacency pairs,* such as a question and its answer, a greeting with a greeting reply, an invite and its acceptance or refusal, and so on. We can usually predict what is coming. What should come after the question "How are you?" spoken by a doctor? We know that an answer about the patient's health should follow. On other occasions, questions are not to be answered. A rhetorical question spoken by a preacher, for example, does not expect a reply from the audience. It is not really a question but an idea or thought for the listeners to consider. If somebody dared to answer, it would be awkwardly disruptive, for both the preacher and everybody else. These established scripts help listeners know what is predictable and expected in such linguistic-act sequences.

7.2.5 Key

Musicians use *keys* to determine what notes are played in a song. The musical key determines the pitch of the song, and to some degree, its mood as well. Similarly, there is a certain key to a speech event that determines the mood and the degree of formality or register of the interaction. Knowing the mood and the register also helps a listener to interpret dialogue appropriately. In a formal encounter, the words "lady" or "young lady" might be interpreted with a positive connotation, but when a mother, who is angry, calls her daughter, "*young lady,*" most people would interpret the phrase as anything but positive. Some common registers are formal, informal, semi-formal, and familiar. *Mood* is used here to mean the tone of a conversation. It does not refer to the technical concept of grammatical mood. The (non-grammatical) mood can include a joke, a heated argument, a serious encounter in a legal court, and so on.

7.2.6 Instruments—nonverbal cues

Another contextual factor guiding language use is knowing the tools used to communicate well. Of course, part of this involves the language variety or code used to communicate. If we do not know Russian, it will be difficult at best for us to communicate with people who speak only Russian. However, beyond the linguistic code itself, there are secondary factors or cues used to communicate, such as images, gestures, body language, tone of voice, volume, facial expression, and so on. In the earlier *young lady* example, to correctly interpret the meaning behind the use of the phrase, it would help to hear the mother's tone of voice, interpret the volume level used, and see her facial expression. Depending on tone of voice and facial expression, the phrase can be understood as a compliment or a reprimand. Likewise, during the pandemic of 2018–2021, while mask-wearing was common, communication became more difficult. More repetition was needed in conversations since masks hid important nonverbal cues such as facial expression, and it restricted lip reading.

7.2.7 Norms

Everyone follows certain norms in everyday life. Our use of language is no different. There are linguistic norms to follow, and here we mean something far beyond grammar rules alone. For example, in Spanish you must know the social status of the hearer in relation to you before you address that person because there are two pronouns for "you," one formal and one informal. You do not want to use informal *tú* 'you' when you address your college professor for the first time, as it can be interpreted as an insult. There are norms about who speaks at what point, about who initiates and who ends the interaction, about how long you are expected to talk, about how to indicate to others that you finished your idea, and so on. Native speakers might forgive you when you break grammatical, lexical, or phonological rules, but what they might never forget is when you violate the SPEAKING (pragmatic) norms.

7.2.8 Genre

Just like literary texts, linguistic interaction also has genre norms. The participants need to know if the interaction is a business meeting, a job-training session, a university lecture, a court trial, a first encounter between strangers in an elevator, informal time with friends, a family reunion, a funeral, story-telling time, and so on. Each genre has an obvious impact on how the participants will interpret what is said. For example, what does "Stop!" mean? It depends. Is it a policeman making an arrest? Is it a girlfriend laughing hard at her boyfriend's jokes? In the first scenario, it *really* means "Stop!", but in the second scenario the pragmatic meaning might actually be, "Keep it up!"

7.2.9 Competent linguistic interaction—Conclusion

Mastery of these SPEAKING factors takes years of repeated interaction with other speakers of the language in a common environment. By living and interacting together, a speaker develops a shared knowledge, understanding, and worldview. They learn what is appropriate in different situations (S) well and get to know the participants (P) in those situations. This extensive interaction trains them in the end goals (E) of everyday interactions, and the expected act sequence (A) of such interactions. They also learn over time about the degree of formality relevant for a specific speech community, and to perceive key moods (K). Of course, they learn more about the words and the grammar, but also become experts in reading non-verbal cues, or instrumentalities (I), like body language, facial expression, and so on. In the same way, they learn the norms of interaction (N) expected and to which they must adhere, and the different genre (G), or types of interactions, in which they can be involved. That is why children, second language learners, machines, and animals have a hard time understanding everything adult native speakers say. They do not have the years of experience and interaction skills required to internalize the contextual cues. They do not have the eyes and ears to perceive non-linguistic information, or the abstract capacity to master this complex communication skill.

7.3 Language use as an inferential process

When you learned of Ripley the Robot, assigned as an exercise in chapter 2, you learned that machines, robots, and computers cannot process language without extensive training and programming. If computer technology is so advanced, what is it they are missing?

There is so much more than grammar rules and a list of sounds and words in the complexity of communication by language. Consider the empathy aspect, worldview, common sense, societal experience, linguistic register, physical context, common needs and expectations,

7.3 Language use as an inferential process

"agreed-upon" social context, time context, and social relationships. All these pragmatic issues are unique to human communication. Processing all these factors in a split second when in a fluid conversation requires the skill of effective *inference.*

One of the first scholars to formally formulate the need for inference in language use was Grice. He stated that in natural human language, "there are very many inferences and arguments ... recognizably valid" (1975:43) that do not follow a formal, mathematical, robotic type of logic. He explained another principle that characterizes human language, what he called the COOPERATIVE PRINCIPLE (CP) (Grice 1975:45). He explained the CP principle in simple terms: "Make your conversational contribution such as is required, at the stage at which it occurs, by the accepted purpose or direction of the exchange" (Grice 1975:45). To comply with this CP principle, Grice recognized that we follow assumed rules or maxims, to be relevant (relevance), orderly, and clear (manner); we shouldn't say more, nor less than is needed (quantity), and should be truthful (quality). People make inferences using these maxims. As an example, the verb "to book" can mean either good news or sobering news. A student explained in a blog that she booked a needed lesson with a driving instructor. The instructor had advised her: "I'll book you in"—that was great news for her! That meant she was on the instructor's calendar and would get her lesson. But if your attorney tells you, "You are booked"—that is not good news. In this case, she is notifying you that you are officially arrested. The most relevant interpretation is what we infer from the situation. The least relevant interpretation is discarded as an unlikely inference.

Figure 43. Grice's Cooperative Principle (CP) of relevance in conversation.

Sperber and Wilson (1986) stated something similar in their Relevance Theory. They argue that of all possible interpretations, especially for expressions with ambiguity or potentially different meanings, we pick the meaning that is based on the most information and that requires the least effort to infer. This tension between cognitive benefit and cognitive effort is what determines relevance. The interpretation with the most benefit and the least effort is the winner. Professor Keris, my colleague, shows this to her class by using the example of someone asking, "Is Julia seeing anyone these days?", and someone replying, "Well, she goes to Cleveland every weekend." If the hearer violates the relevance maxim, then the reference to Cleveland makes no sense, but since the hearer expects the speaker to follow this maxim, the hearer can assume Julia has a boyfriend that she goes to see in Cleveland.

Here is another example: If you say to somebody: "You should be satisfied because now, based on your suggestion, we have an additional crane." the hearer will interpret this only one way based on situation or relevance, and will likely not even perceive the potential ambiguity in the sentence. People disambiguate naturally because ambiguity in meaning requires cognitive effort to interpret. Relevance, that is, the meaning in context, will depend on who you are talking to, and where. Due to RT's principle of relevance, understanding the crane to be a bird requires little effort on the part of a zoologist and it follows up a prior suggestion she made to acquire another crane. These two facts block the "mobile derrick" interpretation and elevate the "bird" interpretation in the speaker's mind. If you were talking to a construction worker, the whole process happens in a similar way, but now the "bird" interpretation is ignored. This inferential process, regardless of which theory you apply (CP or RT), is a fundamental requirement in any human linguistic interaction.

7.4 Dangers in language use

Finally, this chapter raises awareness regarding the potentially damaging or harmful effects of the subtle use of language. Some language uses can be unethical, debatable, or questionable. Some people may deceive others, manipulate, and discriminate, while using language, subconsciously or consciously, covertly or overtly. They can do so through doublespeak, linguistic manipulation, false advertising or claims, and discriminating against others because of their language or choice of code. Let me demonstrate each of these subtle risks. Of course, other uses of language can be equally questionable or damaging, but they tend to be more overt, such as insulting, offending, criticizing, or other similar face-threatening acts. Because people tend to be more aware of these overtly damaging uses of language, there is not as much need to focus on them, so we will discuss the more subtle dangers in language use.

7.4.1 Doublespeak

Using one more-seemingly-acceptable word or expression for another is something we all do. Euphemisms, for example, are sometimes used to ameliorate or ease a difficult situation, such as death. But other times, these linguistic resources are used to manipulate or deceive. Wasserman and Hausrath refer to *doublespeak* as "saying one thing and meaning another" or as "distortions and obfuscations and marketplace flim-flam" (Wasserman and Hausrath 2006:xi). Noted linguist William Lutz illustrates how many times government officials, business leaders, reporters, advertisers, even the average person, use language to mislead their readers or listeners, typically for the benefit of the speaker or his group, alone. In the abstract of his illuminating book on how doublespeak is used, Lutz articulates that "the goal of doublespeak is 'to distort reality and corrupt thought.'" He identifies the most common types of doublespeak as "euphemism, jargon, gobbledygook or 'bureacratese,' and inflated language." It is "the language of non-responsibility, carefully constructed to appear to communicate when it [sic] fact it doesn't" (Lutz 2016). Some examples include "revenue enhancements" instead of "new taxes," "human kinetics," in place of "physical education," "pavement deficiencies" instead of "street potholes". My colleague Keris suggests that some may refer to a marital disagreement as "an intense moment of fellowship." Hospital staff may disguise a doctor's malpractice by calling it "a diagnostic misadventure of a high magnitude." The military may report the killing of their enemies as "servicing the target." Even though doublespeak can have a humorous function, a goal of politeness, or be used to save face, the potential dangers are also obvious (*L.A. Times Archives* 1989).

The opening ceremony for the Paris Olympic Games in July of 2024 appeared to parody Leonardo da Vinci's "The Last Supper" painting, a scene sacred in the minds of Christians. *Reuters*' Grohmann covered the story, the backlash, and the "apology":

7.4 Dangers in language use

> The segment, which resembled the biblical scene of Jesus Christ and his apostles sharing a last meal before crucifixion and featured drag queens, a transgender model and a naked singer made up as the Greek god of wine Dionysus, drew dismay from the Catholic Church and the religious right in America. ...
>
> After angry reaction ... Paris 2024 organisers apologised on Sunday to Catholics and other Christian groups. ...
>
> "Clearly there was never an intention to show disrespect to any religious group. (The opening ceremony) tried to celebrate community tolerance," [the] Paris 2024 spokesperson told a press conference.
>
> "We believe this ambition was achieved. If people have taken any offence we are really sorry." (Grohmann 2024)

In separate interviews by Reuters, "Thomas Jolly, the artistic director behind the flamboyant opening ceremony, said the scene had not been inspired by 'The Last Supper'"; yet, "Hugo Bardin, whose drag queen character Paloma took part in the tableau," acknowledged that they were "reproducing this painting'" (Grohmann 2024).

Were they or weren't they? Was the artistic ceremony "community tolerance," or an elevation of one group over others? It is difficult to conclude that a goal of community tolerance was achieved. Doublespeak leaves the hearer with contradictory messages and confusion.

This type of euphemistic and manipulative speech can be heard in many contexts. A month or so after the COVID-19 outbreak in 2020, a friend of the author's was told by his employers: "Due to unusual financial strains on the company, we need to have you take a rest for now. If the situation moves in our favor in the future, we may call you." Should my friend have waited to be called? Would it be a temporary break—or did they just fire him? Chances are he really was released, though he could not have been sure of that. His company would likely not have been sure of that either at the time, so they used doublespeak to "let him go" until the situation clarified.

The Washington Post reported about a student at a public university some years ago to whom a professor suggested: "If you'd be willing to get involved in some extracurricular activities, it could improve your grade." When she asked him directly about these "extracurricular activities," he told her she could meet him at his apartment at eight pm (Epstein 1981). Covert messages and doublespeak are used to manipulate. In many cases, doublespeak is used by people in roles of power to influence others under their supervision, to their own advantage.

7.4.2 Unwarranted assumptions

Another type of linguistic manipulation is communicating with hidden assumptions. One person makes a claim that presupposes an idea that may, or may not be, true. Approaching this from a logical standpoint, if Jack says, "Peter's brother arrived," the listener assumes the existence of Peter's brother. The claim, whether the listener affirms it or negates it, assumes it to be fact. This sentence and its negation (Peter's brother didn't arrive) both presuppose, as common knowledge, the existence of Peter's brother.

Another claim may be discarded out of hand: "The king of the United States arrived." Since the claim presupposes the existence of a king of the U.S., which, based on real-life experience, and logic, can be assumed to be false. However, sometimes this type of claim is used to manipulate people into assuming to be true, ideas that the speaker wants the listener to believe, even if the idea is illogical. For example, *The New York Times* reported in October of 2020 on the Senate race in South Carolina. The report first reminded readers that South Carolina has not had a Democrat as senator. Then the article reported that the Democratic candidate was "betting that immigration and growing support will change that" (Fausset 2020). The unwarranted assumption was that immigrants vote Democratic. The *Times* article seemed to suggest to immigrants an underlying assumption that, "if you're an immigrant, you vote Democratic." Yet other reports during the 2020 election gave clear evidence that immigrants in Florida voted strongly Republican.

Sometimes subtle little words carry a lot of meaning. The simple word "but" is a contrasting conjunction and is used to contrastive effect in a 2020 newspaper in Spain, *El Dia*. The name of the article was *"Es negro pero tiene la cara simpatica?"* [He's black but has a handsome face?] (Ruiz 2020). The online article told of a friend of the author who, a few years back, was discussing the imminent wedding of a relative to an Afro-Cuban man, that is, a black Cuban. The mother of this young bride opposed the mixed wedding, and the father, the author's friend, said, "He's black but has a handsome face." This *but* suggests to the readers either that black men normally do not have a handsome face or, having a handsome face makes his being ethnically black, excusable. Similarly, a few years ago, I was talking to a person who said something like this: "I met [such-and-such a person], from [such-and-such] country, but a really smart man." Again, the unspoken assumption was that people from that country are usually not smart, which is noticeable by use of the contrasting conjunction, "but." The word may be little, but the implications are huge.

Orvell et al. (2017) open their "How 'You' Makes Meaning" paper citing the following statement by Donald Trump in a CBS, Face the Nation interview during the 2015–2016 campaign: "I fight ... to pay as little [in taxes] as possible ... I'm a businessman. And that's the way you're supposed to do it." Focus on the generic *you* pronoun here. Orvell et al. propose that this *unwarranted assumption* in the use of the "generic you," influences people by "normalizing" their experience, extending it to others beyond oneself. It is easy to agree that paying less taxes is positive. However, making a claim using the generic *you* and the follow-up, *are supposed to* ... makes the individual speaking sound credible, more widely accepted, and more broadly general than the perspective being only what is the speaker's opinion for himself. It is like saying "everybody else and I," even though it is really just "I." This is a way to normalize a practice beyond oneself (Orvell et al. 2017).

Consider the illustration in figure 44 and reflect on the following questions: Who does the speaker refer to by use of the pronoun *we*? How about the pronoun *you*? Ask yourself the same questions the audience is asking in the image. In real life situations, by asking those questions, you can protect yourself and others from linguistic manipulation. After you have asked the questions and answered them yourself, see if you agree with the "person" at the far right of the image.

7.4 Dangers in language use

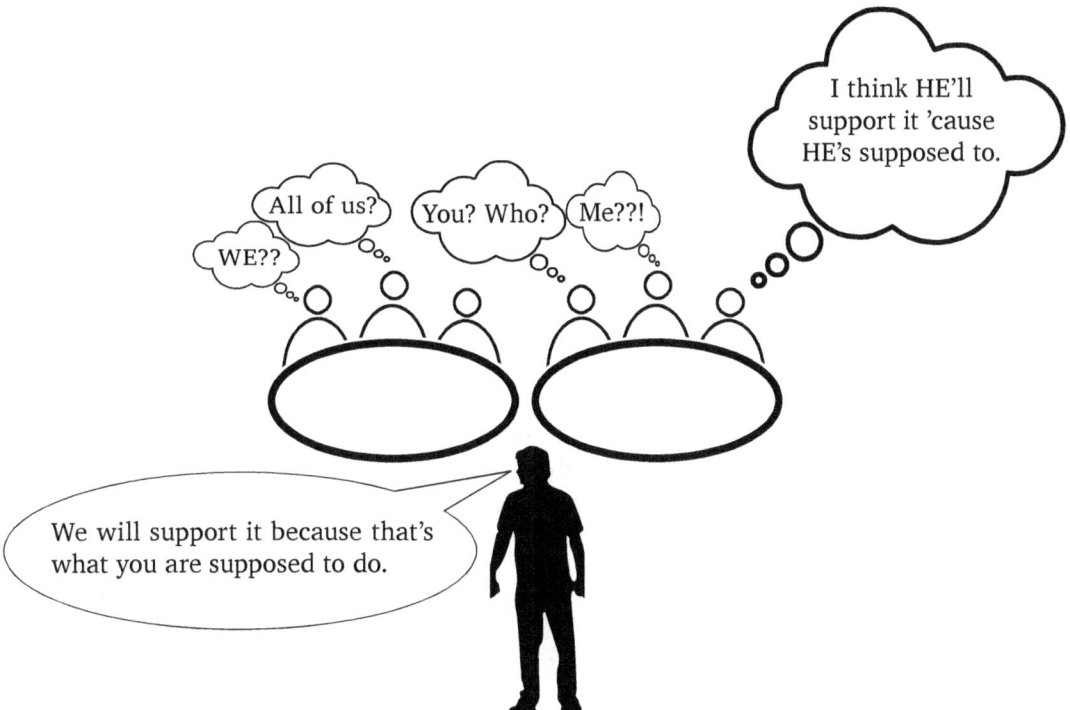

Figure 44. Subtle linguistic manipulation using pronouns.

As shown in figure 44, the pronoun *you* is not the only pronoun used to manipulate. *We* can also be used to negative effect. Imagine a bank manager telling you, "We can't serve you at this point," when she really means "*I* can't serve you at this point," but you would leave the bank depressed, thinking that the whole bank staff has something against you. The current APA Publication Manual calls this the "editorial *we*." It is also called the "author's *we*" or, archaically, *nosism*. The *Merriam-Webster* dictionary (2024d) defines this as "the practice of using we in giving one's opinions." It probably comes from the "royal we". Kings and people of high rank or authority may refer to themselves as *we*. The idea is that *we* sometimes simply means *I*. Sometimes in a research paper or speech, the presenter may use *we* instead of *I*, representing the voice of many, even though it may be just the author or speaker's opinion. A writer or speaker might even use *we* to convince the audience that his is a commonly accepted view, which may not be true.

The pronoun *they* can also be used as a "segregating *they*." *Us* versus *them* alienates the one labeled with the pronoun *they* or *them*, and is often used in a pejorative sense, to belittle or disparage. It can distinguish *us* from *them*, even unintentionally establishing oneself, or one's own group, as superior.

Conscious language beyond pronoun use is important to consider in any type of communication, opening one's thinking to recognize how the listener or reader might interpret the choice of words. Unwarranted assumptions on the part of the one initiating the narrative, which may at first seem innocuous to the speaker, can have problematic results. *Politically correct language* (see also in section 6.1.5) is terminology, especially in matters of race and sex, which is used to avoid offending others.[1]

---

[1] One list of conscious language: https://aceseditors.org/news/2021/conscious-language-a-to-z-of-terms-to-consider.

7.4.3 False advertising

The world of advertising has been notorious for linguistic manipulation, a strategy which seems to be a norm in persuading the public to buy the product they promote. A popular bank has this ad on their website: "Refer your friends. GET A CASH BONUS UP TO **$500**." In this ad, "$500" is highlighted in the ad with a type size four times larger than the rest of the message. How much money do you expect to receive if you refer friends to this bank? $500, of course! However, if you receive $50 you cannot complain to the bank management since the ad offered "up to" $500, and $50, $10, or even $1, is within that range.

The Dannon Company, producers of the popular *Activia* yogurt, advertised in 2007 that "Activia is scientifically proven to help [with digestion issues]." In an interview with Business Wire News, The CEO of the Dannon Company said that "the successful launch of *Activia* in the United States proved to us that Americans are looking for healthier food choices with clinically proven, peer-reviewed, functional benefits" (Progressive Grocer 2007). The price of Activia yogurt was 30 percent higher than comparable yogurts, and clients seemed to have accepted paying more for it because of this "scientific" evidence. In 2010, however, Troy McMullen of *ABC News,* reported that a judge found these claims to be false, and Dannon ended up paying consumers $45 million in damages. It turned out that Dannon had never done scientific and clinical experiments on these products to sustain the results they were falsely claiming. The prosecutor in this class-action suit against Dannon said that legal suits help ensure accuracy in food labeling and avoidance of false advertising (McMullen 2010).

7.4.4 Language-related discrimination

Another danger in language use relates to discrimination due to the language used by someone who speaks a language other than English in public, or because they speak English with a noticeable accent. Chapter 10 will elaborate further on this latter type of discrimination. For now, let us focus on the first type of discrimination: when our speech discriminates against others, for whatever reason; in other words, when language is used as a tool of discrimination. We will clarify this with real-life twenty-first century examples.

Think of the now infamous media-popularized phrase, "Some Mexicans are good people." The logical potential conclusion of a phrase like this is that the majority of the Mexican people are not good people. Imagine the potentially catastrophic outcome in the minds of our children if for years the media and others continue to depict Mexicans this way. In the earlier example about black Cubans, a person "defended" a black groom as being "black but handsome" in section 7.4.2. The implication is that people of that ethnic group are generally *not* handsome, which is an obviously discriminatory statement. The most damaging threat in that assumption is that it is very subtle, and listeners may be only half-aware of the negative implication and subconsciously accept it. This subconscious acceptance is similar to how the media conveys ideas via subliminal or hidden messages in children's movies (Hodge 2018:115).

In 2020, the Dior perfume company released a video to promote their *Sauvage* perfume. The video portrays Native Americans in the mountains, with actor Johnny Depp, allegedly with Native American ancestry, performing as one of the protagonists. At some point, you can hear the phrase, "We are the land. The new sauvage." And the Sauvage perfume appears on the screen. The motto for this *Sauvage* (French for 'savage') perfume, based on the brand name, is "wild at heart."

7.4 Dangers in language use

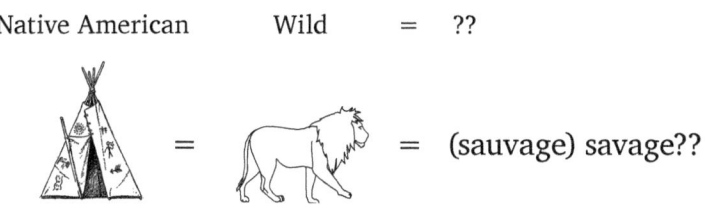

Figure 45. Subtle, or not-so-subtle, implications?

The controversy that the ad provoked had to do with the subtle connection of Native Americans with the label "savage" and "wild at heart." Many criticized this and the Dior company quickly pulled the ad with a formal apology. Whether you agree with this criticism or the outcome of this issue, the point is that our language can embed unwarranted or false claims, like: "Black people are not handsome," "Hispanics are not good people," or "Native Americans are savage."

This chapter discussed in detail the beauty and marvel of human language use, unparalleled in the animal or machine worlds. But we have also observed examples of language use in which this awesome communication tool is misused, abusing other members of society. Take time now to observe and critically consider how language is used in the world around you.

Exercises

1) Describe one real-life example of a communication misunderstanding (different from those in this book). It could be between children and adults or between speakers of ESL and native speakers of English.
2) Describe two examples of linguistic manipulation (different from those in this book), one with non-advertising double-speech, and one in advertising.
3) Other than the examples in this book, present two other words or expressions in their context, which may discriminate against others.
4) Using Grice's CP, Sperber and Wilson's Relevance Theory, or Hymes' SPEAKING, explain how English speakers can solve the ambiguity in this sentence: "Let's stop nagging people."
5) Based on what you learned here, what can you answer to the following hypothetical question of a child: "Why don't adults always say what they mean, or mean what they say?"

8

Is Language in Our Heart or Our Brain?

A [computer] comes closer to being a brain that thinks than any machine ever did before 1940. ... [They are] machines that can handle information with great skill & speed; [with] power very similar to the power of a brain.

– Edmund Callus Berkeley (1949:Preface)

In the fall of 1970, "Genie," an unusual 13-year-old girl, and her mother entered the Los Angeles County welfare office by mistake. Even though she was 13, Genie, who looked like she was six or seven, salivated and spat repeatedly, could not fully focus her eyes, and astonishingly, seemed to have no ability to talk. These factors caught the attention of some of the welfare office employees who decided to take her case. After investigating, they found out her deranged father had kept Genie tied to a potty chair, constrained by a home-made straitjacket, and isolated most of her life. He did not allow her to cry, speak, or make any noise. Additionally, he had punished her and would growl at her like a mad dog. The case made the news, caught the public attention, and drew the interest of scientists, linguists, psychologists, and other researchers. Genie was analyzed from different perspectives: linguistically, neurologically, socially, physically, and mentally. They tried to teach her language and social behavior. She was taken from foster home to foster home, and from researcher to researcher. She learned some level of language and her social interaction dynamics improved, but never to the level of an average person. Curtis (1977) was the linguist who made this case well known in the linguistics field. Unfortunately, many people do not know much about Genie today. It seems this was not a story with a happy ending.

Like Genie and other so-called "wild children" or "feral children," Victor of Aveyron, in the late eighteenth century in France, was also deprived of language use (Lane 1976), and the question was similar: were these children brain damaged? This question has never really been answered. Those studies and many others do, however, show us the strong brain-language connection.

Figure 46. Victor, the "Wild boy of Aveyron": A language-deprived child.

The primary purpose of this chapter is to elucidate the brain-language connection. With this purpose in mind, we will use the computer-brain analogy to illustrate critical issues about the brain. In the next section, we will briefly discuss some basic information about computers with the goal of illustrating key features of language structure and dynamics. This may help us see the fundamental importance of the brain in the storage and processing of language.

8.1 The brain as language storage

The epigraph at the introduction to this chapter tells us a little about the state of affairs of computers in 1949. The brain-computer connection expressed by Berkeley seems obvious. Even from the very early stages of computer technological novelty, the invention of computers or similar machines seems to have resorted to the structure and dynamics of the human brain. The human brain is an amazing "machine," an amazing "computer", a computer like no other. It is in this "human machine" that we find answers regarding the storage and processing of language. As previously explained, language consists, at a minimum, of a small number of phonemes or speech sounds (typically around 40, but up to 100), grammatical rules, multiple thousands of words and affixes, idioms, and so on. In normal circumstances, these sounds, rules, expressions, and words are readily available to people every hour of the day and every day of the week. How is this possible?

One essential aspect to enable this process is the ability to store this information somewhere so people can access those sounds, rules, and words at any given time. All this information is stored in the greatest natural computer of all time: the brain. Based on Berkeley's words in the epigraph, we know that computers were thought of as something like, "Giant brains or machines that think," as he entitled his book. In the 1940s, when the very first computer was invented, computers were enormous machines, sometimes occupying a whole room; that is why he calls them "giant."

Kachur, a molecular geneticist and syndicated science columnist, believes the structure and the dynamics of the human brain is inspiring AI. In a 2017 article on this subject, she writes: "The human brain is the most powerful supercomputer on earth"; and she defines AI as, "a system of computing that aims to mimic the power of the human brain" (Kachur 2017). Goel agrees, observing that the newest generation of computing, what she calls the "fifth generation," is based on AI. AI is an effort to "simulate the human way of thinking and reasoning" (2010:7). Goel explains that the computer system consists of a device that accepts data or input, processes this input by performing mathematical operations (*algorithms*), and produces a certain result or output. This system has four major components: hardware,

8.1 The brain as language storage 97

software, data, and users (2010:10). So then, let us review what we know about computers, with the intention of understanding more about the brain, and eventually of seeing how this human organ stores and processes language. We will consider the hardware component first. See the image of a computer hardware setup, figure 47.

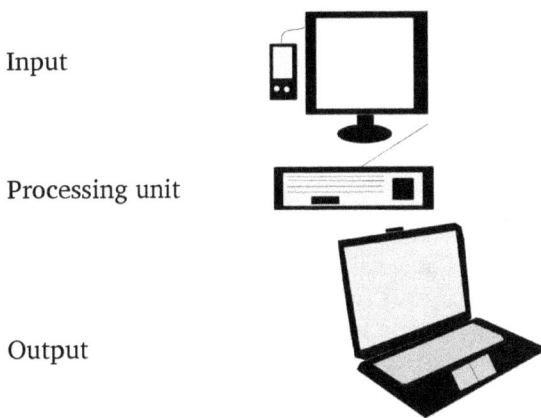

Input

Processing unit

Output

Figure 47. Computer hardware components.

Computer hardware consists of the mechanical, tangible parts of a computer, what you see and touch when you use a computer: the keyboard, mouse, screen, chips, and other physical parts. The software refers to the applications or set of instructions built into the computer. Data consists of the different pieces of information entered into the computers. The users are the people accessing the computer, touching the hardware, writing or using the rules, inputting or extracting the data, and making use of the machine.

We also learn from Goel about the most basic and crucial dynamic in this computing machinery: the *input-process-output*. Data is input into the computer, the computer processes this data using rules written to do so, and produces an output result, a computation that the user expects. For example, if I want the computer to tell me the current interest rate I will have to pay this year on my mortgage, I need to input some data into the computer. I have to give it the percentage for the interest rate, the price of the mortgage, and the dates. Then, I tell the computer to compute this for me by pressing the right keys on the keyboard. The computer takes my input or data, uses its "interest calculation rule," and gives me a result on the screen, in a printout, or as a voice message, as is illustrated in figure 47.

Now, what about the brain? The brain functions in a similar fashion. From cognitive psychology we learn that human information processing happens "in much the same way that a computer takes in information and follows a program to produce an output" (McLeod 2008). Figure 48 illustrates that the brain is like a computer memory board, an information processor.

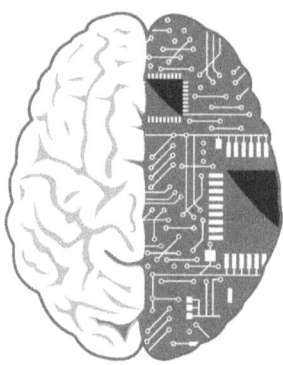

Figure 48. Information processing paradigm.

People have senses such as sight, hearing, touch, smell, and taste. The first two are the most crucial for language. We also have body organs or sensing organs associated with each one of these senses. For example, we typically use our eyes for visual stimuli, our ears for auditory stimuli, and our hands for tactile stimuli. Now, around us are an incredible number of stimuli such as noises, words, images, pictures, and smells. All of these constitute some type of input in our brains. Then in a very complex cognitive process, we primarily focus on some part of this input content, and we do not focus on other parts. Somehow, our brains inhibit some types of stimuli and elevate or excite some others. Lakunina et al. show some aspects of this complex process in the case of auditory stimuli. They state that the nervous system separates auditory stimuli that are just "noise" from stimuli that are signals or key perceptions to be processed. They recognize that this process is not clearly understood, but they suggest that the answer may be in the functions of different cell types. They suggest that certain types of inhibitory cells may reduce the activity of a neuron in response to a stimulus, or what they call, *spectral surround suppression* (Lakunina et al. 2020:3,564). The final goal is to generate objects of perception or *percepts* that are coherent.

Thus, we selectively focus on just a part of this input, as explained earlier, and that becomes the focused input for our brain. Whatever we focus our eyes, ears, or hands on becomes the focused input data for our brain. Over the years, our brain stores that information, in the same way that computers over the years store our files and data, or in the same way we store clothes, files, or other items in different cabinets and drawers in our homes. We need to store recollection data so we can rely on that information later, at any given time, if need be. When the time comes, then, we ask or order the brain to take some of this data and process it somehow.

8.2 Brain structure and its relevance for language

The storing of these linguistic pieces occurs in different sections of the brain, in a way that even today experts are not totally capable of explaining. Researchers know it happens; there is evidence of it; they have learned a little bit about the process; but nobody can explain it completely. There are some things their discoveries have shown us, though; for example, that memory occurs in the brain, and memorization is a critical cognitive process when storing language. Again, it makes total sense to conclude that all this linguistic information must be stored somewhere, and it is clear that the brain already stores information (e.g., memorized melodies, images, phone numbers). Thus, language, no doubt, with all its linguistic pieces and all the relevant information, is stored in the human brain, whether you and I understand the whole process behind this or not. In the following pages of this chapter, we present a brief description of the language-relevant things we have learned about this amazing human organ.

8.2 Brain structure and its relevance for language

Today there are neurological techniques and devices to visually observe brain activity. Huang, a neurologist, explains that a technique called fMRI, which stands for "functional magnetic resonance imaging," uses the MRI, "a non-invasive neuroimaging tool to investigate brain activity in terms of large-scale neuron population dynamics across the whole brain" (Huang 2020:1). These neuron-based activities show up on a screen in different colors, making it relatively easy to see what parts of the brain are activated while performing a certain type of task. These techniques are similar to tests used to examine the brain activity of Genie. Among other functions, Huang tested a language-based task, word-reading (2020). Hoyos, Kim, and Kastner (2019) explain that certain activities require more brain activity than others. For higher-level activities, neurons communicate with each other. For this communication to happen, they need oxygen, which is transported by blood. Consequently, there is more oxygen and blood in a certain part of the brain when it is more active. MRI devices use a magnetic system to detect blood and oxygen, and that is how they can detect and show brain activity.

Figure 49 illustrates an MRI image, as researched by Professor Andrew Newberg, Director of Research in the Marcus Institute of Integrative Health at Thomas Jefferson University. He investigated the brain activity of nuns while in prayer, which demonstrated increased activity in the inferior parietal lobes, or the language area, as shown at the left of the brain in figure 49. He reasons that, since nuns use language when praying, those communication centers of the brain become darker, indicating increased brain activity. Many other studies in this line of research demonstrate that varying types of information are processed in different sections of the brain cortex.[1]

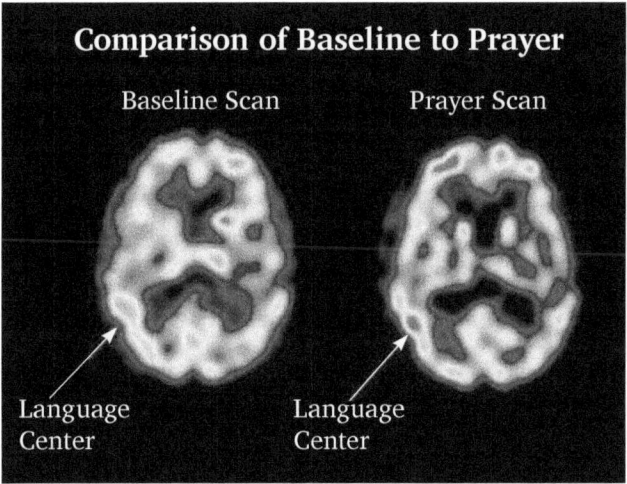

Figure 49. Baseline scan compared with prayer scan.

To further understand this, it is necessary to briefly look at the anatomy of the brain. The sections of the brain, labeled in figure 50, below, are further explained at the Johns Hopkins Medicine website (2024). The brain has three major parts: the *cerebrum*, the *brainstem*, and the *cerebellum*. The cerebrum is the frontal lobe of the brain. It has a right and a left hemisphere. The cerebrum is where movement, the sense of touch, sight, and hearing are controlled. Judgment, reasoning, emotions, and learning are also controlled by the cerebrum. The middle section of the brain is the brainstem. This section controls eye and mouth movement. The cerebellum coordinates and regulates a wide range of functions and processes. Although small, it contains more than half of the neurons that control the nervous system in the body. Other parts of the brain are listed below figure 50, adapted from descriptions on the Johns Hopkins Medicine webpage. (See URL link in references.)

---

[1] The brain *cortex* is the "gray matter" of the brain, or the superficial layer of the brain, full of nerve cells and with billions of neurons. The brain cortex is where cognitive processes take place in the brain.

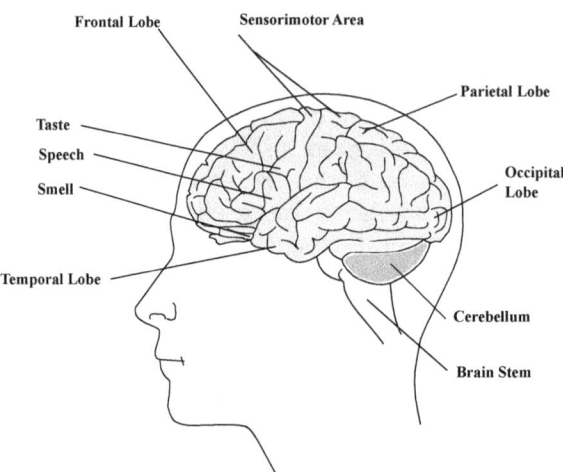

Figure 50. Anatomy of the brain.

- *Pons* (in the brainstem). This deep part of the brain controls much of one's face and eye movement.
- *Medulla* (in the brainstem) This is the lowest part of the brainstem, and it is the most vital part of the brain. It regulates vital organ activities, including that of the heart and lungs.
- *Parietal lobe*. This is the middle part of the brain. It helps in object identification and spatial orientation. It also helps in interpreting pain and body touch sensations.
- *Occipital lobe*. The back part of the brain is involved with vision.
- *Frontal lobe*. The largest section of the brain located in the front of the head, is involved in personality characteristics, movement, and (partially) smell recognition.
- *Temporal lobes*. These are located on the sides of the brain and are crucial for short-term memory, speech, musical rhythm, and (partially) the sense of smell.
- *Spinal cord*. A large bundle of nerve fibers located in the back that extends from the base of the brain to the lower back; the spinal cord transmits messages to and from the brain and to the rest of the body.

Regarding the generation and processing of language, there are sections in the brain typically known as "language centers." Now let's consider how the brain regulates the use of language.

Language centers

Neurolinguists are scientists who study the interface of neurology and linguistics. They have shown that language is controlled by specific areas in the cortex. Friederici credits Franz Gall (1758–1828) as the first researcher to determine that people formulate language in the left hemisphere, frontal lobe (Friederici 2017:5). Friederici also observed that the French scientist Paul Broca (1861) was first to provide empirical evidence that there are "language centers" in the brain; that is, specific areas of the brain that process language. Broca based his conclusions on a late nineteenth-century clinical study of a patient who had a clearly noticeable deficit in language production following a stroke. The patient was only able to produce the syllable "tan," so some called him "Mr. Tan." After "Mr. Tan" died, the autopsy revealed a lesion in the left inferior frontal section of the brain, a section today called BROCA'S AREA (Friederici 2017:6).

Friederici also reported on the fundamental findings of another neurolinguist researcher, Carl Wernicke (1874). Wernicke had observed that patients who had experienced damage to the left temporal cortex had difficulty with language comprehension. That part of the brain is now called the WERNICKE'S AREA (Friederici 2017:7). Language disorders caused by brain damage are defined as APHASIA (*Oxford Reference* 2024a.) So, the disorders occurring in these two areas are known as BROCA'S APHASIA and WERNICKE'S APHASIA.

Many discoveries about the brain have come from autopsies, conducted after a patient is deceased. This was especially true in the past. Friederici explains that with the arrival of the functional neuroimaging technique fMRI, neurologists can now investigate the brain of live patients. Images generated by this neuroimaging technique were used to further understand Broca's area and Wernicke's area. MRI imagery demonstrates that patients with Broca's aphasia not only have difficulties with grammar in language production, as was believed for many years, but also in language perception or comprehension. The activity or inactivity in Broca's area revealed that damage to this language center affects the grammar by inhibited processing especially of function words, both in production and comprehension (Friederici 2017:7). Similarly, Wernicke's aphasia, which was believed to be a language comprehension deficit only, was clarified as a problem with the meaning of words both in comprehension and production. Wernicke's area, then, controls both semantic and lexical processing.

Thus, it has been demonstrated that language functions are processed in the brain—and that the areas of the brain, called LANGUAGE CENTERS, control language production and perception. However, in addition to Broca's area and Wernicke's area, other areas of the brain have also been labeled as language centers. These areas are the *angular gyrus*, the *primary auditory cortex*, the *primary motor cortex*, and the *primary visual cortex*. Friederici reports that the *angular gyrus*, in the *posterior temporal cortex*, is involved with semantic processing (2017:60), and that the primary auditory cortex is involved with speech sound processing (2017:23).

The motor cortex controls muscle movement, which is very important in speech production, whether it is by the mouth, tongue, hands, or face (Coon and Mitterer 2010:63.) The visual area of the cortex processes visual images (Coon and Mitterer 2010:67). It is easy to see how important the visual cortex is for sign language perception, reading, and perception of other non-verbal communication aspects important for language, such as facial expressions.

In figure 51 we can identify the language centers in the brain. The letters A–E identify those language centers.

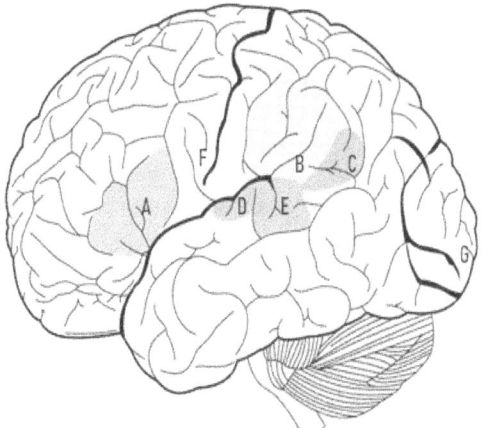

A Broca's area
B Supramarginal gyrus
C Angular gyrus
D Auditory cortex
E Wernicke's area
F Motor cortex
G Visual cortex

Figure 51. Language centers in the brain.

8.3 The brain: Difference between human and animal communication

Previous chapters have indicated that animals and machines lack many attributes innate in people. We have suggested that only humans have a linguistic, communicational ability to such an extremely high degree of ability and creativity. A basic reason for this language disparity between people and non-humans can be explained by differences in our brains. No animal or machine has a brain like ours—or even comparable to it; the human brain is unique. From an evolutionary view, Pinker puts it this way: "In any natural history of the human species, language stand[s] out as the preeminent trait" (1994:16). He sustains that "[language] is man's ... quintessential ... capacity to use symbols, ... irrevocably separating him from other animals" (1994:17). The principal factors distinguishing humans and animals, then, are the dynamic activity and biological structure of the human brain. These differences are evidenced by the human ability to acquire and use language.

Let us consider some basic information about brains in animals. It is widely thought that primates (e.g., gorillas, monkeys, apes, and macaques) are humans' "closest relatives" in the animal world (Redmond 2008:29), so we will focus on the brain of apes or primates.

First, let us contrast what we know about primates' versus humans' brains. "A chimp, roughly the same size as a human, has a brain [only] two-thirds our size" (Patterson and Linden 1981:146–147). The "human cortex has 10 times the surface area of a macaque cortex and plays a key role in many distinctive aspects of human cognition, such as language" (Van Essen 2005:3). Yule further contrasts the human brain with primates. "[The human brain] is not only large relative to human body size, it is also lateralized ... [allowing for] specialized functions in each of the two hemispheres" (2010:5).

The DNA organic chemical structure of the two species points to a higher degree of similarity. The great apes' DNA material and human DNA are 98 percent similar (Boysen 2009:10). Why then is there such a discrepancy in the language ability of the two species?

Another point of comparison is neuronal activity in the brain. "The average number of synapses per neuron increases from 2000–5600 in the monkey, up to 6800–10000 in humans" (Changeux 2005:83). In other words, the connections between neurons are much faster in humans. The great apes are close to the top of Boysen's list of the smartest animals on the planet. He observes that great apes are similar to humans in skills such as problem solving, tools creation and use, and cognitive flexibility (2016:2–3). Even so, authors who defend animals' amazing intelligence, such as Boysen, Patterson and Linden, and others, also, directly, or indirectly, recognize the superiority of human's cognitive ability. Boysen, for example, states that even though great apes present amazing skills in the creation and use of tools, that skill is "still at a very basic level" (2009:10).

Patterson and Linden demonstrated that apes could acquire communication in sign language. Still, this is difficult to analyze and measure. Koko the gorilla has been the most outstanding case, recorded formally and credibly, of an animal trained over a span of years in sign language. (Patterson and Linden 1981). Koko began training in sign language at one year of age. When she died at age 46 in 2018, Koko had developed a vocabulary of over 1,000 ASL signs and could comprehend over 2,000 words of spoken English (Koko.org 2023).

Figure 52. Koko the gorilla is reported to have mastered around 1,000 ASL signs.

For perspective, D'Anna et al. in the *Journal of Literacy Research*, "found that the average number of different words known by a college student is 16,785" (D'Anna et al. [1991] 2024).

Patterson and Linden reported that Koko acquired ASL more slowly than normal speaking children, but they attributed this to the difference between language learning speed of oral language versus sign language, suggesting that acquisition in sign language proceeds more slowly than for oral language. At the date of their study, they did not have access to data comparing oral and sign language acquisition for children of the age at which Koko learned sign language.

Today, we have access to that comparative information, and this new data does not support Patterson and Linden's reasoning for the slower pace at which Koko acquired ASL. Current research demonstrates that there is no significant difference in the rate of language acquisition between Deaf children and speaking children. Lederberg and Beal-Alvarez report (2003:251) that "ranges of lexicon size for DCDP [Deaf children with Deaf parents] and hearing toddlers are similar between 18 and 23 months." Meier (2016:2–3) agrees, showing that children acquiring a spoken language and children acquiring a sign language have a comparable developmental process in their language acquisition. For example, acquiring subject-verb agreement processes and similar grammar rules occur for both types of children by the age of three-and-a-half. D. Anderson concurs: "In general, children acquiring ASL do so in a fashion very similar to their hearing counterparts" (2006:155). Thus, Koko's delayed acquisition cannot be attributed to the nature of sign languages versus oral language, as Patterson and Linden suggested. It is simply a case of Koko having different cognitive and linguistic skills as compared to humans.

Consider the level of language acquisition of children in general, and of Deaf children, using ASL. The Ski-Hi Institute of Utah State University has a scale for the expectations for ASL development. The Language Development Scale Instruction Manual stipulates that a normal Deaf child, growing up in conditions similar to those of hearing children, by the age of four or four-and-a-half knows 3,000 signs and productively uses around 2,000 of those. And, by the age of five, the child understands up to 7,000 signs (SKI-HI 2020). Again, Koko after 46 years mastered only around 1,000 ASL signs. Humans and even the most intelligent of animals demonstrate significantly different cognitive and linguistic skills. There are also differences observed when comparing the vocal tracts of apes and humans, which affects the possibility of producing certain communicative sounds. Apart from the vocal apparatus, and considering the brain structure similarities, however, there is still no explanation for why apes have not developed whole language systems based on sign language like ASL.

In summary, without question, language acquisition for humans, whether of sign language or oral language, is far superior to animals. Some attribute this human-animal disparity and fundamental distinctions to the much larger size of the brain cortex in humans, others, to brain lateralization and the plasticity of the human brain not found in other species, others attribute it to the DNA genetic information or neuronal brain activity in human brains. Any of these, and certainly a combination of them, is key to understanding the linguistic abilities that differentiate humans and animals, and take us back to the primacy of brain differences of the human brain as a key in the linguistic ability people have as compared to apes.

8.4 Brain malfunction and impact on language

Since language is stored and processed in the brain, it is logical to think that, when the brain is damaged, especially at the language centers, it would cause speech or language disorders. For example, we can speculate that if the visual cortex is damaged, the patient would not be able to read well, and for sign language, the patient would not be able to interpret signs well. If the motor cortex is damaged, then we would expect speech articulation to be affected since it would be hard to move the lips, teeth, and tongue, crucial for language production and speech articulation.

In fact, these language deficits have been observed and studied. The most common effect that has been investigated in this regard is *aphasia*. In *The Handbook of Language and Speech Disorders*, Chris Code defines aphasia as "impairments of the *use* of language, the expression and comprehension of language in any modality ... caused by some acquired form of damage to the brain" (2010:317). Code explains that these language disorders normally come after a stroke, dementia, trauma to the head, or similar abnormalities caused by brain damage. Although there are language disorders other than aphasia, here we will focus only on aphasia.

Code (2010:318–325) gives the following types of aphasia:

- *Motor aphasia*: also called "apraxia of speech," this consists of low fluency in speech due to damage to areas of the brain that controls the planning of speech before actually speaking.
- *Fluent aphasia*: speech sounds fluent but there are serious deficiencies otherwise.
- *Non-fluent aphasia*: speech is hesitant and slow, with many pauses; severe problems with clear articulation and prosody.
- *Broca's aphasia*: a type of non-fluent aphasia in which the patient presents a lack of grammar, primarily by skipping function words.
- *Wernicke's aphasia*: a type of fluent aphasia in which the patient's speech sounds fluent but makes no sense, and when the patient has serious difficulty comprehending others' speech.
- *Semantic paraphasia*: when the patient does not use correct wording but gives a semantically related word instead. For example, by saying "chair" instead of "table."
- *Conduction aphasia*: when a patient has a problem with repeating a word or phrase.

Two primary types of aphasia are exemplified in figures 53a and 53b, both inspired by the National Institute on Deafness and Other Communication Disorders (NIDCD 2017).

Figure 53a. Broca's aphasia patients' speech.

8.4 Brain malfunction and impact on language

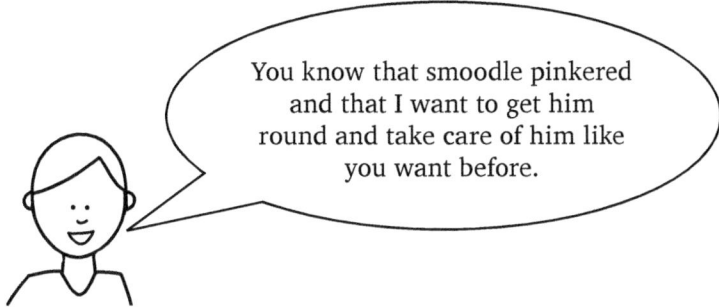

Figure 53b. Wernicke's aphasia patient's speech.

Exercise: The brain and language

Browse the internet, or any other source to answers the following questions:
1) Where are each of the areas of the brain listed in (3) located?
2) What are their language-related functions?
3) What language disorder emerges if they are damaged?
    Broca's area
    Wernicke's area
    Arcuate fasciculus
    Corpus callosum
    Visual cortex
    Motor cortex
    Auditory cortex
4) What are the major differences between the brain of animals and that of humans?

9

Can Anybody Learn a Language?

There are many different languages in the world, yet none of them is without meaning.
– The Apostle Paul (I Cor. 14:10 [*GNT*])

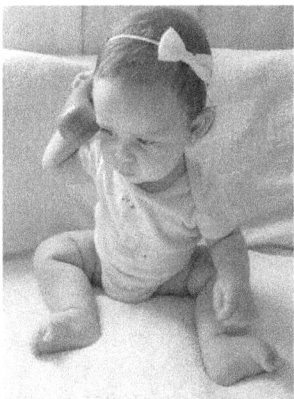

Figure 54. Learning communication skills.

It was a wonderful opportunity for me to watch my son Victor Jr. grow up while I was studying linguistics. He was born the year I started my graduate linguistics program. Because of my linguistics studies I was very aware of language-learning issues and enjoyed watching each stage of language advancement as he developed *coordinate bilingual* speech, or equal proficiency, in English and Spanish.

We expect children to develop crucial skills for life such as walking, eating on their own, and so on; language is one of these critical skills. At times, parents wonder about their children's linguistic development. Some parents may justifiably be very concerned when their children do not form words or sentences by a certain age. This is a valid concern because children are expected to master language at an early age, regardless of the immense complexity of such a task. By three-to-four years of age, a child should have a grasp of conversational speech. If this does not happen, something may be wrong, and parents may want a speech pathologist to analyze the child's speech development. How do we acquire language at such an early age? In section 9.1 we discuss some fundamentals of what is known as FIRST LANGUAGE ACQUISITION or L1 ACQUISITION, which is the primary goal of this chapter.

Observing children learning their first language, often called their *mother* or *native tongue*, is fascinating. However, observing children, even teenagers or adults learn a *second* language, or an L2, is also compelling. I had the experience of learning English as a second language myself, and currently teach language acquisition courses, known as TESOL (teaching English to speakers of other languages) at the university where I am employed and in other contexts.[2] Regardless of the L1 of a student, there are common patterns in the process of learning an L2. Section 9.2 covers some basics about second language acquisition (SLA). After some observations about L1 acquisition in section 9.1, we discuss SLA in section 9.2.

9.1 L1 acquisition: Its nature

My son Victor Jr's is now in his twenties. Language acquisition as he experienced it (although in a bilingual context), is not unique to him. First-language acquisition is the same for everyone, regardless of what their L1 happens to be. We can learn some facts about language acquisition from his and other stories, and from other research.

9.1.1 L1 acquisition is natural

While my son was growing up, he was becoming bilingual in both English and Spanish. However, he would not pronounce the Spanish [r] (trilled r) correctly. As a language teacher, I repeatedly tried to teach him the correct pronunciation, but to no avail; Even for monolingual Spanish-speaking children this sound is difficult to produce. Leacox (2018:81) lists the trilled-r as one of the late sounds acquired by Spanish speakers.

When Victor Jr. was five years old, he ran up to me, all excited and proud of himself, saying, "Daddy, daddy, listen, [ka.ro]," in that way he demonstrated to me that he was pronouncing the trill correctly in the Spanish word for "car." He got it! It was the right time for him. It did not matter how many times I tried to teach him; he could not learn that pronunciation because it is an acquired sound that comes naturally at the right time. We do not need instruction for L1 acquisition, we just need exposure to the language. Pinker put it this way, "Language … is part of our biological birthright; it is not something that parents teach their children or something that must be elaborated in school" (Pinker 1994:19). Roberts says that language "manifests itself in early life with little prompting as long as the human child has adequate nutrition … other basic needs are met … and if exposed to others" who are speaking that language (Roberts 2017:2). The key here is a natural exposure to the language, which is what "Genie," the isolated child who was mentioned in chapter 8, was lacking. Children must be exposed to an environment where the L1 is used naturally; and if so, we can just let "nature" do the rest. At times, adults can give some instructions to a child or help modify his speech, which is not a problem, but the great bulk of the process does not require these coaching efforts.

9.1.2 L1 acquisition is innate

Yule observed that people "are born with a special capacity for language" (2010:6). Humans seem to be wired for language from the time they are born. Chomsky proposed the existence of something in the brain of humans that allows the natural and speedy process of language acquisition, called the Language Acquisition Device or LAD (1965:47). An opposing position posits that humans are born without built-in mental content. For example, Pinker explains

---

[2] For the past twenty-six years the author has had the privilege of teaching both ESL and Spanish in Venezuela, the United States, Spain, and Mexico.

that the philosopher John Locke (1632–1704) hypothesized that humans' minds are like a *tabula rasa* or a blank slate; a sheet of paper without any writing on it (Pinker 2002:5).

For an effective and healthy L1 acquisition process, in addition to needing exposure to a language, children need feedback from people around them, and they need models. However, the exposure of feedback and modeling is not enough; it's not enough to account for all the linguistic evidence observed in children from ages zero-to-three, or to six years of age. Both nature and nurture[3] have roles in language development. Neither alone can explain the whole process of language development.

9.1.3 L1 acquisition is universal

L1 acquisition is true and necessary for every human, barring major brain defects. Roberts states that there are no known ethnic groups that do not speak a language (2017:2). Lenneberg long ago described the characteristics of language as follows: "(i) It is a form of behavior present in all cultures of the world. (ii) In all cultures its onset is age correlated. [And] (iii) [t]here is only one acquisition strategy—it is the same for all babies everywhere in the world" (1969:635).

There are no nationalities or races or ethnicities that can claim, from a linguistic perspective, that they are better than another group. Under normal circumstances, the poorest child in Africa, people of the most ancient culture in the Himalayas, the most educated professor in Europe, the richest person in the U.S.A., the most isolated Indigenous person in the mountains of South America, are equally capable of successful, satisfactory, and full acquisition, honing, and manipulating this complex tool we call language.

If the human brain, as discussed previously, provides the key for language storage and processing, then it is also key for language acquisition. All humans have brains with the structure and dynamics necessary for human language. In this brain structure and dynamics lie the answers to how all humans, unlike animals, acquire this system of verbal communication. Yule asserts that this innate capacity in all humans to acquire or learn language is not found in any species other than humans. (2010:6).

9.1.4 L1 acquisition is gradual and sequential

In 1969 Lenneberg, and four decades later, Clark (2009), summarize the general stages through which children acquire (their first) language.[4]

- *1st stage*: Babbling. Up to six-months old. Children "play" with sounds and syllables.
- *2nd stage*: One-word stage. Around one year of age. One-word utterances instead of a whole sentence, like "water," for "I want water."
- *3rd stage*: Two-word stage, or the start of the *telegraphic* stage. Around two years old. Two or so words for a whole sentence, something like "drink water," for "I want to drink some water."
- *4th stage*: Regular grammar stage, in which the child has incorporated the majority of the rules of their L1 regular grammar systems. Typically three-to-four years of age. The child already has the whole language settled, with its grammar—minus the irregularities of the grammar—and with a less-than robust lexicon. They may say, "I goed to the park yesterday on my two foots."

---

[3] In this case, I use "nature" to refer to what is biologically innate relevant to language development in the gestation months and up to birth. "Nurture" refers to interaction with others and experience with the surrounding world.
[4] 1st, 2nd, 3rd, and 4th stages are also described in Fromkin et al. (2010:334–350); Early Critical Period, in Newport (1988:147ff.); and the Late Critical Period, in Singleton and Ryan (2004:32–33).

- **5th stage**: The *Critical Period*. The *Early* Critical Period occurs around six years of age. All the irregularities are settled. The child's grammar resembles that of an adult. A more robust lexicon will continue to grow over the years, and pragmatic nuances or proper language use according to context will come with biological maturation.

  The *Late* Critical Period occurs around puberty, or what corresponds for many to twelve-years of age. Adolescence and experience settles all the nuances of language. Pragmatic competence is achieved.

The Late Critical Period is so named because it is the "last chance" for people to acquire language. Lenneberg postulated in his Critical Period Hypotheses for language acquisition that there is a period of time within which humans can acquire language successfully. The early part of this period (when it is normally expected to happen) is about the age of six years. If for some reason, it does not happen early, there is a second opportunity for this to happen, which is before the neuromuscular plasticity capacity[5] of humans is critically minimized. This plasticity typically ends with puberty. Typically, after the age of twelve it is very hard to successfully acquire a language smoothly,[6] because neuromuscular plasticity is critically compromised (Rodriguez-Fornells et al. 2009:3713). Figure 55 summarizes these stages, focusing on age with the corresponding linguistic behavior.

Age	Stage name	Language feature	Utterance meaning
Baby. 0-1/2 yr	Babbling	Sound 'play' experimenting	"I want to see all the fish."
Toddler 1 yr old	1-word	1-word sentences	"I want to see all the fish."
2 years old	2-word or telegraphic	2-word sentences or some function words missing	"I want to see all the fish."
3 years old		Full gramar, except irregulars	"I want to see all the fish."
6 years old	Early Critical Period	Full gramar. including irregulars	"I want to see all the fish."
12 years old	Late Critical Period	Similar to adults, with some (not full) figurative play	"I want to see all the fish." or "Show me all the $," etc.

Figure 55. Language acquisition stages.

The ages groups given in figure 55 are debated by some, specifically the level of language acquisition around ages six and twelve. For example, "Zero-To-Three," a Washington DC-based global non-profit organization, combines the Early and Late critical periods: "The critical period for language-learning begins to close around five years of age and ends around puberty." In any case, there is general agreement that the ideal period for effective, natural L1 acquisition is the early period, although there is a "second chance," until puberty. The article "Zero-To-Three" (Zerotothree.org) goes on to say that brain maturation and the reduction of

---

[5] The degree of flexibility of our bodies, muscles, and neurons to adapt and adjust.
[6] This is true for speakers of one's native language—and obviously affects second-language acquisition equally.

9.1 L1 acquisition: Its nature

neuro-muscular plasticity after that point makes it more difficult to learn a language and will affect development of a natural accent.

9.1.5 L1 acquisition is systematic

At times, children may sound humorous when they talk, especially at ages 0–3. They are creative in their use of language at that stage. They may come up with things like, "I goed to my pop's yesterday," or "fourth head" for "forehead," or "I won you," instead of "I beat you." My colleague Keris reports that her three-year-old once said "arm-knee" for "elbow." Even if these sound poorly constructed to a mature speaker, there is a system in place, a logical, grammatical reasoning behind these seemingly disjointed utterances that the child may have not yet assimilated from hearing adult speech.

My son, for several years, referred to every woman as "girl" in Spanish (*niña*). By extension (or overextension, a relatively common phenomenon at this stage of child language acquisition), he transferred the Spanish word for girl to any reference to a female, since it was likely the most common word he heard for a female. At that point, in his mind, the age factor may have been irrelevant since there were no other words in his lexicon for a female. He also kept saying the equivalent of "s/he ached me" instead of "s/he hurt me" in Spanish, probably also because of the translation from English to Spanish of the verb "hurt." As Polonius said in Shakespeare's *Hamlet*: "Though this be madness, yet there is method in it." Yes, there is a method behind this madness; there is a system behind these humorous quirks in language use.

Responding to a question that a parent considered regression of her child's speech, Birner comments on the child's *progression*, not regression:

> Why did my daughter say feet correctly for a while, and then go back to calling them foots?" Birner answers that this is in no way a "going back" in language acquisition but in fact, a "going forward" step. It means the child has learned the rule for use of plural in English—that is progress. (Birner 2021)

Kymissis and Poulson (1990) recount how previous experts postulated that children acquire language through imitation or reinforcement. They, and others, promoted these theories in the twentieth century (Thorndike [1911], behaviorists Pavlov [1928] and Skinner [1936], and Kymissis and Poulson [1990]). In the twenty-first century these theories have been questioned. However, even though the theories of imitation and reinforcement in language acquisition have been discredited as the sole explanation of this language acquisition process, there are undoubtedly some aspects of imitation and reinforcement involved. Children imitate their parents' language to a certain extent, but then they can produce language on their own, even words or expressions they have never heard, such as "foots." The child has been forming grammatical rules in his mind, silently and subconsciously. The daughter referred to, formed a rule of plural in her mind, based on parents' and peers' input, and added an -s suffix to the noun. She went through the imitation stage but, having passed that, she arrived at the stage of grammar regularization. The "irregular grammar" stage will come later. She will then revert to "feet;" but then the utterance, "feet" will be a product of her own grammatical intuition, not solely a product of imitating her parents. Children first observe and listen, then try out new vocabulary by imitation, then repeat. After this, they continue to observe, integrating rules. Then they hypothesize new rules, and assess their success by the feedback they get, observing the expressions and comments of their listeners. They repeat the word or phrase if the feedback was satisfactory or try something different if it wasn't. It is a constant process of trial and error. They continue this process until there is total independence of production that seems to satisfy all. This, then, is a rule-governed process.

The speech bubble in figure 56 illustrates this trial-and-error process that begins at a very young age. Hypothesize, experiment, and confirm-or-reject the hypothesis. Since it worked the first time, the child will add this data to her language rules. If the results are rewarding, the rule or word sticks; otherwise, a new hypothesis is tried.

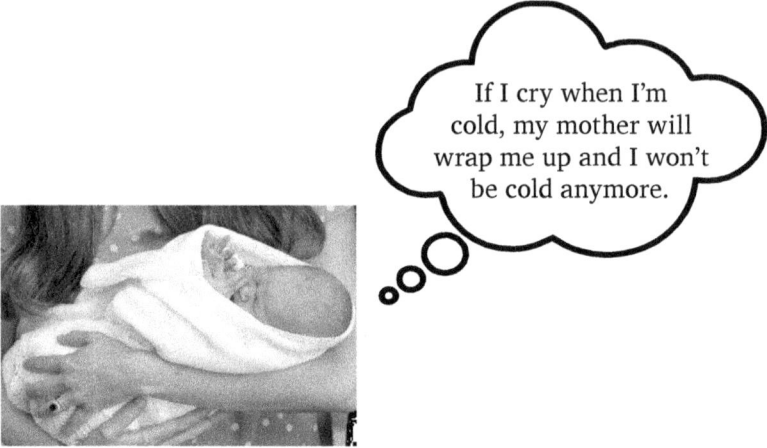

Figure 56. Baby Prince George learns to have his needs met.

Now we will move on to second language acquisition. Are these processes applicable to SLA as well? How similar or how different is L1 acquisition from SLA? Can everyone learn a second language? Are the same principles applied to learning the L2 as when they learned their primary language? Although we do not have all the answers to all these questions, here are important considerations about SLA.

9.2 Second language acquisition (SLA): Its nature

L2 acquisition or SLA, that is, the learning of any foreign language, also involves some important methodologies. At times, L2 acquisition resembles L1 acquisition processes but other times, the two processes are very distinct. We will now consider these similarities and differences. First, to clarify, there are subtle distinctions between *second language learning* and *foreign language learning*. However, for the purposes of this book, we will consider them the same since they share fundamental commonalities. Now, let's consider some features of learning a second language.

9.2.1 L2 acquisition is non-compulsory

Unlike L1 acquisition, SLA may or may not happen. Depending on your circumstances, SLA is not a requisite. This is not to say that it is not necessary under circumstances faced by populations of other countries. According to the Compendium of Language Management of the University of Ottawa, there are fifty-five bilingual or multilingual countries in the world. That means that fifty-five countries have at least two official languages and people in those countries are typically expected to learn those two (or more) languages. In Africa, for example, Equatorial Guinea is listed with Spanish and French as official languages, but there are other local languages recognized as regional languages, such as Fang. India is listed with Hindi and English, but there are additional state languages as well. Canada is officially bilingual, using both French and English. This is especially true in the Province of Quebec. Most citizens of Quebec learn both languages. In India, the average citizen learns three languages. That is not the case in mostly monolingual countries such as the U.S. and most Latino countries in the Americas. However, even in the Americas, bilingualism is more common than most people realize. In bilingual countries, circumstances may mandate the learning of an L2, but that is

9.2 Second language acquisition (SLA): Its nature

mostly for political, professional, and academic advancement. If someone were not to learn a second language, they might lose opportunities in that society. Yet even if they don't advance in society, still the person can communicate within some circles.

9.2.2 L2 acquisition is sequential

Just as the acquisition of a primary language follows certain stages, an effective process of SLA does as well. For example, Dulay and Burt (1973) suggest that there is a certain order in which L2 learners acquire morphemes. This, of course, changes from one language to another, but some morphemes tend to be learned before others. Some sounds are also learned before others. For example, the two fricative interdental sounds in English, [θ] and [ð] (the voiceless and voiced "th" sounds pronounced in English *thigh* and *thy*), are typically some of the last sounds learned in the phonology of English (Crowe and McLeod 2020:2156). Bleile (2018) presents a list of the last eight English consonants acquired by L1 learners of English. Among the "late eight" are: [θ] and [ð] again, in *thanks* and *the*, [š] in *she*, [č] in *chin*, the liquids [l] in *little* and [r] in *riddle*, and the [s] in *sip* and [z] in *zip* (2018:4). Although not necessarily the same last eight for SLA students, as with the order of morpheme acquisition for L2 learners, there are additional rules that affect a logical, sequential methodology of learning an L2.

9.2.3 L2 acquisition is time-constrained

The age of a person when they learn an L2 is crucial. Similar to L1 acquisition, the ideal time for SLA is during childhood and the early teen years before puberty, as discussed regarding the Critical Period hypothesis. Typically, the earlier the SLA process begins, the better to more fully acquire an L2. Krashen (1982) makes the distinction between "learning" and "acquisition," with the former, more like our academic rule-based memorization process, and the latter, a more natural, everyday process. The earlier you learn, Krashen emphasizes, the more natural the acquisition process, the more ideal. Older adults tend to follow rules and attempt to memorize; so, it becomes laborious to learn the language.

In addition to being a more natural process, the younger a child is, the less of a foreign accent (s)he will likely retain. Again, the plasticity of muscles and the brain before puberty permits more adaptability of the tongue and cognitive processes to new challenges. Although typical adults can learn an L2 after puberty, the naturalness of the learning process as a child is more natural, especially in terms of an accent, than for those who learn a second language as an adult.

Genie's case and that of other "wild" or "feral" children, show that being exposed to language for the first time after puberty may imply never acquiring language at the communication ability of other people. Typically, the younger the L2 learner is, the less of a foreign accent they will have. Meanwhile, each L2 learner past the Critical Period must decide how important it is for them to speak without an accent and to sound like the average speaker of that society. It is a case of personal desire and intention to work to achieve that goal of mainstreaming.

9.2.4 L2 acquisition is systematic

Similar to L1 acquisition as a child, there is a system in the process of SLA. There is input exposure, hypothesizing, trial and error, analysis of feedback and input, and there is rule formation. The main difference in regard to L1 acquisition is that now, because there is a full linguistic system already in place in the mind of the learner (their L1), some of the hypotheses (regarding a grammar rule or the pronunciation of a sound, etc.) relate to their L1, whether they depend upon this transfer consciously or subconsciously. For example, a Spanish speaker learning English may say "boy good" instead of "good boy" because they follow word order rules in

Spanish when trying to speak English. This is called LINGUISTIC INTERFERENCE or *L1 transfer* (Odlin 2003:436). Sometimes the hypothesis works, which is *positive transfer*, and sometimes the hypothesis does not work, like in the Spanish earlier example, which then would be *negative transfer*. It might be the case that, if the two languages resemble each other grammatically or phonologically, the learner may have more instances of positive transfer, but this is not really a guarantee. I have seen native speakers of Japanese or Chinese struggling with English as much as native speakers of German. German and English are sister languages from a historical or genetic perspective since they both come from the Germanic languages, they belong in the same linguistic family. However, Japanese and Chinese are not linguistically related to English. In some cases, German speakers may have an easier time with certain sounds or grammatical rules of English, and other times, the Japanese speaker may have an easier time.

What is the hardest second language to learn? This can be answered only relatively speaking. There is no absolute answer. Notice that I did not ask this question for L1 learners since all languages present the same ease or complexity for first-language learners. All people learn the majority of their L1 system by the age of three or four, regardless of the language or linguistic family of their L1. Thus, in this sense, every language is equally difficult and equally easy to learn.

How difficult an L2 is for a person may depend on various factors, one of them being how different the linguistic system is of their L1 compared with the L2. For example, an English speaker learning Hawaiian may have an easier time learning the sounds of Hawaiian than Japanese since Hawaiian only has around fifteen phonemes. Japanese has around twenty phonemes, but English has 40–44. It also depends on the degree of contact between the two languages region-wise and history-wise.

Pimsleur (2013:10) says that "the average American who knows no French can guess" a small percentage of the French written vocabulary since many French words have been borrowed into English or they have the same etymology as English words due to some similarities in the history of English or French. Pimsleur says that the same can be said about related or "nearby" languages such as Spanish, Italian, and German (2013:11). Some important similarities may be seen among Romance languages such as Spanish, French, Italian, and others. The same can be said of Germanic languages such as German and English. Geographic proximity also produces some level of familiarity. All these factors can affect the "ease" or "difficulty" of learning an L2.

I then insist on the following linguistic reality: Every first language is equally difficult and equally easy to learn. They all take roughly an average of three-to-four years to learn. This reality is not the same for second (or third, or fourth, etc.) language acquisition, which depends on many factors. It could take months, or a couple of years, or ten years, or a whole lifetime to learn an L2! I know people who after a few months learning a second language, can communicate at a survival level acceptably well. Likewise, I know people who, after years of studying a language, struggle substantially to communicate in that language.

Figure 57. Every language is equally challenging and accessible to children. L1 acquisition takes three-to-four years.

Thus, deciding which language is the most challenging for you to learn depends on your L1 and your linguistic contacts. It may be Spanish, French, Mandarin, Japanese, or Arabic. Decide based on your interests, your nearness to speakers of other languages, the usefulness of a certain L2 for your future and profession, and other practical criteria. Again, it is impossible to prove that any particular language is the most difficult to learn.

In the last pages of this chapter, we present some suggestions in case you have the chance to learn an L2 or teach English as a second language to others. These suggestions are based on research in the field and the author's experience as an L2 learner, L2 teacher, and L2 teacher-trainer. There are many effective methods, but the points in section 9.3 are ones this author has proven to be effective. These strategies serve as principles to guide the learner and to be adapted according to the specific language you want to learn.

9.3 Suggestions for a better SLA experience

A French proverb says, "A man who knows two languages is worth two men." I can verify that your worldview expands when you learn another language. It becomes easier to see things from a different perspective; this is crucial for adapting in this twenty-first century world. If you offer to teach English to others, you are to be congratulated also. If either category fits you, the following suggestions will help you enjoy your journey.

9.3.1 Focus on communication in SLA

The main purpose of language is to communicate. When you think of grammar rules or vocabulary words to learn or teach, think of what communicative function those words or rules perform. It is best not to teach or learn grammar rules or words in isolation. Think of communicative tasks in which to apply them.

Prabhu (1987) popularized an L2 teaching method based on the principle of communication tasks: The Task-Based Language Learning (TBLL) or the Task-Based Instruction (TBI). Using this method, the students are given activities like those listed here, and the grammar and vocabulary are taught within those tasks:

- Taking someone to the supermarket or to the bank
- Shopping for specific grocery items
- Opening a bank account for the first time
- Starting a conversation with new people
- Reporting on your health to the doctor
- Performing a job interview

TBLL or TBI is part of what has been known as the Communicative Language Teaching approach or the *Communicative Approach*, first introduced in a formal way by Wilkins (1976). In 2013 the American Council on the Teaching of Foreign Languages published their L2 teaching and learning standards for teacher preparation programs in the U.S.A. with a methodology built around the teaching of *Core Standards*. Standard 3, "Language Acquisition Theories and Knowledge of Students and their Needs," establishes that,

> Meaningful classroom interaction is at the heart of language instruction. Candidates engage students in communicative and interesting activities and tasks on a regular basis. All classroom interaction reflects engaging contexts that are personalized to the interests of students and reflect curricular goals." (2013:66–67)

Meaningful classroom interaction is key. Everything is taught with a goal of communication in mind and is heavily dependent on interaction between people and negotiating meaning. It is the opposite approach of grammar-based traditional methods popularly used in many L2 classrooms today.

9.3.2 Contextualize in SLA

Context is crucial for communication, as discussed. It is hard to interpret language correctly out of context. As illustrated by the rhetorical question, "How are you?" the question makes sense only when interpreted in the right context. As Hymes (1974) showed, we need to know about the situation of the speech, the participants, the goals of the interaction, and other extralinguistic factors. This was part of the Hymes' SPEAKING acronym (section 7.2). One strategy is to teach vocabulary and grammar embedded in a dialogue, a story, or a similar contextualized narrative through repetition and memorization. The Audiolingual Method (ALM) of the 1930s uses that approach. I do not support the behaviorist, *tabula rasa*-like philosophy[7] of this method; it is important to contextualize grammar and vocabulary versus teaching by rote memorization.

In addition to this, it is important to keep in mind that each language is used within a particular speech community, with certain dynamics, worldview, and culture. Understanding the L2 speaker's worldview and culture as much as possible helps facilitate learning. For example, if you understand that Jaqaru speakers care about the source of the information you convey, whether it is hearsay or a firsthand account of the message, then you will seek ways in the language to express that. Thus, if you are an L2 learner, try to learn about the culture and worldview of the native speakers of your target language. If you are a teacher of your L1, teach about your culture, and embed grammar and vocabulary in that context. As a part of this, you will also want to learn or teach about the norms of linguistic interactions in the speech community of your L2. There are certain expectations or *scripts* of certain speech events. In a court in the United States, for example, Americans typically know what to say and when, and who says what. By attentively observing the target culture's communicational behavior with an open mind and non-ethnocentric eyes, you can learn a lot about their language. Good L2 learners are good observers and listeners. Likewise, good L2 teachers help their learners notice the patterns taking place both in the target language and in the cultural context.

Figure 58. Effective L2 learners are good observers and great listeners.

9.3.3 Exploit previous knowledge in SLA

Again, people don't come to a language-learning situation with a *tabula rasa,* as some theorists have suggested. Because of that, we cannot consider our students or ourselves (as L2 learners) to be completely ignorant of the L2. In fact, I would suggest that you probably know a little bit about whatever language you might want to study. It is important to be cognizant of that fact and use that previous knowledge wisely. For example, all languages have at least three vowel sounds, including [a]. All languages have adjective-noun connections, and all languages have some type of subject and a predicate, or a topic and comment; these factors can be compared or contrasted with the way English grammar structures its sentences. Start with this general knowledge and build on it. Also, all people share some aspects of worldview regarding their life and the planet on which we live.

---

[7] An opportunity to begin again with no record, history, or preconceived ideas is one kind of *tabula rasa* (Vocabulary.com). Latin for blank slate.

It is important to activate schemas or mind images that can trigger topics or knowledge relevant to whatever needs to be taught or learned. If you want to learn about how to open a bank account, ask questions or show pictures that can trigger bank-related knowledge for the L2 learner. This schema-activation process must occur at the beginning of a lesson. This will help to contextualize the related learning that can occur during the lesson.

Finally, Krashen pointed out the importance of following a step-by-step process in any L2 learning and teaching experience. He calls this *Comprehensible Input* or the "*i+1*" (input plus one-step-higher) hypothesis (1982:33). The idea is that we start off with knowledge already in place in the mind of the learner. For example, if we want to learn how to tell stories or convey past narratives, we start by reviewing how to tell current stories. In other words, assuming the learner knows the present tense best, to teach past tense usage, the instructor starts by reviewing or "re-activating" the present tense.

9.3.4 Orality before writing in SLA

It is equally beneficial, for a better effective L2 learning or teaching process, that all the elements involved focus on oral skills first and later apply reading and writing. Remember that writing is secondary to oral language expression. Languages exist and are used with or without a reading and writing system. We speak first before we write our L1; it makes sense to follow this natural sequence when in the L2 setting. As a teacher, present oral input first and then the written input. Typically, if you do it backwards, the students will use their L1 phonology to "pronounce" that word in their minds, and it might not match the sound system of the L2. Obviously orality is not the only acceptable medium, but the oral presentation should be the first medium taught in SLA. Additionally, oral competence typically requires a higher cognitive effort. It is typical that a student can pass an L2 written test but fail an equivalent test given orally. It rarely happens in reverse order. Mastering oral skills is the best starting point of SLA.

9.3.5 Multi-sensory approach in SLA

Students often protest at being taught oral skills first if they consider themselves visual or tactile learners; they may claim the need to visualize words so they can learn them. However, as discussed in chapter 8, the motor cortex, the visual cortex, and the audio cortex of the brain each contribute to learning. Unless a major injury has occurred that inhibits one of the language centers, all those language centers are active and receptive to learning. The idea of visual learners or auditory learners is more appropriately understood if these are understood as learning *preferences* (Allen et al. 2011:37). Students may *prefer* to learn in a certain way. Certainly, teachers and learners can keep in mind these preferences, but that does not restrict a student from learning in other ways. In fact, I strongly suggest a multi-sensory method of teaching and learning. If the same information is presented visually, orally, and via other modes, more brain centers get activated. (Papadatou-Pastou et al. 2021:514). The more the different brain centers are activated, the more the learning potential because more sections of the brain are involved in the acquisition of a sound, expression, or other linguistic norm.

Figure 59. A multi-sensory approach: (visual-auditory-kinesthetic-tactile).

Students learn more rapidly, more comprehensively, and more effectively when content is presented in different modalities.

Exercises

1) **L1 Acquisition**
   Record at least two expressions or words uttered by children (up to six years of age) that are different from the speech of adults. Use examples not mentioned in this book. First, list the utterances and the age of the child. Then, indicate how it is different from language used by adults. Finally, based on what this chapter covers, provide at least one hypothesis for why this speech difference happens.

2) **L2 Acquisition**
   Record at least two expressions or words uttered by non-native speakers of English that are different from an English native-speaker's language. Use examples not mentioned in this book. First, list the utterances and if possible, the age and country of origin of the ESL speaker. Then, indicate how the expression or word is different from a native English speaker's language use. Finally, based on what this chapters covers, provide at least one hypothesis for why this difference occurs.

10

Does Society Help or Harm Language?

Crime cannot be tolerated. Criminals thrive on the indulgence of society's understanding.
– Ra'as al Ghul, ("Batman Begins.")

Figure 60. Society's effect on language.

Juan, a Mexican young man, native speaker of Spanish, was one of over one hundred respondents to a survey about "dialectos," the word in Spanish for "dialects." Respondents were simply asked to define that word, to which Juan said: "For example, in Mexico the common language is Spanish. Then there are dialects that only a small group of people speak." In conversations afterward, we talked about what a dialect really is and how to properly refer to Indigenous languages in Mexico, North America, and elsewhere. In another set of cellphone texts back and forth, he wrote: "thinking of [Indigenous languages] as other languages [instead of "dialectos"] helps me. Just because [someone] is different does not mean they are less than me. No language is better than another. [Now] I have more respect for them." He recognized that it was not accurate or proper to refer to Indigenous languages as *dialectos* instead of languages. He even asked me, later, "Where did that word even originate from?" showing his frustration, like mine, with the misuse of the term in this context, based on bias, misconception, or ignorance.[1]

---

[1] "FluentU" *Foreign Language Immersion Online* distinguishes *languages* from *dialects* based on national vs. regional and an official written system vs. oral but takes care to not speak of one as substandard or

Juan, like millions of other people, had been indoctrinated with the misconception that the majority language was superior to the minority language. Society, via the media, schools, laws, traditions, common rhetoric, and similar institutions or platforms, tends to shape our thinking this way. Unfortunately, we get wrong ideas about language varieties and the people who speak those languages or language varieties.

In this chapter, I aim to raise awareness of these *society-at-large*-based linguistic issues. This chapter follows the earlier discussion (chapter 5) regarding sociolinguistics; here, particularly in connection with macro-aspects of society, such as the hierarchy and history of society. This chapter elucidates how those macro factors shape language-related issues.

10.1 Awareness of how society interacts with language issues

Should we care how societal structure and dynamics help us or harm us? They inevitably affect each of us for good or for bad. Social norms affect the way we dress, the way we interact, what we buy,—and yes, the way we talk. If we ignore or are blind to currents of social norms we may unknowingly end up promoting them. As the chapter 10 epigram, referring to the Batman movie, says: "...*the indulgence of society's understanding.*" But we do not need a fictional character to remind us of that. George Floyd's murder in 2020 and many historical movements around the world remind us that when we recognize injustice and come together to speak out against it, good can result, if we do so thoughtfully.

Before coming to the U.S., I heard commentaries in Venezuela about the way other segments of society speak Spanish. When I came to the States, similarly I started hearing comments evaluating the way English is spoken. Some comments were neutral, whereas others were harsh and diminishing. I heard: "New Yorkers sound rude;" "Bostonians sound funny;" "Valley girls are always asking questions;" "Southerners sound dumb;" "if you say *y'all* and *fixin' to*, you are Southern"; and so on. Some comments characterized certain groups in America as unintelligent, and some labeled others as inferior—"they don't even speak English!"

In 1988, PBS aired Nicholas Marshall's award-winning sociolinguistic documentary, "American Tongues," which records the story of a young Northeastern woman who broke up with her Southern boyfriend because she did not want her children to "sound Southern" (Marshall 1988).

As was introduced in chapter 5 about language variation, I notice a tendency these days on American TV singing, dancing, and talent competition shows to include a person on the judges' panel who has a British accent. The average TV-viewer seems to think that comments offered by the judge who speaks with a British accent are worth listening to because theirs is "the most intelligent" verdict. The underlying belief seems to be that if you sound British you are intelligent.

Something similar happens in Latin America regarding the accent in Spanish used by people from Spain. The Continental European variety of Spanish is perceived of as high class. In other contexts, people think that those who speak with a French accent are romantic. Some people not only think certain groups of society *sound* intelligent or rude, but also tend to think of that group, even apart from their speech, as inherently intelligent or rude.

People evaluate and critique the way people sound to others. A popular saying goes, "you can judge a man by the company he keeps." but in the same way, you can "judge a man by the way he talks"—or so people think. Another saying is: "Show me your friends and I'll show you who you are." In the same way, Schneider said: "Show me your language and I'll show you who you are" (2000:359–361). Don't forget, though, that sometimes, we may be right, but other times we may be very wrong.

---

qualitatively more elegant or sophisticated than the other. Visit https://www.fluentu.com/blog/learn/difference-between-language-and-dialect/.

Figure 61. Society's judgments based on language used.

So it is that the way people use language in society, their pronunciation, choice of vocabulary, and use of grammar, may deeply shape the way they perceive of others, and the way others see them. People speculate about your age, gender, social class, and level of education simply by the way we talk, even without looking at physical appearance; opinions are formed spontaneously and subconsciously. Based on one's accent or regional speech, people speculate about one's country of origin or about what region they are from within that speaker's country. Categorization *per se* is not negative. How a listener reacts based on that speculation is what may be hurtful, as we will discuss further in section 10.2.

The most important aspect of these perceptions is not the label that people give each other as part of one society or regional group. The most significant result is how this awareness affects how two people relate. Fortunately or unfortunately, fairly or not, the way you talk can bring about inclusivity between people or can alienate people. If you speak with a Southern accent, a classmate from the North may not identify with you and hold you at a distance. He may have preconceived prejudices about Southerners, as did the Northeastern lady who didn't want her children to sound Southern.

Stereotypes, presuppositions, prejudices, myths, formed among your family and peers, and your previous experiences all shape what you believe about other people andthe groups to which you belong. One of the most immediate and superficial ways to identify a person as part of one group or another is their speech. Clothing choice, jewelry, makeup, and other outward appearances play a role. But, one of the strongest group identifiers in society is language.

10.2 Societal macro factors that shape language: Structure, dynamics, history, and beliefs

Chapter 5 discussed issues about dialects, in which sociolinguistic variables were mentioned that impact language, factors such as gender, age, social class, and race. These sociolinguistic variables shape language use. In this chapter we will discuss other society-wide or macro factors that have a similar and even stronger impact. We will call these *macro* factors because they identify the society at large—the hierarchy of society, its history or past experiences, its long-standing norms, interactions with other societies, and its prejudices.

10.2.1 Societal hierarchy

The island of Java in Indonesia is Indonesia's political, historical, and economic core, containing 60 percent of the total population and most of its wealth. Here we find a clear example of how societal hierarchy affects language choices. Robson and Wibisono (2002:3-4) explain that Javanese has two main speech levels: *Ngoko* and *Krama*. The basic level is Ngoko, and the ceremonial level is Krama. Many Ngoko words have Krama equivalents. The authors explain that Krama words are used if speakers need to show respect based on hierarchical differences and social distance. Speakers need to be aware of the relation between self and the hearer before they choose a speech level. *Madya*, an in-between level, is a "compromise between Ngoko and Krama."

More specifically, the sublevels High Krama and Low Krama, are used to express honorifics and humility. High Krama expresses respect to the hearer or referent and can never be used to refer to oneself. Low Krama, on the other hand, expresses humility and thus can be used only in reference to oneself (2002:3-4).

Figure 62 illustrates these societal strata. The top section of the pyramid represents the king, with the highest status. At the base of the pyramid are those with the lowest social status—the proletariat or working class. In between are mid-level groups such as the king's servants, and middle-class citizens, up to the status of the princely class. The Sentono Dalem (princely) class uses the High Krama speech of Javanese among themselves and to address the king, but address proletarians with Ngoko. Royalty uses Madya Ngoko to address servants. The Priyavi (palace servants) address underlings using Ngoko. (Poedjosoedarmo 1968:58-59).

Proletarian class

Figure 62. Social and linguistic hierarchies.

Worldwide, there is a hierarchy of strata of society within countries, within regions of a country, or based on other structural elements within society. Although there exist social classes in the U.S. and the Western world, they are minimal when compared with other nations. There is the well-known social caste system in India, and other types of societal hierarchy in all countries, whether classified as such, or not. In all parts of the world, people organize themselves in societies or communities with a hierarchy of some sort, which affects language distinctions.

Societal hierarchy shapes language, but conversely, language choice shapes at least part of our perception of society. Brown and Gilman (1968) explain that in some languages like Classic Latin and French, at least two pronouns are used for the pronoun you; The French pronoun vous (formal) implies that the addressee has a higher social status than the speaker, whereas tu (informal) implies a lower or equal status of the addressee. Spanish, of the same language family as Latin and French, makes this distinction too, as described in section 7.2.7. This formal—informal pronoun difference was once marked in OE but LME has lost this distinction.

Different segments of society, with both high and low status, shape the development of language. Vocabulary, grammar, even accents used by people from a prestigious class of society may become the standard for other groupings of society. At times, lower-status groups may set standards for language change. However, in other cases, two standards exist side-by-side. Myhill reports that in Norwegian there are two norms for the official writing of the Norwegian language: Bokmål and Nynorsk. Bokmål "book language" is written by the high-prestige group and Nynorsk "new Norwegian" is standard language used in the western areas (Myhill 1999:42; Norwegian Academy). "Both forms are taught in schools, [and] used in official documents and media. ... So, it comes to your preferences and your place of living. It might be hard to learn writing Bokmål in an area where everyone uses Nynorsk" (Norwegian Academy).

10.2.2 History or past experiences

In 2015 I visited the former Soviet country of Georgia, in Eurasia. While walking around the streets of a small town in that country, I noticed that the older people spoke Russian and Georgian, but the younger generations spoke only Georgian. I asked around and found out that it was a way to become more independent from Russia. Georgia was ruled by Russia during the time of the Soviet Union. They became independent of the Soviet Union in 1991 after 70 years under their control. The Russian language was a symbol of that dominance. Georgia's independence was reflected in a conscious shift from the use of Russian to the Georgian language.

The murder of George Floyd in May of 2020 is a reminder of decades-old tensions between races in the U.S.A. Floyd, an African American man was murdered by white police officers, causing heated debates, riots, and the implementation of new measures to avoid police brutality and systemic racism. That incident may have impacted our English language use, particularly in our understanding of the word "racism" and other words related to this issue.

Webster's New World College Dictionary in 1996 gives two entries for the word *racism*, defined in six lines (Neufeldt and Guralnik 1996). Over twenty years later, the online version of this dictionary gives nine entries, requiring 18 lines to define (*Merriam-Webster* 2024e). Since dictionaries reflect the use of our language, reporting what is happening in the language of communities they describe, today, undoubtedly due to racially affected incidents, nuances have been added to the word *racism*, including "microaggressions," "police profiling," "systemic oppression," "White Supremacy," and "redlining." The same source says that "Racism and racist appear to be words of recent origin, with no citations known that would suggest these words were in use prior to the early 20th century" (*Merriam-Webster* 2024e). Much of the George Floyd reactionary movement was led by the younger generation, which was also true of the intentional shift from Russian to Georgian language use. What that means is that whatever is achieved by that movement will, most likely, become the linguistic norm of the coming generation.

10.2.3 Social etiquette

Politically correct language is an example of how society norms, expectations, or etiquette determine what we can say or not say.

It is customary to name sports teams using mascots: "Detroit Lions," "Carolina Panthers," "Florida Marlins," and so on. Some team names have been given that conjure up race distinctions as well: "Washington Redskins," "Cleveland Indians," "Atlanta Braves," "Florida Seminoles," "Kansas City Chiefs," among others. Political correctness has been called into question in connection with names that could be construed as offensive to Native American peoples. Journalist Jeff Kerr, for CBSsports.com reports that the Washington "Redskins" name was coined in 1933 but increasingly became compared to racist slurs of African Americans, and in 2020 was retired (Kerr 2020). Later it was changed to the Washington Commanders.

As explained in sections 5.2 and 6.1.5, political correctness shapes language. What is now called INCLUSIVE LANGUAGE is a movement toward tailoring language to not exclude others. If the vocabulary you use can be perceived as inappropriate by others in society, the best practice is to avoid using that stigmatized language. CNN.com reported in 2021 that the "Aunt Jemima" name brand and logo of pancake and waffle syrup, founded in 1888, has been replaced for having been "long criticized as a racist caricature of a Black woman stemming from slavery." Parent company PepsiCo says they want to be in line with the company's "values of diversity and inclusion and support of the Black community" (Alcorn 2021).

Racial overtones also have affected rice brand "Uncle Ben," which illustrates an aged African American male restaurant server or host. Some people no longer accept the term "master bedroom," changing the name of the main bedroom in a house to less racially charged "primary bedroom." The conflict with this designation is that the etymology of the term contrasted a master's bedroom from slave quarters.

Similarly, but unrelated to racial discrimination, it is a well-known taboo to ask a woman about her age, or to ask about someone's salary or weight. Additionally, instead of speaking about death directly, people prefer to euphemistically say, "passed away" instead of "died," or "he is an aged gentleman" instead of "he is old," and so on. Many unacceptable words or phrases in today's society are either not addressed or, if verbalized, are couched in an expression that softens the message. Figure 63 illustrates euphemisms on a sign for an aisle in a pharmacy. I am sure you can think of many other examples.

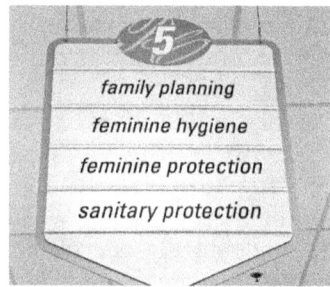

Figure 63. Sign in a pharmacy using euphemistic terminology:
How societal norms shape language.

10.2.4 Steady cross-linguistic interaction (languages in contact)

Sometimes two or more groups who speak different languages find themselves living among or near each other and with the need to interact with the people who speak those other languages. The speech that results from this cross-linguistic interaction illustrates how pidgins and creole languages emerge. Examples of these are Haitian Creole, or Hawaiian Pidgin (which is not really a pidgin, but a creole language). Gullah is another English creole spoken in the Southeastern states of North Carolina, South Carolina, and Georgia. When Africans from different language groups were brought from Africa to the Caribbean and the Americas they were forced to work as slaves alongside other slaves who often were from a different language group. French was the majority language used in work and trade in Haiti and Louisiana, and so they learned a version of French that overlaid their native language. This was a pidgin French. The same happened in English-speaking areas like Jamaica and the Americas, where pidgin English became the common language. The pidgin language spoken

10.2 Societal macro factors that shape language

by the first generation became more standardized when the next generation learned the amalgamated language as their first language. That new emergent language, influenced by both the African languages and the majority language, became solidified as *creole* languages. The English variety used by many African Americans on the Southeast coast, near the Charleston port, has obvious influences from Gullah (Kaye and Tosco 2001:95). Similar creole languages, unrelated to imports from African slaves, are the Chabacano language, a Spanish-based creole in the Philippines, and the English-based creole in Hawaii, Hawaiian Pidgin.

After extended contact, a language influences the language of their neighbor; and that second language influences the first. English and Spanish have been in close contact on the American continent for many years. This close contact between Spanish-speaking countries in the Americas and the English of the U.S. resulted in loan words borrowed by both languages. In American English the Spanish words, "siesta" and "fiesta," are now universally understood; while in Spanish, the English word baseball, written as "beisbol," is commonly used.

Different from two languages in contact, Ferguson (1959) describes those situations in which one language is expressed in two ways as *diglossia*. Within a single language, two or more varieties co-exist, one variety that is more prestigious is used in school, church, and formal situations; the other variety used in everyday interactions. Diglossia is clearly observable in Arabic-speaking countries. Classical Arabic "is primarily used for religious purposes, ... [whereas] Modern Standard Arabic is the opposite end of the spectrum. ... [It] is the primary form of the Arabic language that is spoken" (Live Lingua 2024); that is, Arabic used in formal and literary religious contexts versus vernacular, common Arabic, spoken in the home. Figure 64 illustrates some of the contexts in which diglossia is practiced in most languages.

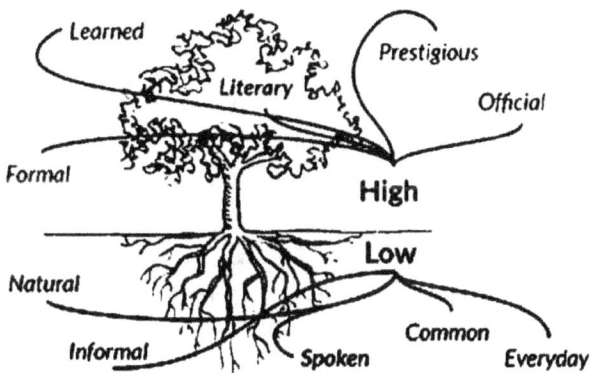

Figure 64. Living diglossia.

Thus, due to regular contact between languages, a new language may evolve (a pidgin, evolving into a creole); or more than one variety may develop out of the same language contact and be used differently under certain conditions, often by the same speakers and within the same community (diglossia), as is the case for formal and colloquial Arabic. Both language contact and language context matter.

10.2.5 Beliefs and prejudices

Beliefs and prejudices are one of the least investigated of the societal issues listed here, so we give more space to this topic. The critical importance of this topic is that societal prejudice threatens social justice. Prejudice affects our use of language and our attitudes toward both our own and others' language, and that has the effect of creating social injustice that permeates society.

Social justice is an expected ideal in the societies of the world, both today and in the world in which we grew up. We are given to believe that at least, based on religious creeds, governmental constitutions, and other public official documents. Pound quotes Plato, saying that justice implies harmony among all, and that the law should provide accountability for the equal treatment of individuals (1912:7).

The Preamble to the United States Constitution begins like this:

> We the People of the United States, in Order to form a more perfect Union, establish Justice, insure domestic Tranquility, ... promote the general Welfare, and secure the Blessings of Liberty to ourselves and our Posterity ...

The first ideal prescribed for a "more perfect union" in the Preamble is for U.S. citizens to "establish justice." Historically, then, the ideal of justice for the United States, is expressed in the introduction to our first nation-wide declaration of standards. We see this idealized concept "on the books," and also central to the Pledge of Allegiance to the United States of America: "liberty and justice for all." Thus, key codified records and guiding principles of the United States outline the spirit of the Constitution at the highest level, although they cannot ensure protection for citizens from social injustice and prejudice.

The aspiration of social justice is not a cause just for the United States. Many countries strive for this ideal, often in a similar fashion. The Preamble of the 1999 Constitution of Venezuela establishes that the People of Venezuela seek to form a society that guarantees "... the right to life, to work, to culture, to education, to social justice, and to equality without discrimination nor subordination [by any authority]."[2]

Not only do country-wide constitutions proclaim this human ideal of social justice, but documents with global reach do so also. As early as the mid-1800s French ethicist Pierre-Joseph Proudhon "identified ... social justice with respect for human dignity" (Proudhon 2006:12). In the United Nations (UN) *Universal Declaration of Human Rights*, social justice is given international recognition: "The inherent dignity and of the equal and inalienable rights of all members of the human family is the foundation of freedom, justice and peace in the world." The UN celebrates social justice yearly on February twentieth, as the "World Day of Social Justice."

The *Oxford Reference* defines SOCIAL JUSTICE as, "The objective of creating a fair and equal society in which each individual matters, their rights are recognized and protected, and decisions are made in ways that are fair and honest" (*Oxford Reference* 2024c). In religious contexts, the Bible also expresses the expectation of social justice: "See that justice is done—help those who are oppressed, give orphans their rights, and defend widows." (Isa. 1:16 [*GNT*]). Jesus said he would "bring good news to the poor ... proclaim liberty to the captives ... set free the oppressed." (Luke 4:18–19 [*GNT*]).

Historically, ethically, and socially, we have the mandate to eliminate prejudice and strive for social justice. British Prime Minister Sir Winston Churchill, in a eulogy of President Roosevelt, recognized his life devotion to human freedom and social justice which fortified and enhanced his presidency during the tumultuous days of World War II. Churchill said:

> But all this [achievement by President Roosevelt] was no more than worldly power and grandeur, had it not been that the causes of human freedom and social justice, to which so much of his life had been given, added a lustre to this power. (17 April 1945)[3]

The high goal to achieve justice is not easy because, as Sonia Nieto says, fighting for social justice may deeply "challenge, confront, and disrupt misconceptions, untruths, and stereotypes that lead to structural inequality based on race, social class, gender, and other social

---

[2] "...el derecho a la vida, al trabajo, a la cultura, a la educación, a la justicia social y a la igualdad sin discriminación ni subordinación alguna..." (Preamble to the Constitution of Venezuela [1999]), country of birth of this author. (Translated from Spanish by the author.)

[3] http://www.ibiblio.org/pha/policy/1945/1945-04-17a.html.

and human differences" (2006:2). In the use of language, misconceptions are obvious that result in undervaluing of some groups in society, as was shown in the example of Juan and what he was led to believe about the inferior nature of *dialectos* at the beginning of chapter 10.

The Charter for Compassion of the Council of Conscience, unveiled at the National Press Club in Washington DC in 2009, put it this way:

> To become aware of injustice in our world, we must become aware of the words we use, how we use them and the meanings we assigned to them. In many ways, the way we use language is completely unconscious. Because our language use is mostly invisible, we sometimes continue to reinforce stereotypes, bias and norms that create barriers for others to try to overcome. (Charter for Compassion 2009)

Although social injustice is revealed in the words we use, i.e., in linguistic discrimination, "language discrimination" is difficult to challenge legally. There is a discrepancy between moral justice in our society and the legal guarantees that might protect that sense of justice. In fact, James Leonard, former Vice Dean of the University of Alabama School of Law, objects to the concept of "language discrimination" from a legal perspective (2004:62–63). However, Roberts, Davies, and Jupp (1992:10) argue that there is a "relationship between language and discrimination." They, and more recently Kibbee (2016), recognize that this is one of the least visible and recognized aspects of discrimination. Lippi-Green (2012) agrees that there is discrimination on the basis of language but amplifies that this is not discrimination against one language or a language variety *per se* but has more to do with the social circumstances and perceptions around that language variety.

If there was any doubt, Pauwels explains how language can be a vehicle for discrimination (1991:3), and Skutnabb-Kangas, Rannut, and Phillipson link the idea of *linguistic discrimination* with the "violation of linguistic human rights". They clarify what they mean by relating a dozen current examples worldwide of such cases (1995:18–22). One example is in the case of a Kurdish mother in Turkey who visits her son in prison but is prohibited from speaking to her son. The guard forces them to speak only Turkish and the mother does not speak Turkish. Thus, language discrimination, in Skutnabb-Kangas et al. (1995), involves the different treatment of a person because of the language they speak. Other examples of linguistic discrimination include immigrants who are sometimes treated poorly and sidelined at their workplace simply due to their language barrier or a strong foreign accent. They may even be denied government services because of their inability to communicate well in English. This behavior would be considered rude and unacceptable if it involved native speakers of English, but it demonstrates a root of prejudice may be evident when an American treats a foreign-born person with that disrespect simply because their primary language is speech other than English.

Miller explains that often these prejudices, and damaging stereotypes do not show up in reference to skin color, physical appearance, or similar traits. Many times these are subtle embedded references to certain groups that imply a level of pronoun degradation of *us* vs. *them*. They appeal to underlying stereotypes, sometimes subconsciously, that make people unfairly perceive of certain groups as threatening. Miller calls this *coded language*, a type of language or linguistic expression that spreads racism and hatred more subtly (2019:37).

In election campaigning, some well-known candidates for high-ranking offices have categorized immigrants as perpetrators of crime as a way to promote their own platform as intolerant of undocumented immigration. However, in "Debunking the Myth of the 'Migrant Crime Wave,'" the data shows otherwise: "The research does not support the view that immigrants commit crime … at higher rates than native-born Americans" (Seid et al. 2024). Despite the fact checking, prejudice and malcontent is stirred up by the candidates' rhetoric. In the process, people who speak a primary language other than English are sometimes regarded with suspicion and are marginalized. For many, then, this prejudice may shape or perpetuate a misconception about non-native speakers of English in the U.S.A.

The image in figure 65 illustrates the coded language mentioned earlier. The sign is impactful in terms of prejudice and disdain. Similar to signs in Southern states that restricted access to African Americans, this bleak notice in a border state illustrates hurtful prejudice toward a people group and their language.

Figure 65. Sign in a Texas restaurant in 1949.

This evidence of prejudices against Latinos illustrates a sad era in the United States. Whether this prejudice remains in our minds, although no longer on our walls, remains unclear.

Two other clear examples, near me and current, of how societal prejudices affect language and language perception is the conception many people have about minority languages, Indigenous languages, and sign languages. Regarding sign languages, many people still struggle with the idea that sign languages such as American Sign Language (ASL) are real and fully descriptive languages. However, linguists have clearly demonstrated that ASL and other sign languages have a complete grammar and lexicon, as much as do English, Spanish, or any other language. More specifically, Brentari suggests that we need to recognize that "sign language are ... natural languages" (Brentari 2010:21). They are the natural language of Deaf people. Why do so many people still have misconceptions about ASL? Is it due to prejudices about the Deaf community and misconceptions about what many call language? For example, if we understand language only based on our own verbal expression of English, which is both oral *and* written, we may not perceive of ASL as a language because it is not oral and it is not written in the way we write English. Also, the Deaf community is a minority, and it may suffer the same issues as many minority languages and people groups in the world. On top of that, many conceive of people who cannot hear as people who have a disability. All of these perspectives are prejudices.

Christopher Rim wrote in an online Forbes magazine editorial about his experience in which ASL was not considered a viable language. Around seven years ago, Rim went to an Ivy League university after graduating from high school and wanted to study a language other than Spanish, which he had taken in high school. He decided to learn ASL. He went to the administrators to request an ASL class, and they said they could accommodate him by providing an independent-study class. However, Rim reports, they told him that "studying ASL would not count towards meeting the language study requirement because there is no written component" (Rim 2019). Fortunately, Rim's article continues to share how this preconception has changed in Ivy League schools, and now more and more universities are accepting ASL as a valid language of study, just like English, Latin, or Spanish.

There are similar misconceptions about Indigenous and minority languages. Recently, I interviewed 109 native speakers of Spanish and asked them to define *dialect*. Over 30 percent of the respondents defined *dialect* as something inferior or less than a language. Twenty percent of the respondents, all of them within the group that defined dialect with an inferior status, expressed that dialect is what they call Indigenous languages in the Americas, and in that way they distinguish those languages from majority languages such as English, French, or Spanish. Thus, an important segment of Spanish speakers in the world seems to consider Indigenous languages as inferior when compared to languages such as English or Spanish. They do not assign the label *language* to these minority languages because they do not consider them to be valid languages.

Just recently, while talking to a Guatemalan friend who speaks English, Spanish, and K'iche', I asked how his last trip to Guatemala went with his young daughters. He said the girls, who don't speak K'iche', were a little confused because all they heard around them was Spanish and *dialecto*; by 'dialect' my friend was referring to the K'iche' language. The *Ethnologue* of SIL Global describes K'iche' as a Mayan language of Guatemala with over a million speakers (Eberhard et al. 2025). Even this K'iche' man devalued his primary language by categorizing it as secondary in status to Spanish.

If *dialect* is rated inferior to *language*, or spoken of in a pejorative sense as a secondary means of communication, then the "so-called" dialects shelf should be empty, as in figure 66. There is no such thing as an inferior language.

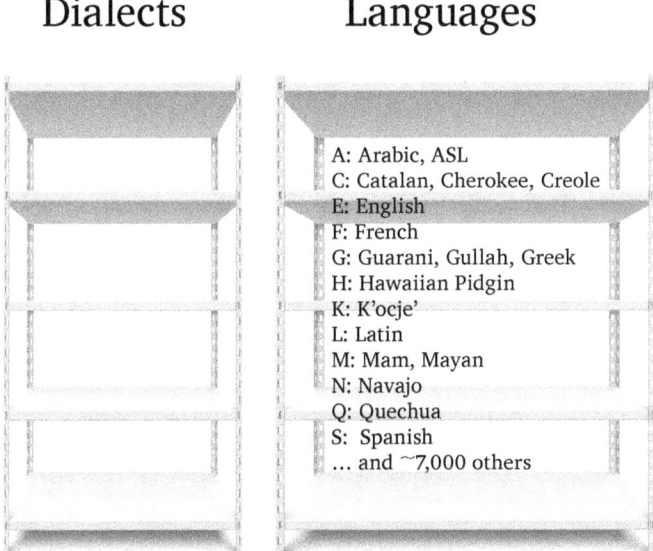

Figure 66. Languages and dialects.

In conclusion, society's history and experiences, beliefs and prejudices, and its structure and dynamics affect the way we use language for good or bad, and the way we perceive of our own and others' languages, whether these are biased perceptions or not. It is a moral responsibility for every member of society to be well informed about these issues and to contribute to an appreciation of others, respecting the various linguistic norms and systems described here. Ignoring this ethical responsibility can be the cause of social injustice and a license for the continuation of those injustices, with tragic consequences to the dignity of other human beings.

Exercises

1) Survey on language attitudes
   Ask ten people (native speakers of English) if they think that in some region of the U.S. they speak better or worse English than in other regions. Ask them which regions, and why they think they speak "good" or "bad" English.
2) Write an email to one of these people who thought a certain region spoke better/worse than another. Explain in that email, based on what you have learned, why some languages are not superior to others.

3) While reading current news or watching TV programs or on your social media network, pick at least one word/expression that exemplifies the impact of society on language. Indicate the word/expression, its context, and the source. Indicate why you think this illustrates what society's impact on language has been.
4) Words/expressions as "distinguishers." Write down:
   One word/expression that distinguishes between genders _____
   One that distinguishes between age groups _____
   One that distinguishes between social class _____
   One that distinguishes between regions _____
   One that distinguishes between races or ethnicity _____

   Were you able to fill out all these blanks? Why or why not?
5) "The media helps perpetuate stereotypes/social prejudice using language."
   Do you agree? Explain.
6) Record real examples (while interacting with others, your social network time, the media, etc.) of prejudice that some of those words or expressions (exercise [4]) may show. Indicate the word or expression and explain the prejudice. If you can't find any, write a paragraph about what you think the current status of societal prejudice is in your generation (as exemplified in this chapter).

Conclusions

Yes! Your language matters! It is part of who you are—your identity—and has life implications. It is beautiful and marvelous. And we can say the same thing about the language or language variety of any person in the world! In addition, the way you use language can build others and yourself up or demoralize and tear down. Because of this, it is important to ask critical questions about language, questions such as those addressed in this book. It is equally necessary and helpful to search for well thought-out answers to those questions. Following is a review of those ten questions and answers I believe concord with linguistic research and discoveries, and day-to-day experiences. Although not an exhaustive list of the fundamental questions to consider related to language and communication, it is sufficient as an introduction to a serious study of language.

1) Do we really know what language is?
   No, I do not think we really understand what language is. The fact that a person says that they speak a dialect—not a language—or that ASL or Indigenous languages are not competent languages, tells me there is still much ignorance about what language is, even in our twenty-first century world.

   So, what is it?
   Language is the most important and effective system of human communication, that helps us express ourselves and interrelate. Fundamentally, it is a system that consists of a set of words or morphemes, a lexicon formed by sounds or signs, and a set of rules that organizes these (grammar) in a logical, consistent way. These sets of rules are very complex; yet any three-year-old, for any language worldwide, masters these rules.

2) Can animals or machines speak in the true sense of the word?
   No. Contrary to what TV cartoons or sci-fi programs show, cartoons, animals, and machines cannot talk, not in the same way that humans can generate creative communication. Features such as displacement, infinite creativity, and duality of patterning are distinctive characteristics of only human communication. Animals and machines do have a system of communication but not with the unlimited creativity and interactivity of human language.

3) Is your grammar good?
   Yes! Your intuitive grammar is good, valid, useful, and complex. The fact that you were able to read this book, understand it, and respond to these exercises demonstrates that you have mastered grammatical skills to an awesome level of ability. Even preliterates master the phonology, lexicon, and grammar of their language to be able to communicate with others. Perhaps not everyone can pass an English grammar exam at school, but that does

not mean they have not mastered the grammar rules intuitively that are necessary to communicate in English.

4) What do we mean when we talk?

We talk in order to communicate our ideas, our thoughts, our feelings. We aim to convince others, to inform others, to entertain others. What we want to do is to connect with others by means of language. In the process we can play with language and communicate secondary concepts, even using the same vocabulary in figurative speech. Communicating with other people and connecting with them through speech is the fundamental aspect of talking.

5) Who speaks English better?

Nobody and everybody; all normal native speakers of a language speak well and can communicate. They may sound different; some people may like how others sound or may despise it, but that is just personal taste. Different varieties of English (across time, across regions, across societal groups) are just that: different varieties of the English language. This is true not just for English. Who speaks Spanish better? Or French? Or Chinantec? Or Creole? And so on. It is the same answer for every language in the world.

6) Did King Alfred really speak English?

Yes, he did. The history of the English language started about the year 500 AD. King Alfred ruled in a part of Sub-Roman Britain sometime during the Early Middle Ages (400–1000 AD). He spoke OE. Every language has older versions and a modern version, because languages change. Language change is a natural process because other languages affect it and life circumstances change, and one's vocabulary and grammar adapt to those changes. There is no linguistic measure or evidence to conclude that a former version of a language is better than a later one, or vice versa. They are simply different stages of the same language. Each version achieves its purpose in its historical context.

7) Do we mean what we say?

Yes and no. No doubt we as language users clearly have a set goal when we talk. As mentioned, we intend to convince, to inform, or simply to entertain. We use words with that purpose. We choose our words to achieve what we want to convey. In that sense, yes, we mean what we say. But the words we say cannot always be taken at face value or literally by our audience. People play with language, exaggerate, joke, use irony, figurative language, and even silence to express creative meaning. Even if I ask you, "How are you?" you know I do not always expect a content answer to inform me about your health or what's going on with you, but even in the context of a passing greeting, there is nothing wrong with my asking that question. Amazingly, both you and I, and native speakers of English understand that, within context. We use the world around us, our common background and knowledge, our understanding of society, and similar factors to interpret meanings correctly. Those contextual clues help avoid ambiguity or enable us to disambiguate effectively most of the time.

8) Is language in your heart or in your brain?

Even if we love our language and prefer to express ourselves in what we call the "language of our heart," we really store and process language in our brains. The term "heart language" is the common way to refer to the first language we learned, also known as our mother tongue, or our native or primary language. It metaphorically refers to the reality that language is ingrained in our sense of identity. But, from a scientific perspective of our anatomy, the brain is where language acquisition, language storage, and language processing happen.

9) Can everybody learn a language?

Yes, all normal people do—and they must! Normal children, in any corner of the world, are born wired for language acquisition. Learning a first language is a natural process that begins almost effortlessly, starting at birth, a process that continues until about the age of six. All people under normal conditions just need to be exposed to language naturally, without needing formal instruction.

Now, acquiring a second language is slightly different. In theory, anybody can learn a second language. If exposure to the second language happens before puberty, the learning process will be easier. Learning a second or a foreign language after this critical period can still be successful but the learner may always have a foreign accent, influenced by their first language. To sound more like a native speaker depends, in part, on how hard the learner works to not only acquire the grammar and vocabulary, but also the accent, stress, and pitch patterns of that second language.

10) Can society help, or harm, language?

Both are true. On one hand, there is what I call a "neutral" effect of societal structure and dynamics on language. For example, social hierarchy may affect the grammar and vocabulary of a language by establishing different ways to refer to others using honorifics or formal versus informal pronouns. This is a way language speakers respond within that structure, and it may be neither negative nor positive. However, the way society is structured and its effect on language and language use depends more on a person's *use* of the power structure, resulting in the way they treat others. An example of how society can help to diminish harmful use of language is to discourage the use of words that discriminate, that alienate and promote an "us versus them" dynamic. Due to social pressure, English speakers are attempting to bring into disuse words that have been offensive to other members of society. For example, a disuse of the "N" word by White people out of respect for African Americans. At the same time, a bias or prejudice within a society against another group of people can generate discriminatory language, resulting in stigmatizing and degrading them.

What we say (or express) matters!
(A bride saying, "*I do*" in a wedding, makes her a "Mrs.".)
How we say what we do matters!
(A professor's sarcastic "*Well, hello!*" to a late student, is not a greeting.)
Who says what we do matters!
(Which carries weight? A doctor, or the dictator, saying, "*I declare war.*")
To whom we say what we do matters!
("*You're heavier*" sounds good to the emaciated but not to a dieter.)
When we say what we do matters!
(Saying, "good *evening!*" to a latecomer at 9:00 AM, we're making a point.)
Where we say what we do matters!
(Saying, "*How are you?*" in a busy school hall versus in a doctor's office.)
Why we say what we do matters!
(Is saying "*It's hot!*" to inform or to ask others to adjust the AC?)
What we do *not* say may also matter!
(A husband to his wife, "*I'm home!*" Her stony silence means something!)

In short, people have a unique, incredible, highly complex, and effective device for communication—our language. This human ability is what has allowed us to travel together through this journey. I hope you will value your own language and the language of others even more; and I also hope you will use this valuable tool for good, because, as this book clearly demonstrates, *your language matters*!

Appendix A:
The International Phonetic Alphabet

THE INTERNATIONAL PHONETIC ALPHABET (revised to 2020)

CONSONANTS (PULMONIC)

©℗© 2020 IPA

	Bilabial	Labiodental	Dental	Alveolar	Postalveolar	Retroflex	Palatal	Velar	Uvular	Pharyngeal	Glottal
Plosive	p b			t d		ʈ ɖ	c ɟ	k ɡ	q ɢ		ʔ
Nasal	m	ɱ		n		ɳ	ɲ	ŋ	ɴ		
Trill	ʙ			r					ʀ		
Tap or Flap		ⱱ		ɾ		ɽ					
Fricative	ɸ β	f v	θ ð	s z	ʃ ʒ	ʂ ʐ	ç ʝ	x ɣ	χ ʁ	ħ ʕ	h ɦ
Lateral fricative				ɬ ɮ							
Approximant		ʋ		ɹ		ɻ	j	ɰ			
Lateral approximant				l		ɭ	ʎ	ʟ			

Symbols to the right in a cell are voiced, to the left are voiceless. Shaded areas denote articulations judged impossible.

CONSONANTS (NON-PULMONIC)

Clicks	Voiced implosives	Ejectives
ʘ Bilabial	ɓ Bilabial	ʼ Examples:
ǀ Dental	ɗ Dental/alveolar	pʼ Bilabial
ǃ (Post)alveolar	ʄ Palatal	tʼ Dental/alveolar
ǂ Palatoalveolar	ɠ Velar	kʼ Velar
ǁ Alveolar lateral	ʛ Uvular	sʼ Alveolar fricative

OTHER SYMBOLS

ʍ Voiceless labial-velar fricative
w Voiced labial-velar approximant
ɥ Voiced labial-palatal approximant
ʜ Voiceless epiglottal fricative
ʢ Voiced epiglottal fricative
ʡ Epiglottal plosive

ɕ ʑ Alveolo-palatal fricatives
ɺ Voiced alveolar lateral flap
ɧ Simultaneous ʃ and x

Affricates and double articulations can be represented by two symbols joined by a tie bar if necessary. t͡s k͡p

VOWELS

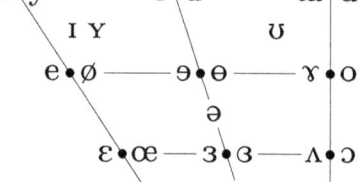

Where symbols appear in pairs, the one to the right represents a rounded vowel.

SUPRASEGMENTALS

ˈ	Primary stress	ˌfoʊnəˈtɪʃən
ˌ	Secondary stress	
ː	Long	eː
ˑ	Half-long	eˑ
̆	Extra-short	ĕ
ǀ	Minor (foot) group	
ǁ	Major (intonation) group	
.	Syllable break	ɹi.ækt
‿	Linking (absence of a break)	

TONES AND WORD ACCENTS

LEVEL		CONTOUR	
e̋ or ˥	Extra high	ě or ˩˥	Rising
é ˦	High	ê ˥˩	Falling
ē ˧	Mid	e᷄ ˦˥	High rising
è ˨	Low	e᷅ ˩˨	Low rising
ȅ ˩	Extra low	e᷈ ˧˦˨	Rising-falling
↓ Downstep		↗ Global rise	
↑ Upstep		↘ Global fall	

DIACRITICS

	Voiceless	n̥ d̥		Breathy voiced	b̤ a̤		Dental	t̪ d̪
	Voiced	s̬ t̬		Creaky voiced	b̰ a̰		Apical	t̺ d̺
ʰ	Aspirated	tʰ dʰ		Linguolabial	t̼ d̼		Laminal	t̻ d̻
	More rounded	ɔ̹	ʷ	Labialized	tʷ dʷ	̃	Nasalized	ẽ
	Less rounded	ɔ̜	ʲ	Palatalized	tʲ dʲ	ⁿ	Nasal release	dⁿ
	Advanced	u̟	ˠ	Velarized	tˠ dˠ	ˡ	Lateral release	dˡ
	Retracted	e̱	ˤ	Pharyngealized	tˤ dˤ	̚	No audible release	d̚
	Centralized	ë	̴	Velarized or pharyngealized	ɫ			
	Mid-centralized	ẽ		Raised	e̝ (ɹ̝ = voiced alveolar fricative)			
	Syllabic	n̩		Lowered	e̞ (β̞ = voiced bilabial approximant)			
	Non-syllabic	e̯		Advanced Tongue Root	e̘			
˷	Rhoticity	ɚ ɝ		Retracted Tongue Root	e̙			

Some diacritics may be placed above a symbol with a descender, e.g. ŋ̊

Appendix B:
Body-based Figurative Language

- "In the same vein"
- "The head of a department"
- "A body of water"
- "By the skin-of-my-teeth"
- "the teeth of a comb"
- "A leg up"
- "The heart of the city"
- "The life-and-soul of the party"
- "Blood, sweat, and tears"
- "Get it off your chest"
- "At someone's heels"
- "A joint venture"
- "All hands on deck"
- "My knees are knocking"
- "My lips are sealed"
- "At the top of your lungs"
- "Traffic on the central artery"
- "I don't have the guts"
- "Keep your eyes on the prize"
- "The legwork of a task"
- "She's the brains of the operation"
- "That's a no-brainer"
- "Nosy"
- "Hand it to her"
- "Elbow your way out"
- "Take the task upon your shoulder"
- "The backbone of the operation"
- "They are backing me up"
- "A cigarette butt"
- "To stick your neck out"
- "Losing the game was a kick in the shins"
- "To knuckle under"
- "That movie is a real nail biter"
- "Politics is a cut-throat business"
- "Go toe-to-toe"
- "Shoot from the hip"
- "Win something by a hair"
- "Fight tooth and nail"

References

Acosta, Teresa Palomo. 2003. We serve White's only: No Spanish or Mexicans. *Las Tejanas: 300 years of history*. 116. In Hilary Mac Austin and Kathleen Thompson, (2022), Latinx discrimination. Digital Collections for the Classroom. Chicago: The Newberry. https://dcc.newberry.org/?p=20692.

Aikens, N. L., and O. Barbarin, 2008. Socioeconomic differences in reading trajectories: The contribution of family, neighborhood, and school contexts. *Journal of Educational Psychology*, 100:235–251. http://dx.doi.org/10.1037/0022-0663.100.2.235.

Aikhenvald, Alexandra. 2004. *Evidentiality*. Oxford University Press.

Alcorn, Chauncey. February 2021. Aunt Jemima finally has a new name. CNN Business. https://www.cnn.com/2021/02/09/business/aunt-jemima-new-name/index.html.

Allen, Kelli, Jeanna Scheve, and Vicki Nieter. 2011. *Understanding learning styles: Making a difference for diverse learners*. Huntington Beach, CA: Shell Educational Publishing.

American Council on the Teaching of Foreign Languages. 2013. *Program standards for the preparation of foreign language teachers*. Alexandria, VA: ACTFL.

Anderson, Diane. 2006. Lexical development of Deaf children acquiring signed languages. In Brenda Schick, Marc Marschark, and Patricia E. Spencer (eds.), *Advances in the sign language development of Deaf children*. New York: Oxford University Press.

Anderson, E. G. 2017. The X-files' transregional South. In Lisa Hinrichsen, Gina Caison, and Stephanie Rountree (eds.), *Small-screen Souths: Region, identity, and the cultural politics of television*. Baton Rouge, LA: LSU Press.

AP News. 2020. 1 ad, 3 accents: How Democrats aim to win Latino votes. https://apnews.com/article/nv-state-wire-joe-biden-az-state-wire-cuba-miami-4bee1e65617262bddceee0c5c2b1c254.

APA. 2023a. Inclusive language guidelines. American Psychological Association. https://www.apa.org/about/apa/equity-diversity-inclusion/language-guidelines.

APA. 2023b. Social instinct. American Psychological Association. https://dictionary.apa.org/social-instinct.

Austin, John Langshaw. 1962. *How to do things with words.* Cambridge, MA: Harvard University Press.

Barcelona, Antonio, ed. 2003. *Metaphor and metonymy at the crossroads: A cognitive perspective.* New York: Mouton de Gruyter.

Barker, Richard. 2024. Old English (c. 500–1100). History of English. https://www.thehistoryofenglish.com/old-english.

Berkeley, Edmund Callus. 1949. *Giant brains or machines that think.* New York: John Wiley. archive.org/details/in.ernet.dli.2015.285568/page/n9/mode/2up?q=computer.

Bernstein, Basil. 1960. Language and social class. *British Journal of Sociology* 11(3):271–276. London: Wiley. https://www.jstor.org/stable/586750.

Bernstein, Leandra. 2019. *The 2020 election could solidify a new standard of political incivility.* https://nbcmontana.com/news/nation-world/the-2020-election-could-solidify-a-new-standard-of-political-incivility.

Bernstein, Theodore Menline. 1958. Watch your language: A lively, informal guide to better writing, emanating from the news room of the *New York Times.* New York. The Channel Press.

Bhat, D. N. S. 1999. *The prominence of tense, aspect, and mood.* In Studies in Language Companion Series 49. Amsterdam: John Benjamins.

Birner, B. 2021. Language acquisition. Facebook, CR-Sharing-Knowledge https://www.facebook.com/CRsharingknowledge/posts/langauge-acquisition-why-did-my-daughter-say-feet-correctly-for-a-while-and-then/104036141811509/.

Bleile, Ken M. 2018. *The late eight.* Third edition. San Diego, CA: Plural Publishing.

Bloomfield, Leonard. 1933. *Language.* Chicago: The University of Chicago Press.

Boas, Franz. 1911. *Handbook of American Indian languages.* Part I. Washington, D.C.: Government Printing Office.

Bonnice, S. 2014. *Computer programmer.* Broomall, PA: Mason Crest Publishers.

Boysen, Sally. 2009. *The smartest animals on the planet: Extraordinary tales of the natural world's cleverest creatures.* Buffalo, NY: Firefly Books.

Brentari, Diane. 2010. *Sign languages.* Cambridge Language Surveys. Cambridge University Press.

Brown, Penelope, and Stephen C. Levinson. 1987. *Politeness: Some universals in language usage.* Studies in Interactional Sociolinguistics 4. Cambridge University Press.

Brown, Roger, and Albert Gilman. 1968. The pronouns of power and solidarity. In Joshua A. Fishman (ed.), *Readings in the sociology of language*, 252–275. New York: Mouton.

Bull, Tove. 1995. Language contact leading to language change: The case of northern Norway. In Jacek Fisiak (ed.), *Linguistic change under contact conditions.* 15–34. Berlin, New York: Mouton de Gruyter.

Candland, Douglas K. 1993. *Feral children and clever animals: Reflections on human nature.* New York: Oxford University Press.

Carroll, John B., ed. 1956. *Language, thought, and reality: Selected writings of Benjamin Lee Whorf.* Cambridge, MA: MIT Press.

Carroll, Lewis. 1872. *Through the looking-glass.* London: Macmillan.

Chafe, Wallace. 1994. *Discourse, consciousness, and time: The flow and displacement of conscious experience in speaking and writing.* Chicago: University of Chicago Press.

Chambers, Jack, and Peter Trudgill. 1998. *Dialectology.* Cambridge Textbooks in Linguistics. Second edition. Cambridge University Press.

Changeux, Jean-Pierre. 2005. Genes, brain, and culture: From monkey to human. In Stanislas Dehaene, Jean-Rene Duhamel, Marc Hauser, and Giacomo Rizzolati (eds.), *From monkey brain to human brain: A Fyssen Foundation symposium.* Cambridge, MA: MIT Press.

Charter for Compassion. [2009] 2024. https://charterforcompassion.org/who-we-are/mission.html.

Chomsky, Noam. 1965. *Aspects of the theory of syntax.* Cambridge, MA: MIT Press.

Chomsky, Noam. 2006. *Language and mind.* Third edition. Cambridge University Press.

Churchill, Winston. 1945. Prime minister Churchill's eulogy in Commons for the late president Roosevelt. http://www.ibiblio.org/pha/policy/1945/1945-04-17a.html.

Cillizza, Chris. 2018. The dangerous consequences of Trump's all-out assault on political correctness. CNN: The Point, with Chris Cillizza. https://www.cnn.com/2018/10/30/politics/donald-trump-hate-speech-anti-semitism-steve-king-kevin-mccarthy/index.html.

Clark, E. V. 2009. *First language acquisition.* Second edition. Cambridge University Press.

Code, Chris. 2010. Aphasia. In Jack Damico, Nicole Muller, and Martin Ball (eds.), *The handbook of language and speech disorders,* 317–330. Oxford: Wiley-Blackwell.

Collins, Wesley M. 2016. *The heart of the matter: Seeking the center in Maya-Mam language and culture.* Dallas, TX: SIL International.

Compendium of Language Management of the University of Ottawa. n.d. https://www.uottawa.ca/about-us/official-languages-bilingualism-institute/clmc.

Cook, Albert S. 1891. The evolution of the Lord's Prayer in English. In *The American Journal of Philology* 12(1):59–66. https://archive.org/details/jstor-287989/.

Coon, Dennis, and John O. Mitterer. 2010. *Introduction to psychology: Gateways to mind and behavior.* Twelfth edition. Belmont, CA: Wadsworth Cengage Learning.

Critica Sur. 2018. El lunes arranca baja cero: El pronóstico del tiempo para la semana en Río Grande. *Critica Sur.* https://criticasur.com.ar/nota/17258/el_lunes_arranca_bajo_cero_el_pronostico_del_tiempo_para_la_semana_en_rio_grande.

Crowe, Kathryn, and Sharynne McLeod. 2020. Review of Children's English consonant acquisition in the United States. *American Journal of Speech-Language Pathology* 29(4):2155–2169. https://doi.org/10.1044/2020_AJSLP-19-00168.

Curtis, Susan, and Harry A. Whitaker. 1977. *Genie: A psycholinguistic study of a modern-day "wild child."* New York: Academic Press. Also in Eirlys E. Davies, *Perspectives in neurolinguistics and psycholinguistics: A series of monographs and treatises* (1986). https://search.worldcat.org/title/1455709351.

D'Anna, Catherine A., Eugene B. Zechmeister, and James W. Hall. (1991) 2024. Toward a meaningful definition of vocabulary size. *Journal of Literacy Research* 23(1). https://psycnet.apa.org/record/1992-41749-001.

De Leon, Virginia. 2007. Spreading the word. *The Spokesman-Review.* Spokane, WA. https://www.spokesman.com/stories/2007/feb/04/spreading-the-word.

Deutscher, Guy. 2005. *The unfolding of language: An evolutionary tour of mankind's greatest invention.* New York: Henry Holt.

Devlin, Thomas Moore. 2024. The United States of accents: Hawaii English and Pidgin. *Babbel Magazine.* https://www.babbel.com/en/magazine/the-united-states-of-accents-hawaiian-english/.

Dobrow, Julia R., and Calvin L. Gidney. 1998. The good, the bad, and the foreign: The use of dialects in children's animated television. In *The Annals of the American Academy of Political and Social Science,* vol. 557, Children and Television (May, 1998):105–119. Sage Publications, Inc. https://www.jstor.org/stable/1049446

Dockrill, Peter. 2020. There's a "desert" in the middle of the Pacific, and we now know what lives there. *Science Alert.* https://www.sciencealert.com/there-s-a-desert-in-the-middle-of-the-pacific-and-we-now-know-what-lives-there.

Dragojevic, Marko, Howard Giles, and Bernadette M. Watson. 2013. Language ideologies and language attitudes: A foundational framework. In H. Giles and B. M. Watson (eds.), *The social meanings of language, dialect, and accent: International perspectives on speech styles,* 1–25. New York: Peter Lang.

Dulay, H. D., and M. K. Burt. 1973. Should we teach children syntax? Language Learning 23(2):245–258.

Durkheim, Emile. 1915. Sociology and philosophy. New York: Free Press.

Eberhard, David M., Gary F. Simons, and Charles D. Fennig, eds. 2023. *Ethnologue: Languages of the world.* Twenty-fifth edition. Dallas, TX: SIL International.

Eberhard, David M., Gary F. Simons, and Charles D. Fennig, eds. 2025. *Ethnologue: Languages of the world.* Twenty-eighth edition. Dallas, TX: SIL Global. https://www.ethnologue.com.

Epstein, Noel. 1981. When professors swap good grades for sex. *The Washington Post* September 6, 1981. https://www.washingtonpost.com/archive/opinions/1981/09/06/when-professors-swap-good-grades-for-sex/dae0ace9-58e0-4dc8-bdf2-a271c1245d9a/.

Ertel, Wolfgang. 2018. *Introduction to Artificial Intelligence.* Second edition. New York: Springer.

Fausset, Richard. 2020. South Carolina is changing. Is it enough to put Jaimie Harrison in the Senate? *The New York Times.* October 13, 2020. https://www.nytimes.com/2020/10/13/us/politics/jaime-harrison-south-carolina.html.

Farlex Partner Medical Dictionary. n.d. Gyrus. https://medical-dictionary.thefreedictionary.com/gyrus.

Fattal, Isabel. 2018. Why do cartoon villains speak in foreign accents? *The Atlantic* January 2018. https://www.theatlantic.com/education/archive/2018/01/why-do-cartoon-villians-speak-in-foreign-accents/549527.

Ferguson, Charles A. 1959. Diglossia. *Word* 15(2):325–340. https://www.tandfonline.com/doi/abs/10.1080/00437956.1959.11659702.

Filipović, Luna. 2007. *Talking about motion: A cross-linguistic investigation of lexicalization patterns.* Studies in Language Companion Series 91. Amsterdam: John Benjamins.

Fischer, O., and H. Olbertz. 2019. The role played by analogy in processes of language change: The case of English "have-to" compared to Spanish "tener-que". Nuria Yáñez-Bouza, Emma Moore, Linda van Bergen, and Willem B. Hollmann (eds.), *Categories, constructions, and change in English syntax,* 253–282. Studies in English Language 63. Cambridge University Press. Doi:10.1017/9781108303576.

Förster, Frank, Joe Saunders, Hagen Lehmann, and Chrystopher L. Nehaniv. 2019. Robots learning to say "No": Prohibition and rejective mechanisms in acquisition of linguistic negation. *Association of Computing Machinery Transaction on Human-Robot Interactions* 8(4):23. https://doi.org/10.1145/3359618.

Freedman, Glenn, and Elizabeth G. Reynolds. 1980. Enriching basal reader lessons with semantic webbing. *The Reading Teacher* 33(6):677–684.

Friederici, Angela. 2017. *Language in our brain: The origins of a uniquely human capacity*. Cambridge, MA: MIT Press.

Friedrich, Paul. 1971. *The Tarascan suffixes of locative space: Meaning and morphotactics*. Bloomington, IN: Mouton.

Fromkin, Victoria, Robert Rodman, and Nina Hyams. 2010. *An introduction to language*. Ninth edition. Independence, KY: Wadsworth CENGAGE Learning.

George, Timothy. 2014. The nature of God: Being, attributes, and acts. In D. Akin (ed.), *Theology for the church*. Revised edition. 157–203. Nashville, TN: B&H Publishing.

Goel, A. 2010. *Computer fundamentals*. Delhi: Pearson.

Goffman, Erving. 1955. On face-work. Cited by C. Lemert. 2010. *Social theory: The multicultural readings*, 338–343. Philadelphia: Westview Press.

Goffman, Erving. 1956. The nature of deference and demeanor. *American Anthropologist* 58(3):473–502.

Goffman, Erving. 1967. *Interaction ritual*. Garden City, NY: Anchor Books.

Grohmann, Karolos. 2024. Olympic ceremony's 'Last Supper' sketch never meant to disrespect, says Paris 2024. *Reuters*. https://www.reuters.com/sports/olympics/paris-2024-apologises-any-offence-caused-by-last-supper-sketch-2024-07-28/.

Grondelaers, Stefan, Roeland van Hout, and Paul van Gent. 2019. Re-evaluating the prestige of regional accents in Netherlandic Standard Dutch: The role of accent strength and speaker gender. *Journal of Language and Social Psychology* 38(2):215–236.

Hagura, Nobuhiro, Patrick Haggard, and Jörn Diedrichsen. 2017. Perceptual decisions are biased by the cost to act. eLife. University College London. https://elifesciences.org/articles/18422.

Hardman, M. J. 1988. Fuente de datos y persona gramatical en las lenguas Jaqi. *Dialogo Andino* 7/8:121–134. Arica, Chile: Universidad de Tarapaca.

Henderson, Anita. 2001. Put your money where your mouth is: Hiring managers' attitudes toward African-American Vernacular English. PhD dissertation. University of Pennsylvania.

Hockett, Charles. 1960. The origin of speech. *Scientific American Journal* 203:89–97.

Hodge, Matthew. 2018. Disney "World": The westernization of world music in EPCOT's "IllumiNations: Reflections of Earth." In Lauren Dundes (ed.), The psychosocial implications of Disney's movies. *Social Sciences* (special issue) 7(8):112–122. https://www.mdpi.com/2076-0760/7/8/136.

Hoyos, Patricia Maria, Na Yeon Kim, and Sabine Kastner. 2019. How is magnetic resonance imaging used to learn about the brain? *Frontiers for young minds*. https://kids.frontiersin.org/article/10.3389/frym.2019.00086.

Huang, Jie. 2020. Dynamic activity of human brain task-specific networks. Scientific Reports. 10(1):7851. https://pubmed.ncbi.nlm.nih.gov/32398669/.

Hymes, Dell. 1974. *Foundations of sociolinguistics: An ethnographic approach.* Philadelphia: University of Pennsylvania Press.

Ide, Nancy, and Jean Veronis. 1998. Introduction to the special issue on word sense disambiguation: The state of the art. *Computational Linguistics Special Issue on Word Sense Disambiguation* 24(1):1–40.

Jacob, Sandra. 2014. "Kernel" lexicon of languages remains stable in the long run. Max Planck Society. https://phys.org/news/2014-10-kernel-lexicon-languages-stable.html.

John A. Hartford Foundation, The. 2013. *Dissemination Center* (online). New York: JAHF. https://www.johnahartford.org/dissemination-center/view/us-hhs-releases-new-national-standards-for-culturally-and-linguistically-ap.

Johns Hopkins Medicine. 2024. Brain anatomy and how the brain works. https://www.hopkinsmedicine.org/health/conditions-and-diseases/anatomy-of-the-brain

Kachur, Torah. 2017. Human brain structure inspires artificial intelligence. *Technology and Science*, Q&A. CBC News. https://www.cbc.ca/news/technology/human-brain-inspires-artificial-intelligence-1.4183556.

Kasper, Gabriele. 1997. Linguistic etiquette. In Florian Coulmas (ed.), *The handbook of sociolinguistics* 374–385. Oxford: Blackwell.

Kaye, Alan S., and Mauro Tosco. 2001. *Pidgin and creole languages: A basic introduction.* Second edition. Munich, Germany: Lincom Europa.

Kelly, Laura. 2021. Do Inuits really have 50 words for snow? The readable blog. https://readable.com/blog/do-inuits-really-have-50-words-for-snow/.

Kerr, Jeff. July 13, 2020. CBS sports digital. https://www.cbssports.com/nfl/news/washington-redskins-name-change-heres-a-timeline-detailing-the-origins-controversies-and-more/.

Kibbee, Douglas A. 2016. *Language and the law: Linguistic inequality in America.* Cambridge University Press.

Koko.org. 2023. Why Teach American Sign Language (ASL) to a Gorilla? The Gorilla Foundation. https://www.koko.org/about/programs/project-koko/interspecies-communication/sign-language/.

Krashen, Stephen. 1982. *Principles and practice in second language acquisition.* Oxford: Pergamon.

Kurath, Hans, and Raven I. McDavid, Jr. 1961. *The pronunciation of English in the Atlantic states.* Ann Arbor, MI: University of Michigan Press.

Kwong, Oi Yee. 2012. Psycholinguistics, lexicography, and word sense disambiguation. *The 26th Pacific Asia Conference on Language, Information and Computation*, 408–417. Bali: Univesitas Indonesia. https://aclanthology.org/Y12-1044.

Kymissis, Effie, and Claire L. Poulson. 1990. The history of imitation in learning theory: The language acquisition process. *Journal of the Experimental Analysis of Behavior* 54(2):113–27. https://pubmed.ncbi.nlm.nih.gov/2230633/.

Labov, William. 1994. *Principles of linguistic change. Vol. 1: Internal factors.* Language in Society 20. Oxford: Blackwell.

Labov, William. 2009. *Dialect diversity in America: The politics of language change.* Charlottesville, VA: University of Virginia Press.

Labov, William, Sharon Ash, and Charles Boberg. 2006. *The atlas of North American English: Phonetics, phonology, and sound change*. New York: Mouton de Gruyter.

Lakoff, George. 1987. *Women, fire, and dangerous things: What categories reveal about the mind*. Chicago: Chicago University Press.

Lakoff, George, and Mark Johnson. 1980. *Metaphors we live by*. Chicago University Press.

Lakunina, Anna A, Matthew B. Nardoci, Yashar Ahmadian, and Santiago Jaramillo. 2020. Somatostatin-expressing interneurons in the auditory cortex mediate sustained suppression by spectral surround. *Journal of Neuroscience* 40(18):3564–3575.

Lambrecht, Knud. 1994. *Information structure and sentence form: Topic, focus, and the mental representation of discourse referents*. Cambridge Studies in Linguistics 71. Cambridge University Press.

Landsman, Robert E. 2005. *RIP-ing through scientific inquiry: Critical thinking and effective decision making skills for middle school and high school science education*. Honolulu, HI: ANOVA Science Publishing.

Lane, Harlan. 1976. *The wild boy of Aveyron*. Cambridge, MA: Harvard University Press.

Langacker, Robert W. 1987. *Foundations of cognitive grammar: Theoretical prerequisites*. Vol. 1. Redwood City, CA: Stanford University Press.

Langacker, Robert W. 1990. *Concept, image, and symbol: The cognitive basis of grammar*. Cognitive Linguistics Research 1. New York: Mouton de Gruyter.

Lange, Carol, ed. 2023. Newspaper in education : A classroom resource. *The Washington Post*. https://nie.washingtonpost.com/node/483.

Leacox, L. R. 2018. The late eight en Espanol. In Kenneth Bleile (ed.), *The late eight*. Third edition, 59–91. San Diego, CA: Plural Publishing.

Lederberg, Amy R., and Jennifer S. Beal-Alarez. 2003. Expressing meaning: From prelinguistic communication to building vocabulary. In Marc Marschark and Patricia E. Spencer (eds.), *Oxford handbook of Deaf studies, language, and education*, 258–275. New York: Oxford University Press.

Lehmann, Winifred P. 1978. *Syntactic typology: Studies in the phenomenology of language*. Austin: University of Texas Press.

Lehmann, Winifred P. 1992. *Historical linguistics*. Third edition. New York: Routledge.

Lenneberg, Eric H. 1969. On explaining language. *Science, New Series* 164(3880):635–643. https://www.science.org/doi/10.1126/science.164.3880.635.

Leonard, James. 2004. Bilingualism and equality: Title VII claims for language discrimination in the workplace 38(1):56–140. *University of Michigan Journal of Law Reform* 57. https://repository.law.umich.edu/mjlr/vol38/iss1/3.

Lippi-Green, Rosina. 2012. *English with an accent: Language, ideology, and discrimination in the United States*. Second edition. London: Routledge.

Live Lingua. 2024. The differences between Classical Arabic and Modern Standard Arabic. https://www.livelingua.com/arabic/the-differences-between-classical-arabic-and-modern-standard-arabic.

Lust, Barbara. 2006. *Child language acquisition and growth*. Cambridge Textbooks in Linguistics. Cambridge University Press.

Lutz, William. 1989. The dangers of doublespeak. *L.A. Times Archives.* November 5, 1989. https://www.latimes.com/archives/la-xpm-1989-11-05-op-1763-story.html.

Lutz, William. [1989] 2016. *Doublespeak: From "revenue enhancement" to "terminal living": How government, business, advertisers, and others use language to deceive you.* New York: Ig Publishing. (Citing William Lutz, The dangers of doublespeak.) https://bookshop.org/p/books/doublespeak-william-lutz/571532?ean=9781632460172.

Lyons, John. 1968. *Introduction to theoretical linguistics.* Cambridge University Press.

Lyons, John. 1977. *Semantics.* Vol. 2. Cambridge University Press.

Marshall, Nicholas. 1988. American tongues. YouTube: https://www.youtube.com/watch?v=k5IUmHVj-H8.

McLeod, Saul. (2008) 2014. Information processing. *Simply Psychology.* https://www.simplypsychology.org/information-processing.html.

McMullen, Troy. 2010. Dannon to pay $45M to settle yogurt lawsuit. *ABC News*, February 25, 2010. https://abcnews.go.com/Business/dannon-settles-lawsuit/story?id=9950269.

Meier, Richard P. 2016. Sign language acquisition. *Oxford handbooks online.* Oxford University Press. https://doi.org/10.1093/oxfordhb/9780199935345.013.19.

Merriam-Webster. 2024a. Ergonomics. Merriam-Webster.com dictionary. https://www.merriam-webster.com/dictionary/ergonomics.

Merriam-Webster. 2024b. How many English words. Merriam-Webster.com dictionary. https://www.merriam-webster.com/help/faq-how-many-english-words.

Merriam-Webster. 2024c. Literally. Merriam-Webster.com dictionary. https://www.merriam-webster.com/help/faq-how-many-english-words.

Merriam-Webster. 2024d. Nosism. Merriam-Webster.com dictionary. https://www.merriam-webster.com/dictionary/nosism.

Merriam-Webster. 2024e. Racism. Merriam-Webster.com dictionary. https://www.merriam-webster.com/dictionary/racism.

Meyers, Miriam Watkins. 1990. Current generic pronoun usage: An empirical study. *American Speech* 65(3):228–237.

Miller, George A., Richard Beckwith, Christiane Fellbaum, Derek Gross, and Katherine J. Miller. 1990. Introduction to WordNet: An on-line lexical database. *International Journal of Lexicography*, 13(4):235–312.

Miller, Michael. 2019. *Exposing hate: Prejudice, hatred, and violence in action.* Minneapolis, MN: Twenty-First Century Books.

MLA Style Center. 2020. How do I use singular *they*? March 4, 2020. https://style.mla.org/using-singular-they/.

Morgan, Paul L., G. Farkas, M. M. Hillemeier, and S. Maczuga. 2009. Risk factors for learning-related behavior problems at 24 months of age: Population-based estimates. *Journal of Abnormal Child Psychology* 37:401–413. https://link.springer.com/article/10.1007/s10802-008-9279-8.

Myhill, John. 1999. Rethinking prescriptivism. In Rebecca Wheeler (ed.), *Language alive in the classroom*, 37–46. London: Praeger.

Netiquette. 2023. California State University, Fullerton. Canvas Resource Center. https://canvashelp.fullerton.edu/m/Student/l/1336786-student-what-is-netiquette.

Neufeldt, Victoria, David Bernard Guralnik. 1996. *Webster's New World College Dictionary.* Third edition. New York: Macmillan.

Newport, Elissa. 1988. Constraints on learning and their role in language acquisition: Studies of the acquisition of American Sign Language. *Language Sciences* 10(1):147–172.

Nieto, Sonia. 2006. *Teaching as Political Work: Learning from courageous and caring teachers.* The Longfellow Lecture. Child Development Institute, Sarah Lawrence College. Institute of Educational Sciences. https://eric.ed.gov/?id=ED497692.

NIDCD 2017. National Institute on Deafness and Other Communication Disorders, U.S. Department of Health and Human Services. https://www.nidcd.nih.gov/health/aphasia.

Nordquist, Richard. 2019. Speech acts in linguistics. ThoughtCo. https://www.thoughtco.com/speech-act-linguistics-1692119.

Norwegian Academy. n.d. Norwegianacademy.com. https://norwegianacademy.com/nynorsk-or-bokmal/.

O'Grady, W. D. 2005. *How children learn language.* Cambridge University Press.

Odlin, Terence. 2003. Cross-linguistic Influence. In C. J. Doughty and M. H. Long (eds.), *The handbook of second language acquisition.* Malden, MA: Blackwell.

Orvell, A., E. Kross, and S. A. Gelman. 2017. How "you" makes meaning. *Science* 355(6331):1200–1302. https://www.science.org/doi/10.1126/science.aaj2014.

Oxford English Dictionary. 2024. Language. Oxford University Press. https://www.oed.com/search/dictionary/?scope=Entries&q=language.

Oxford languages. 2023. Effable. https://www.google.com/search?q=effable&rlz=1C1GCEA_enUS1039US1039&oq=&aqs=chrome.0.69i59i45018.426691j1j7&sourceid=chrome&ie=UTF-8.

Oxford reference. 2024a. Aphasia. Oxford University Press. https://www.oxfordreference.com/display/10.1093/acref/9780199661282.001.0001/acref-9780199661282-e-1338.

Oxford reference. 2024b. Communication. Oxford University Press. https://www.oxfordreference.com/display/10.1093/oi/authority.20110803095627847.

Oxford reference. 2024c. Social justice. Oxford University Press. https://www.oxfordreference.com/display/10.1093/acref/9780198609957.001.0001/acref-9780198609957-e-7514.

Oxford reference. 2024d. Word. Oxford University Press. https://www.oxfordreference.com/search?q=word&searchBtn=Search&isQuickSearch=true.

Papadatou-Pastou, Marietta, Anna K. Touloumakos, Christina Koutouveli, and Alexia Barrable. 2021. The learning styles neuromyth: When the same term means different things to different teachers. *European Journal of Psychology of Education* 36:511–531.

Papafragou, Anna. 2018. Pragmatic development, language learning and development. *Journal of Language Learning and Development: Pragmatic Development* 14(3):167–169. https://www.tandfonline.com/doi/full/10.1080/15475441.2018.1455791.

Patterson, Francine, and Eugene Linden. 1981. *The education of Koko.* New York: Holt, Rinehart, and Winston.

Pauwels, A. 1991. *Non-discriminatory language.* Canberra: Australian Government Publishing Service.

Pimsleur, Paul. 2013. *How to learn a foreign language.* New York: Simon & Schuster.

Pinker, Steven. 1994. *The language instinct.* New York: Penguin Books.

Pinker, Steven. 2002. *The blank slate: The modern denial of human nature.* New York: Penguin Books.

Poedjosoedarmo, Soepomo. 1968. Javanese speech levels. *Indonesia* 6:54–81.

Polomé, Edgar C. 1967. Swahili language handbook. Language Handbook Series. Washington DC: Center for Applied Linguistics. https://archive.org/details/swahililanguageh0000polo/page/n7/mode/2up.

Pound, Roscoe. 1912. Social justice and legal justice: Address delivered before the Allegheny County Bar Association, Pittsburgh, Pa., April 5th, 1912. Pittsburgh: Allegheny County Bar Association. https://search.worldcat.org/title/60731859.

Prabhu, N. S. 1987. *Second language pedagogy.* Oxford University Press.

Prieto, Victor M. 2005. Spanish evaluative morphology: Pragmatic, sociolinguistic, and semantic issues. PhD dissertation. University of Florida.

Prieto, Victor M. 2015. The semantics of evaluative morphology. In N. Grandi and L. Körtvélyessy (eds.), *Edinburgh handbook of evaluative morphology*, 21–31. Edinburgh: Edinburgh University Press.

Progressive Grocer. 2007. Dannon expanding probiotic portfolio. Progressive Grocer, January 22, 2007. https://progressivegrocer.com/dannon-expanding-probiotic-portfolio.

Proudhon, Pierre-Joseph. 2006. Social justice in an open world: The role of the United Nations. The International Forum for Social Development: UN Department of Economic and Social Affairs. https://digitallibrary.un.org/record/567990?v=pdf.

Redmond, Ian. 2008. *Primates of the world: The amazing diversity of our closest relatives.* London: New Holland.

Rim, Christopher. 2019. How ASL is conquering the Ivy League. *Forbes Magazine.* https://www.forbes.com/sites/christopherrim/2019/01/25/how-asl-is-conquering-the-ivy-league/#6a9e839e7ec7.

Roberts, C., E. Davies, and T. Jupp. 1992. *Language and discrimination: A study of communication in multi-ethnic workplaces.* New York: Longman.

Roberts, Ian, ed. 2017. *The Oxford handbook of universal grammar.* Oxford University Press.

Robson, S., and S. Wibisono. 2002. *Javanese English dictionary.* Singapore: Periplus Editions.

Rodríguez-Fornells, Antoni, Toni Cunillera, Anna Mestres-Missé, and Ruth de Diego-Balaguer. 2009. Neurophysiological mechanisms involved in language learning in adults. Philosophical Transactions of the Royal Society of London. Series B, *Biological Sciences*, December 27, 2009; 364(1536):3711–35. https://pubmed.ncbi.nlm.nih.gov/19933142/.

Rosengren, Karl Erik. 2000. *Communication: An introduction.* London: SAGE Publications.

Rowe, Bruce M., and Diane P. Levine. 2018. *A concise introduction to linguistics.* Fifth edition. New York: Routledge.

Ruiz, Juan Cruz. 2020. Es negro pero tiene la cara simpática? *El Dia* (newspaper). Tenerife, Spain. 7 June 2020. https://www.eldia.es/opinion/2020/06/07/negro-cara-simpatica-22395651.html.

Sadeghi, McKenzie, and Sudiksha Kochi. 2022. Fact check roundup: Debunking false narratives about the Jan. 6 Capitol riot two years later. *USA Today*. (Updated Jan. 5, 2023).

Sanchez, Rosa. 2020. NFL's Washington Redskins to change name following years of backlash. *ABC News*, July 13, 2020.

Sapir, Edward. 1921. *Language: An introduction to the study of speech*. New York: Harcourt Brace.

Saussure, Ferdinand. 1916. *Course on general linguistics*. New York: McGraw-Hill.

Schank, Roger C., and Robert P. Abelson. 1977. *Scripts, plans, goals, and understanding: An Inquiry Into human knowledge structures*. Hillsdale, NJ: Earlbaum.

Schlegloff, Emanuel A., and Harvey Sacks. 1973. Opening up closings. *Semiotica* 8(4):289–327.

Schneider, Edgar W. 2000. From region to class to identity: Show me how you speak, and I'll tell you who you are. *American Speech* 75(4):359–361. https://www.muse.jhu.edu/article/2785.

Searle, John. 1969. *Speech acts*. Cambridge University Press.

Seid, Brianna, Rosemary Nidiry, and Ram Subramanian. 2024. Debunking the myth of the "Migrant Crime Wave". Brennan Center for Justice. https://www.brennancenter.org/our-work/analysis-opinion/debunking-myth-migrant-crime-wave.

Shannon, Claude Elwood, and Warren Weaver. 1949. *The mathematical theory of communication*. Vol. 1. Champaign, IL: University of Illinois Press.

Shapiro, Lawrence. 2011. *Embodied cognition*. New Problems in Philosophy. New York: Routledge.

Singleton, David, and Lisa Ryan. 2004. *Language acquisition: The age factor*. Second edition, revised. *Second Language Acquisition* 9. Buffalo, N.Y.: Multilingual Matters. https://books.google.com.au/books?id=M2XeLjlTl-0C&printsec=frontcover&source=gbs_ge_summary_r&cad=0#v=onepage&q&f=false.

SKI-HI Institute. 2020. Assessment of language skills for children who are Deaf or hard of hearing from infancy to five years of age: Instructions and test form. In *SKI HI language development scale: An instruction manual and test form*. Third edition. Logan: Utah State University. https://hopepubl.com/product/ski-hi-language-development-scale-individual-test-forms-3rd-edition-2020-english/.

Skutnabb-Kangas, Tove, and Robert Phillipson. 1995. *Linguistic human rights*. In Tove Skutnabb-Kangas, M. Rannut and Robert Phillipson (eds.), Contributions to the Sociology of Language, 1–25 Berlin: De Gruyter.

Sperber, Dan, and Dierdre Wilson. 1986. *Relevance: Communication and cognition*. Oxford: Blackwell.

Swadesh, Morris. 1952. Lexico-statistic dating of prehistoric ethnic contacts. In *Proceedings of the American Philosophical Society* 96:452–463.

Tannen, Deborah. 1990. *You just don't understand: Women and men in conversation*. New York: William Morrow.

Thorsen, Donald A. D., and V. Becker. 1996. *Inclusive language handbook: A practical guide to using inclusive language in college writing*. Azusa, CA: Azusa Pacific University.

Toribio, Almeida Jacqueline. 2011. Code-switching among U.S. Latinos. In Manuel Diaz-Campos (ed.), *The Handbook of Hispanic Sociolinguistics*, 530–552. Malden, MA: Wiley Blackwell.

Traugott, Elizabeth C., and Richard B. Dasher. 2004. *Regularity in semantic change.* Cambridge Studies in Linguistics 97. Cambridge University Press. https://doi.org/10.1017/CBO9780511486500.

Trier, J. 1931. *Der deutsche Wortschatz im Sinnbezirk des Verstandes.* Hoboken, NJ: Heidelberg.

Van Essen, David C. 2005. Surface-based comparisons of macaque and human cortical organization. In Stanislas Dehaene, Jean-Rene Duhamel, Marc Hauser, and Giacomo Rizzolatti (eds.), *From monkey brain to human brain: A Fyssen Foundation Symposium.* Oxford University Press.

Velupillai, Viveka. 2012. *An introduction to linguistic typology.* Philadelphia: John Benjamins.

Vocabulary.com. n.d. Tabula rasa. https://www.vocabulary.com/dictionary/tabula%20rasa.

Wang, Feng, and William S-Y. Wang. 2004. Basic words and language evolution. *Language and Linguistics* 5.3:643–662.

Weinreich, Uriel. 1968. *Languages in contact: Findings and problems.* The Hague: Mouton.

Whitney, William Dwight. 1875. *Life and growth of language: An outline of linguistic science.* New York: Appleton.

Wierzbicka, Anna. 1996. *Semantics: Primes and universals.* Oxford University Press.

Wilkins, D. A. 1976. *Notional syllabuses: A taxonomy and its relevance to foreign language curriculum development.* Oxford University Press.

Wilson, John, and Diana Boxer, eds. 2015. *Discourse, politics, and women as global leaders.* Philadelphia: John Benjamins.

Yule, George. 2010. *The study of language.* Fourth edition. Cambridge University Press.

Zenner, Eline, Laura Rosseel, and Andreea S. Calude. 2019. The social meaning potential of loanwords: Empirical explorations of lexical borrowings as expression of (social) identity. *Ampersand* 6. https://doi.org/10.1016/j.amper.2019.100055.

Zero-to-three. 2020. What is a "critical period" in brain development? Washington, DC: Zero to Three. https://www.zerotothree.org/resources/1368-what-is-a-critical-period-in-brain-development.

Zwicky, Arnold, and Ann Zwicky. 1982. Register as a dimension of linguistics variation. In Richard Kittredge and John Lehrberger (eds.), *Sublanguage: Studies of Faroese language in restricted semantic domains*, 213–218. New York: Walter de Gruyter.

Illustrations Credits

Figure #	Owner, license, URL
Half title	Openclipart.org/Presentation icon, by ousia; Excited smiley face, by GDJ; Headphones icon, by pnx
Figure 1	Openclipart.org/Nuclear family silhouette without ground, by GDJ; Cartoon thought bubble, by purzen
Figure 2	© 2025 Pixabay, CC0, https://pixabay.com/photos/young-woman-phone-girl-female-4681512/. Adapted by author.
Figure 3	Openclipart.org/BW retro boy, by liftarn; Bedroom eyes, by FEN; Siamese cat, by papapishu; Cartoon thought bubble, by purzen
Figure 4	Openclipart.org/book, by gingercoons
Figure 5	Openclipart.org/Collie dog, by johnny automatic
Figure 6	Openclipart.org/Siamese cat, by papapishu Wikipedia.org/Sign_language_C; Sign_language_A; Sign_language_T, public domain, by wpclipart.com
Figure 7	Openclipart.org/Unicorn, by GDJ; Reindeer line art, by GDJ; Cloud, by cinemacookie
Figure 8	© 2022 Linguistic Society of America, Public domain, https://web.archive.org/web/20220208131649/https://www.linguisticsociety.org/what-linguistics
Figure 9	© 2022 Janson G. (Pixabay.com), Public domain, https://www.needpix.com/photo/1103639/
Figure 10a	© 2008 Wanderingstan, Public domain, https://commons.wikimedia.org/wiki/File:Shannon_communication_system.svg
Figure 10b	© 2012 Rahulkepapa, CC By-SA 3.0, https://commons.wikimedia.org/wiki/File:Communication_process.jpg
Figure 11	Clipart-library.com/cartoon judge, Free for commercial use Cliparts, https://clipart-library.com/search1/?q=cartoon+judge
Figure 12	© 2022 Vivianlee2005, CC BY-SA 3.0, https://commons.wikimedia.org/wiki/File:Email_final.jpg
Figure 13	Openclipart.org/Capuchin monkey 01, by papapishu; Capuchin monkey 02, by papapishu; Cartoon thought bubble, by purzen; Thumbs up, by SavanaPrice; Banana bunch line art, by Child_of_Light
Figure 14	© 2014 Kalhh (Pixabay.com). Public domain, https://www.needpix.com/photo/627562/binary-digitization-null-one-pay-internet-www-numbering-system-security
Figure 15	Openclipart.org/Laptop, by jlmrtinez; Minimal desktop computer with optical drive and power button, by qubodup; Gorila, by Siddymcbill
Figure 16	Openclipart.org/Robotic arm, by Inkie30
Figure 17	© 2011 PictureYouth, CC By-SA 2.0, https://commons.wikimedia.org/wiki/File:Young_girl_with_smart_phone.jpg Openclipart.org/Cartoon thought bubble, by purzen
Figure 18	Openclipart.org/Chess coloring book, by DG-RA; Temple icon, by oksmith
Figure 19	Openclipart.org/Apple-lineart, by frankes; Three legged stool outline, by rygle; Sun, by Issi
Figure 20	Openclipart.org/Presentation icon, by ousia; Health education, by j4p4n; Cartoon thought bubble, by purzen
Figure 21	© 2025 Bobek Ltd., Public Domain Pictures.net, https://www.publicdomainpictures.net/en/view-image.php?image=40413&picture=keep-calm-and-carry-on
Figure 22	Openclipart.org/Top hat white, by cschreuders; Simple ear, by rematuche; Feet. pies, by mediobit
Figure 23	© 1871 John Tenniel, Public domain, https://commons.wikimedia.org/wiki/File:Humpty_Dumpty_Tenniel.jpg
Figure 24	Openclipart.org/Loaf of sliced bread, by j4p4n; yam, by johnny_automatic
Figure 25	Openclipart.org/laptop, by jlmrtinez; Minimal desktop computer with optical drive and power button, by qubodup
Figure 26	Created by Global Publishing Services

Illustrations Credits

Figure 27 Openclipart.org/Crane, by ShannonW © 2020 bsd studio, iStock-1254597558_Crane
Figure 28 Openclipart.org/Old couple walking silhouette, by GDJ; Telescope, by Sev
Figure 29 Openclipart.org/Mountain, by kasahorow; SUN(black&white), by yodomark
Figure 30 Openclipart.org/Pointing finger (#7), by oksmith
Figure 31 © 1960 Rogers & Cowan, Beverly Hills-publicity agency, https://commons.wikimedia.org/wiki/File:Andy_Griffith_Don_Knotts_Andy_Griffith_Show_1960.jpg
Figure 32 Openclipart.org/Élève lisant, by Improulx; Retirement home, by j4p4n; Cartoon thought bubble, by purzen; and ghost, by jbruce
Figure 33 Openclipart.org/Cartoon thought bubble, by purzen; Presentation icon, by ousia; Online presentation, by ousia
Figure 34 © 2023 GreekApple123, CC By-SA-4.0, https://commons.wikimedia.org/wiki/File:States_of_South_Asia_by_language.png
Figure 35 © 2007 nakedcharlton, https://commons.wikimedia.org/wiki/File:King_Alfred_the_Great.jpg
Figure 36 © 2009 Hogweard, https://commons.wikimedia.org/wiki/File:Her_swutela%C3%B0_seo_gecwydr%C3%A6dnes_%C3%B0e.jpg
Figure 37 Openclipart.org/Élève lisant, by lmproulx
Figure 38 Openclipart.org/Teaching, by ousia; Health education, by j4p4n; Court gavel outline, by j4p4n
Figure 39 Openclipart.org/Nuclear family silhouette without ground, by GDJ; 1277949122, by horse50; Cartoon thought bubble, by purzen; Feet, by Firkin
Figure 40 Openclipart.org/Nuclear family silhouette without ground, by GDJ; Retirement home, by j4p4n; Cartoon thought bubble, by purzen
Figure 41 Openclipart.org/Nuclear family silhouette without ground, by GDJ; Cartoon thought bubble, by purzen; Plan of a house in 3D perspective, by DG-RA; Temple icon, by oksmith
© 2020 bsd studio, iStock-1254597558_Crane
Figure 42 Openclipart.org/People talking, bubbles, by palomaironique; Interview-without-speech-bubbles, by GDJ
Figure 43 Openclipart.org/BW retro boy, by liftarn; Cartoon thought bubble, by purzen
Figure 44 Openclipart.org/Nuclear family silhouette without ground, by GDJ; Cartoon thought bubble, by purzen
Figure 45 Openclipart.org/Lutz - tepee outline, by pitr; Lion line art, by horse50
Figure 46 © c. 1801 Anonymous (B.R.) Source: Gallica Digital Library, digital ID: btv1b8626267t/f8, https://en.wikipedia.org/wiki/Victor_of_Aveyron#/media/File:Victor,_the_savage_of_Aveyron,_end_XVIIIe.jpg
Figure 47 Openclipart.org/icono-pc, by juanvelezm98. Adapted by author
Figure 48 Openclipart.org/cybernetic-brain from Pixabay, by GDJ
Figure 49 © 2019 Andrew Newberg, Thomas Jefferson University, http://www.andrewnewberg.com/research
Figure 50 Openclipart.org/human-brain, by ozhank
Figure 51 © 2007 James.mcd.nz. CC By-SA-4.0, https://commons.wikimedia.org/wiki/File:Brain_Surface_Gyri.SVG. Adapted by author
Figure 52 Openclipart.org/Gorila, by Siddymcbill; Cartoon thought bubble, by purzen; Pointing Finger (#7), by oksmith; Human Hand line art, by GDJ; Simple palm, by qubodup
Figure 53a Openclipart.org/Élève lisant, by Improulx; Cartoon thought bubble, by purzen
Figure 53b Openclipart.org/Élève lisant, by Improulx
Figure 54 © 2020 Courtesy of Rafsil Prieto
Figure 55 Openclipart.org/Baby Icon, by GDJ; Baby silhouette, by gringer; Nuclear family silhouette without ground, by GDJ; Presentation icon, by ousia; Health education, by j4p4n
Figure 56 © 2016 UK Crown, Open Government license 3.0, https://commons.wikimedia.org/wiki/File:Prince_George_best_2013.jpg
Figure 57 Openclipart.org/Father and toddler silhouette, by GDJ
Figure 58 Openclipart.org/Excited smiley face, by GDJ; Headphones icon, by mlampret
Figure 59 Openclipart.org/Loud Megaphone, by qubodu; Woman-playing-lute, by papapishu; Human hand line art, by GDJ; sketch eyes, by naoshika; Simple lips, by Tavin; Simple ear, by rematuche; Excited smiley face, by GDJ; Headphones icon, by mlampret; File or document icon, by tsaoja; Music notes, by Ehecatl1138
Figure 60 © 2025 Sapesaje (Pixabay), https://www.needpix.com/photo/download/347398/costume-batman-model-free-pictures-free-photos-free-images-royalty-free-free-illustrations
Figure 61 Openclipart.org/Woman shouting through megaphone silhouette, by GDJ; Mike the mic listening, by Bibbleycheese; Retirement home, by j4p4n; Excited smiley face, by GDJ; Élève lisant, by lmproulx
© 2024 milkghost, istockphoto.com/vector-caveman-with-a-club-doodle-illustration-gm2187827882-606386145
Figure 62 Author creation, based on data from Poedjosoedarmo 1968:58–59
Figure 63 © 2013 Daniel Case, CC By-SA 3.0, https://commons.wikimedia.org/w/index.php?curid=36868915
Figure 64 © 2018 Dirk Schmidt, Public domain, esukhia.xyz/blog/2018/4/27/diglossia-language-change-standardization (discontinued)
Figure 65 © Wikimedia.com, CC By-SA 4.0, https://commons.wikimedia.org/wiki/File:We-Serve-White%27s-Only-No-Spanish-or-Mexicans.jpg (discontinued)
Figure 66 © 2025 pialhovik, iStock-473089128_empty-shelf

Scripture quotations marked (*GNT*) are from the Good News Translation in Today's English Version-Second Edition. Copyright © 1992 by American Bible Society. Used by permission.

Victor M. Prieto is a bilingual, binational university professor of languages and linguistics. Born in Venezuela, he obtained a BA in Foreign Language Education (with specializations in both English and Spanish) and a second bachelor's degree in theology, with a minor in music.

Prieto and his wife Monica moved to the United States in 1998 and he began graduate studies in linguistics at the University of Florida (UF). There, he was granted an MA in Linguistics and Teaching English to Speakers of other Languages (TESOL). He also obtained a PhD in Linguistics. His dissertation was on the semantics and morphopragmatics of the Spanish language evaluative affixes (that is, the diminutive, augmentative, and pejorative).

From 1999–2005, while a student at UF, he taught undergraduate courses in linguistics, English as a Second Language (ESL), and Spanish. He also taught ESL at Santa Fe Community College.

Upon graduation, Prieto was hired as an assistant professor of Spanish at North Greenville University (NGU) in South Carolina. While at NGU he was promoted to full professor of Linguistics, TESOL, and Spanish. He was part of a team who brought Spanish and Spanish Education as majors to NGU. He was named Chair of the Linguistics and Modern Languages Department in 2017. His 16 years at NGU included four years as Department Chair.

During this time, Prieto published a chapter in the *Handbook of Evaluative Morphology* (2015), Edinburgh Press. He also earned an MA in Theology and completed half of an EdD program for Higher Education Leadership.

In 2021, he was hired as a professor of Spanish at Cabrillo College in Santa Cruz, California. He is currently Chair of the Department of World Languages at Cabrillo, overseeing the language programs of Spanish, French, German, Italian, Japanese, and American Sign Language. He also teaches ESL.

Prieto has given professional conferences in El Salvador, England, and Poland; and in the states of Florida, South Carolina, North Carolina, and New Jersey. Due to his involvement in college leadership, in the summer of 2024 he received a Certificate of Program Management from the Harvard Graduate School of Education in Cambridge, MA.

Prieto has been highly involved in community service through church ministries for 30 years, both in Venezuela and the U.S. He is currently Music Director and teacher at a small church in California and the Chairman of the Board of the Great Commission Association of Churches in Central California.

He loves traveling with his wife and son. They have visited over 20 countries, including Spain, Portugal, Belgium, Peru, Colombia, Morocco, Georgia, Canada, Mexico, and Cuba. He also loves involvement in most sports, and recently participated in recreational Pickleball tournaments.

In these diverse experiences, Prieto has seen the value and importance of language. This gave birth to the work you have in your hands, because he is convinced that "your language matters!"

Publications and honors

Prieto, Victor M. 2005. Spanish evaluative morphology: Pragmatic, sociolinguistic, and semantic issues. PhD dissertation. University of Florida.

Prieto, Victor M. 2015. The semantics of evaluative morphology. In N. Grandi and L. Körtvélyessy (eds.), *Edinburgh handbook of evaluative morphology*, 21–31. Edinburgh: Edinburgh University Press.

Certificate of Program Management. 2024. Harvard Graduate School of Education. Cambridge, MA: Harvard University.

www.ingramcontent.com/pod-product-compliance
Lightning Source LLC
Chambersburg PA
CBHW060513300426
44112CB00017B/2657